Critical Care Ethics

Treatment Decisions in American Hospitals

David F. Kelly

Wipf and Stock Publishers
EUGENE, OREGON

Wipf and Stock Publishers
199 West 8th Avenue, Suite 3
Eugene, Oregon 97401

Critical Care Ethics
Treatment Decisions in American Hospitals
By Kelly, David F.
©1991 Kelly, David F.
ISBN: 1-57910-992-6
Publication date: June, 2002
Previously published by Sheed and Ward, 1991.

To my Mother,
Cecelia M. Kelly

Contents

Preface vii

Chapter One
Forgoing Treatment:
The Catholic Tradition and the American Consensus . . 1
    Theological Basis: Divine Sovereignty and
        Human Stewardship 2
    Sanctity and Quality of Life 4
    Ordinary and Extraordinary Means 6
    Killing and Allowing to Die—Euthanasia 8
    Privacy, Autonomy, and Liberty 13
    Discussion Questions 15
    Endnotes 16

Chapter Two
Forgoing Treatment:
Nutrition and Hydration 20
    The Basic Consensus 20
    The Problem of Nutrition 21
    The *Brophy* Case 22
    Four Questions 24
    Consensus on Nutrition 28
    Discussion Questions 29
    Endnotes 29

Chapter Three
Forgoing Treatment:
The *Cruzan* Decision and Advanced Directives 36
    Part One: The *Cruzan* Decision 36
    Part Two: Advanced Directives 48
    Discussion Questions 54
    Endnotes 55

Chapter Four
Forgoing Treatment: Some Specific Questions 57
    Part One: Medical Futility 57
    Part Two: Mistakes and Conflicts 63
    Part Three: Brain Death 68
    Discussion Questions 70
    Endnotes 70

Chapter Five
Whatever Happened to the Good Old Medical Ethics? . . 73
    Part One: Intraprofessional Medical and Nursing Ethics . 75
    Part Two: Metaethics 78
    Conclusion 84
    Discussion Questions 85
    Endnotes 86

Chapter Six
Catholic Medical Ethics 88
    Part One: History 89
    Part Two: Material Definition 91
    Part Three: Method 92
    Part Four: Authority 98
    Discussion Questions 102
    Endnotes 102

Chapter Seven
Pain and Pain Management 105
    Introduction 105
    The Problem of God and Suffering 106
    Christian Answers 108
    Helpful Ideas 111
    Anger 112
    The Ethics of Pain Management 113
    The Role of the Clergy and the Chaplain 114
    Discussion Questions 117
    Endnotes 117

Chapter Eight
Ethics Committees 119
    Introduction 120
    Part One: Makeup 121
    Part Two: Function 128

Conclusion 136
Discussion Questions 136
Endnotes 137

Chapter Nine
Allocating Health Care Resources 138
Introduction: The Problem 139
Part One: Allocation and Forgoing Treatment 142
Part Two: The Problem with Allocation Arguments . . 144
Part Three: Competing Visions of Who People Are . . 146
Part Four: Rationing on the Basis of Age 147
Part Five: Toward a Better Health Care System 152
Conclusion 153
Discussion Questions 154
Endnotes 154

Chapter Ten
The Use and Misuse of the Allocation Argument . . . 159
Resistance to Allocation Arguments 160
Problems with the Allocation Argument 162
Improving the Allocation Argument 169
Artificial Heart Implants 170
Conclusion 173
Discussion Questions 173
Endnotes 173

Appendix A
Forgoing Treatment Policy 177

Appendix B
Making Difficult Choices About Treatment 192

Appendix C
Guidelines for Ethics Consultations 197

Appendix D
Condoms and AIDS in Catholic Hospitals 204

Bibliography 209

Preface

Except for the last chapter, which was originally delivered at a meeting of the College Theology Society, all the chapters of this book are revised versions of talks I gave to hospital personnel. The first six chapters were delivered as "Grand Rounds" lectures over a six month period at St. Francis Medical Center, a 750-bed tertiary care facility in Pittsburgh, Pennsylvania. The chapter on the meaning of pain was part of a talk at St. Francis for a symposium on pain management. The chapter on ethics committees was delivered at Sewickley Valley Hospital in Sewickley, PA. The chapter on allocation is a talk I delivered at a conference on medical ethics at Mount Aloysius Junior College in Cresson, PA; earlier versions were given at various medical conferences.

In revising the talks for this book, I have tried to keep the flavor of their original context, in order to keep them accessible to those who are familiar with the daily procedures of hospital work but who are not schooled in the more theoretical aspects of moral theology or moral philosophy. For those who are interested in specific theoretical issues, I have adopted the European practice of carrying on certain conversations in the reference notes. These notes also refer the reader to other sources for further analysis.

It is also for the sake of practical accessibility that I have decided on the order of the chapters. The first four chapters address the issue of forgoing treatment. Chapter one talks about the bases for the present American consensus on this question. Chapter two deals with the problem of nutrition and hydration, and offers a chance to review and apply the principles presented in chapter one. Chapter three addresses the implications of the Supreme Court decision in the *Cruzan* case, and describes advanced directives. Chapter four introduces three areas of some importance: medical futility, brain death, and the problem of mistakes and conflicts.

I had considered beginning the Grand Rounds lectures (chapters one through six) with more theoretical concerns, but decided to start with the issue which St. Francis Medical Center was addressing in developing a new policy on forgoing treatment. I was frankly afraid that I might lose part of the audience were I to start, as many lecture series do, with questions of method. I have decided to keep the same order in this book, for the same reasons.

It would be easy, however, for a teacher to use this book in the more usual way. The two chapters which deal most with history and with theory are chapters five and six. Chapter five looks at the history of medical ethics within the medical profession and moves from there to a consideration of metaethics (relativism, emotivism, natural law theory). Chapter six overviews the development of Catholic medical ethics and moves to a consideration of ethical method (physicalism and personalism, with some affinity to deontology and consequentialism) and, again, metaethics (ecclesial authority and natural law). Teachers could easily begin with these two chapters and then return to the others.

Chapters seven though ten return to more practical questions. Chapter seven is about pain; chapter eight gives some suggestions about starting ethics committees; chapter nine introduces the thorny issues of resource allocation within a just health care delivery system; the final chapter is a somewhat more theoretical look at some of the problems connected with allocation arguments.

The first three appendices come from St. Francis Medical Center. The first is the Forgoing Treatment Policy of that hospital. The second is a brochure written for patient education by Dr. Stacey Hinderliter. The third appendix is a series of guidelines written by the St. Francis Ethics Committee as helps in calling ethics consultations and carrying them out.

Appendix D is a brief essay on the ethics of condom education for AIDS prevention. Because this is not directly germane to the principle focus of the book and is of importance only for Catholic hospitals, I have included it as an appendix.

I have chosen the title of the book for three reasons. First, much of my work at St. Francis was in the Critical Care Unit, and that naturally came to form the context and inspiration for some of the issues I addressed in the Grand Rounds lectures there. Second, I have spoken on two occasions to meetings of the Society of Critical Care Medicine, and a number of physician members have noted how much this specialization has increased its attention to ethics over the past several years. Third, the word "critical" comes from the Greek "to cut," hence "to judge or to discern," "to choose in an important way." It thus has not only the more common meaning of seriously unfortunate situation, but the equally important meaning of medical and moral discernment.

Duquesne University and St. Francis Medical Center made this book possible. Duquesne supported and funded a sabbatical year and St. Francis hired me as "ethicist-in-residence." Funding for the work at St. Francis came from a number of sources, among them Glaxo Pharmaceutical Corporation and the St. Francis Auxiliary.

Many persons have helped support the project. Dr. John W. Hoyt, Director of Critical Care Medicine at St. Francis and chair of the Hospital Ethics Committee, initiated the idea of an ethicist-in-residence and secured much of the necessary funding. He has consistently supported the ethical dimensions of health care at St. Francis and in the medical societies with which he is associated. Without him this project, as well as many others of ethical importance at St. Francis, would not have happened.

Chapter One

The Catholic Tradition and the American Consensus

This chapter will describe the present American consensus concerning the ethical and legal status of forgoing medical treatment. It will trace as well the basic Roman Catholic teaching on this question, which is the source for much of the American consensus.

Over the past twenty years or so, a consensus has gradually emerged in the United States concerning the moral and legal rightness of forgoing certain medical treatments in some circumstances. This consensus is based first on a recognition that not all treatments which prolong biological life are humanly beneficial to the patient, and second on the general agreement that there is a moral difference between killing (active or direct euthanasia) and allowing to die. In the American legal system, these two ethical bases have been combined with the legal concepts of autonomy, privacy, and liberty. Together these three bases are the pillars on which a growing consensus concerning the moral and legal rightness of forgoing treatment has been built. It is true that this consensus is not yet completely accepted in all states, that some ethicists and jurists oppose certain aspects of it, and that the recent Supreme Court decision in the *Cruzan* case, while legally supporting the consensus in important ways, has also opened the door to possible changes (later chapters will return to this in greater detail). Nonetheless, the consensus has emerged within our nation to the point that it clearly represents the most widely accepted approach to the moral rightness and the legality of forgoing treatment. It is gain-

1

ing more and more support from theological, philosophical, legal, and medical communities, as well as from the general public.

The first two pillars supporting the growing consensus, that is, the distinction between morally ordinary (or mandatory) and morally extraordinary (or optional) means of treatment, and the distinction between killing and allowing to die are well established within the Roman Catholic tradition, the only tradition, religious or secular, where medical ethics was developed at any depth prior to the 1960's.[1] Indeed, it is probable that the growing American consensus would have been impossible had these concepts not already been developed.

Theological Basis: Divine Sovereignty and Human Stewardship

We can begin with a few remarks on theological context. This will be particularly helpful for Catholic hospitals, where this theological context is explicitly important, but it must be stressed at the outset that in this issue there is no major point of disagreement between the Catholic tradition and the emerging American consensus, so that those who do not accept the theological vision of the meaning of human life on which the consensus is based need not for that reason question or reject the consensus itself.

God is the creator of life. To human persons, created in God's image, God gives a responsibility of stewardship which is to be exercised in a creaturely and a co-creative manner. Human life is a gift of God, over which God, and God alone, retains ultimate sovereignty. This means that as human persons we do not have total control over the gift of life, so that we might destroy it or alter it at whim. It means also, however, that we are called to exercise initiative in our stewardship, to act courageously in relieving that human suffering which degrades, while actively accepting the pain which ennobles and the suffering which cannot rightly be avoided.

The questions of care for the dying, of prolongation of life, of prolongation of the dying process, of forgoing treatment, and of euthanasia must be seen in this context. Modern medical techniques make possible magnificent human achievements in healing.

They also make possible a lengthening of the natural process of dying, sometimes accompanied with dehumanizing sufferings. Human intervention in caring for life is governed by a concern for the value of women and men in their total human existence, as created and loved and saved by God.

I have already mentioned at least two theological principles which have often been applied to questions of care for the dying: first, God's sovereignty or control over human life; second, the meaning of human suffering as redemptive. These need some further development before we go on to more immediately practical concerns.[2]

What does it mean to say that God is sovereign over life, and that human suffering has meaning when it is joined to the redemptive suffering of Jesus? In some text books of Catholic medical ethics in past years, theological principles like these were often used as a sort of proof for the ethical judgments which the authors made. Those judgments were made for other reasons, some good, some bad. Then the fact that God is author and sovereign of life, or the idea that sometimes suffering can be humanly and supernaturally meaningful, were added as supportive reasons for the judgment. As a quick example, authors might say that abortion was wrong, and add that this is true because only God is sovereign of human life; we cannot take life ourselves. But the same authors would defend capital punishment and the just war, and in these cases God was said to delegate authority to human beings. Or, those abortions said to be indirect were permitted, even encouraged, in order to save the life of the mother, and God's sovereignty was not said to forbid them. Similarly, if a sterilization was direct it was forbidden because God alone has sovereignty over life; a woman whose health might thus be endangered was urged to accept her suffering as ennobling and redemptive. But if the sterilization could be seen as indirect, then the physician was told to go ahead and relieve the woman's suffering, since in this case God wants us to exercise some degree of active intervention in human life.[3]

Recently Catholic moralists have criticized this way of making moral judgments.[4] They have tended to be less clear about how to distinguish direct from indirect. They have also been slower to claim to know exactly what it means to say that God is sovereign over human life. Does it mean that God wants us to do nothing at all about human life? Surely not. Does it mean that God wants us never to kill, that all killings are morally wrong? Some think this is true, but most of us accept the moral rightness of killing in self-defense, for example. And what does it mean to say that suffering is redemptive? Surely not that we ought never try to alleviate it— Jesus Himself did this often. So today we are less apt to apply this kind of theological concept simplistically or directly to a medical-ethical question, as if these quite important theological principles could solve our ethical dilemmas.

Yet the principles remain important. How? I would argue that they tell us something about the way we, as human beings, are related to God as Creator. But when we use them this way, we see that our Faith-tradition is clearly ambi-valent, or bi-valent, in what they mean. They pull us both ways. We are, after all, both crea-tures and co-agents with God. We are created in God's image, with at least a partial dominion (stewardship may be a better word) over life and over the world we live in. We are called both to find meaning in human suffering and to alleviate it when it is right to do so. Theological principles like these are helps for us to understand what human life means. They ought to keep us from easy answers and urge us to realize that we are asked by God to do some things and not to do others. They help us know what kind of "thing" the human person is in relation to God. They do not give us answers to our ethical questions.

This is important when it comes to dealing with dying patients. We are asked to do some things, but not all things. God gives us some authority, but not total authority. We are asked to find meaning in suffering, but not to worship it. We are not called merely to sit back in resignation to God's will, but are called to co-operate with God in alleviating human misery. Theology thus provides a base for understanding who we are, even when theological principles like these cannot give clear answers to our dilemmas.

Sanctity and Quality of Life

Thus many of today's Catholic moralists argue, and I agree, that it is not ethically responsible to attempt an answer to the serious questions of care for the dying on the basis of simplistic or one-rubric ethical arguments. This is to disrespect the magnificence of human life as created and sustained by God. The moral approach which I propose is a critique of two positions which occupy opposite ends of a spectrum, and which both tend to be reductionist—that is, to reduce what is complex to what is facile. The first of these positions is an extreme version of the "sanctity of life" position, a version which permits no cessation of efforts to prolong life, and which supports "vitalism," the theory that life itself is the greatest possible value, to be sustained at all costs. Catholic moral theology has seldom if ever embraced this position. I have found it in some approaches to dying, and surveys have indicated that some physicians find this approach compatible with what they perceive as their medical role, though this is far from universal among doctors and has clearly changed over the past two decades.

The second position is a totally lax version of the "quality of life" position, a version which permits cessation of treatment, and even active killing, for the most trivial and even hedonistic of motives. No Catholic moralist to my knowledge has accepted this position, nor has the Catholic tradition. The reductionist argument that the morality of abortion depends solely on the woman's choice, the argument that infants with virtually any handicap should be let die, the approach to suffering which denies it human value, and the position that the morality of suicide is purely a personal matter are typical of the other extreme view, where nearly any reduction in the quality of our lives is seen as a morally valid reason for ending them.

The Roman Catholic tradition has recognized *both* the sanctity of life—life is indeed sacred—*and* the ethical import of at least some degree of quality of life—life need not be prolonged under all circumstances, that is, at some point a lack of the ability to carry out the humanly meaningful purposes of life, which some would call a lack of quality of life, means that life can be let go.[5] Thus Catholic moralists who argue against a one-rubric approach to these questions find ourselves in continuity with the Catholic tradition, though some of us would question that tradition when it absolutely forbids certain kinds of intervention under all circumstances. We will return to this last question later.

When we move from the general context to specific questions, we find that examination of these complex questions by Catholic medical moralists has not led to any one, universally accepted set of answers, and moralists differ among themselves concerning specific points in both their argumentation and their conclusions. There are, however, general directions shared by most ethicists, and I think it accurate to say that the vast majority of Catholic moralists agree that the Catholic tradition supports the basic American consensus on forgoing treatment.

We will prescind here from the question of the "definition" of death, more accurately named the problem of the "moment of death." Chapter four will address this question in the context of brain-death. For now we can assume that we are dealing with living, though sick and probably dying people, not the already dead. In those cases where respiration and heartbeat are maintained by machines, if the criteria of total brain-death are met, there is not a dying person, but a corpse. No treatment is required; indeed, none is permitted. The only responsibility is that of the respect due the body of what was a human person.

Ordinary and Extraordinary Means

Now we can turn to the two pillars found in Roman Catholic ethics on which the emerging American consensus is based.

First, the Roman Catholic tradition has long recognized a distinction between ordinary and extraordinary means of prolonging or preserving life. The distinction, at least implicitly, goes back several centuries,[6] though it is most often attributed to Pope Pius XII, who repeated it and stressed it during his pontificate in the 1940's and 1950's.

According to this tradition, it is never obligatory to make use of medical measures which are morally "extraordinary" in order to preserve life. The distinction between ordinary and extraordinary is a useful one within the Catholic tradition, and I am hesitant to abandon it even in the face of some criticism. Critics do have a point, however, when they argue that the words used, "ordinary" and "extraordinary," are open to misinterpretation if the distinction is understood as a medical one.[7] It is rather a moral distinction, and there are no simple technical or statistical criteria for determining the difference.

Means that are usually thought of as *medically* ordinary (no longer experimental, normal hospital procedures in some cases, not requiring IRB protocol approval) may be *morally* extraordinary. Thus what would be an ordinary or reasonable means when used in caring for a person whose chance of renewed health is great would become extraordinary in the care of a patient who has no chance or possibly even little chance of recovery. There is no moral obligation to preserve life at all costs.

Many factors must be weighed in this decision: the chance of success, the degree of invasiveness, pain, and patient fear, the patient's readiness for death, the needs of others, and even the financial cost to family and society (the context in all of this, of course, is that the patient decides to forgo these extraordinary means—using financial and social criteria is very risky when surrogates make the decision[8]). Even the sense of modesty or shame that women of previous centuries were said to have felt when being examined by male physicians was sufficient reason, for some moralists of past centuries, to call such an examination an extraordinary means, and to permit these women to neglect all medical treatment. We need here to remember, of course, that in those days doctors were as apt to kill as to cure, and there was far less likelihood that the examination and treatment would do any good. The point is, however, that the distinction between ordinary and extraordinary means as developed and applied within the Catholic tradition is very wide and very flexible.

This, then, is the first pillar on which the current American consensus is based. People do not have a moral obligation to preserve their lives if the means needed to do so offer little benefit or impose significant burden. The moral obligation to which this principle speaks is, of course, that of the patient. The patient is morally obliged to use ordinary or reasonable means of preserving life and not morally obliged to use extraordinary ones. But it clearly has implications for hospital practice. If a patient is not obliged to use every possible means of preserving life, then hospitals and health care practitioners may not impose them on patients. The fact that such a distinction was developed within Catholic medical ethics has been important in support of the consensus now emerging in our country.

Killing and Allowing to Die—Euthanasia

The second pillar on which this consensus is based is the distinction between killing and allowing to die, which, in the medical ethics context, has been provided by the Catholic tradition in its analysis through the principle of double effect.

According to this distinction, the direct killing of an innocent person is never morally right, but allowing to die is sometimes morally right. Some would now question the absoluteness of this distinction; that is, some now argue that direct killing (active euthanasia or assisted suicide) may be morally right in some cases. But the acceptance until recently of this basic distinction has helped form both American medical practice and American law.

The word "euthanasia" generally means doing something which brings about a "good" death in a person who is hopelessly ill and/or who is suffering pain or other burdens from an illness. There are five different kinds of actions to be considered.

First, one may decide not to use certain medical means which would prolong life (for example, not to use a ventilator for a terminally ill patient or not to resuscitate a patient who suffers from some severe illness). If the means in question is indeed "extraordinary," the act (the decision not to use the means) is generally accepted as moral.

Second, one may decide to stop the use of a means which has already been begun (to turn off the ventilator, to "pull the plug," to "do a terminal wean"). Catholic moral tradition has generally seen this action to be the equivalent of the first. Morally, assuming the treatment can rightly be called "extraordinary," it is the non-use of extraordinary means, and is normal procedure in many hospitals. Legally this second kind of action is sometimes considered more dangerous, more open to legal repercussion or at least to malpractice litigation, as it is physically the actual doing of something, rather than the simple non-doing of it. But morally it is indeed the non-doing of extraordinary treatment, and in most American jurisdictions the courts are now recognizing that the second action is legally the equivalent of the first. This has been supported by the Supreme Court in the *Cruzan* decision.

Unfortunately, the word "euthanasia" is sometimes applied to the second case, and even to the first. Though moralists often speak of "negative euthanasia" or, more technically within Roman Catholic moral theology, "indirect euthanasia" to refer either to the first or the second case, it seems to me far better not to use the word "euthanasia" to apply to either of them. It is less confusing if we reserve this word for the actual killing of patients. Neither withholding nor withdrawing morally extraordinary (that is, morally optional) medical treatments are acts of killing. Rather they allow the patient to die of the underlying disease when treatment is of great burden or of little benefit. The Catholic tradition considers them morally equivalent, all other things being equal. The emerging American ethical and legal consensus agrees with this judgment.

Third, one may take positive means aimed at relieving the patient's suffering, but not directly intended to cause death. The distinction is sometimes medically difficult to make, as increasing doses of a sedative may shorten life. But it is certainly a moral act to relieve pain, again all things being equal, and this sort of medication cannot be considered ethically wrong. Consideration must be given, however, to the patient's wishes, ability to stand pain, desire for consciousness, and readiness for death. The Catholic tradition would tend to call this third kind of action, like the first two, indirect euthanasia. It is sometimes called "double effect euthanasia." The act itself is not a killing, but a giving of medication which relieves pain. The intention is not to relieve pain by bringing death, by killing, but rather to relieve pain even though death may "indirectly" result. This act, like the first two, may well be morally right, according to the Catholic moral tradition. And, in the American legal and ethical consensus, the same judgment is made.

Fourth, one may act in conjunction with the patient by assisting the patient in active euthanasia. The patient wishes to kill him or herself, and makes this known to the health care practitioner, asking the practitioner to provide the necessary means. The patient actually consumes the drug. This is assisted suicide in the strict sense. It is active euthanasia, and involves direct killing. In the

Catholic tradition, and until recently in the American moral consensus, it is judged to be always morally wrong. In addition, assisting in suicide is illegal in most, though not in all, American jurisdictions.[9]

Fifth, the health care practitioner may take action directly intended to bring about death. This, like the fourth action, is referred to as "positive euthanasia," "active euthanasia," or, within the Catholic tradition, sometimes as "direct" euthanasia. It is a "direct" killing according to the principle of double effect as that principle was developed by moralists up to the middle of this century, and is illegal in all American jurisdictions.

A further analysis of the distinction between killing and allowing to die will be helpful, especially in the current American context, since the absoluteness of this distinction is being more and more questioned by Americans, and even by some Catholic ethicists. This discussion does not pertain directly to current hospital practice, since the policy at all American hospitals, at least publicly, is that killing, or "active euthanasia," is never permitted. It will nonetheless be helpful to deal briefly with this issue since citizens will need to make political decisions about this question, and these decisions will have serious implications for American hospitals.

In my judgment, and in the judgment of most ethicists, there is an important moral difference between the fourth and fifth kinds of actions and the first three. But there is some question as to whether or not this distinction is sufficient by itself to make all acts of positive or active euthanasia morally wrong. Many ethicists think that the distinction can carry this weight. According to this position, the first three kinds of actions, withholding and withdrawing treatment and sedating from pain, are considered morally right in those cases where it is reasonable to do so. But actual killing, either in patient suicide or by the killing action of the physician or other practitioner, is judged to be always morally wrong.

The Catholic tradition has made this difference definitive and has argued consistently, and, until recently, rather universally against such direct killing. I will not attempt here an analysis of the double effect principle, detailing the exact specifications of how the direct-indirect distinctions were made, though an understanding of that principle is necessary for a grasp of the official Catholic position on this and on many other issues.[10]

However, a fair number of today's Catholic moralists would argue that this difference between direct and indirect, as specified by the principle of double effect, is not important enough to warrant the conclusion that all such direct actions are intrinsically immoral. Some now argue that once the dying process is irreversibly begun the difference loses some of its moral weight, so that distinctions between forgoing treatment or sedation and positive euthanasia are no longer of themselves morally definitive. The difference is still of moral importance, but it cannot be the sole criterion for the absolute forbidding of "positive euthanasia." To do so is to reason from one-rubric arguments, to limit the process of moral reasoning to one set of criteria which cannot of themselves carry the burden.[11]

This opening to the possible moral rightness of active euthanasia is, of course, a quite restricted one. In theological terms positive euthanasia as morally right would be limited to those cases where the process of dying has become the person's vocation, where cooperation with the call of the creating and loving God means a positive human co-creative joining with the letting-go of physical life. God's basic gift to us is life, not death. We should hesitate lest we accede too easily to a letting-go of this gift.

But what about the legalization of "active" euthanasia? Even those who argue that in some cases active euthanasia may be morally right do not necessarily want it to be made legal. There are still valid reasons for insisting on very strict legal limitations to the practice, and possibly for insisting that no changes in the law be made in this regard. Any increase in the number of exceptions to the general principle against killing makes other exceptions easier. Human life is of great value. When a society decides to legalize certain kinds of killing, there is an ever-increased chance that the society will extend such permission even further. Our nation has decided that killing is legally permitted in properly declared wars (and often in never-declared "actions" of various kinds), in court-ordered capital punishment, in abortion, in self-defense, and in some circumstances in defense of private property attacked criminally. Active euthanasia is not the same kind of killing as these others, but to permit it legally would add one further allowable exception to the law forbidding killing.

In addition, it must be emphasized that the distinction between killing and allowing to die has been one of the pillars on which the present American consensus which legally permits the forgoing of treatment is based. The absolute legal prohibition of active euthanasia thus serves as one protective barrier against going too far and stands as a valid argument against those who think that forgoing treatment is itself euthanasia. If we remove that barrier, there may be fear on the part of some that we have gone too far already. There may, in other words, be a backlash against the present consensus that forgoing treatment is in many cases legally and morally right. The legalization of active euthanasia may actually lead politically to a restriction of the present consensus. Furthermore, it is very likely that the conditions placed on active euthanasia, similar to those in effect in the Netherlands, would require legal involvement in the clinical decision, something which the present consensus is trying to avoid.[12]

Another reason against the legalization of active euthanasia concerns the integrity of the medical profession. Doctors are not now allowed to kill their patients. Permission to do this might well lead to mistrust on the part of some patients.

But there are arguments on the other side. The principal one is that if euthanasia is morally right in some cases, it ought to be legally right as well. We often hear of court cases where juries find family members innocent of killing their suffering relatives even though they admit having done so. And some are jailed for actions which seem to most of us to be those of a distraught and loving relative and possibly even acts of moral courage. It is clear that the law is not able to deal adequately with certain exceptional cases. If legislation is ever enacted legalizing positive euthanasia, it must limit the practice to those cases where the patient has entered the dying process, has become terminally ill in the immediate sense and in such a way that recovery is virtually impossible. Given the dangers even of this kind of legislation, however, it may be better to leave the law as it now is concerning positive or active euthanasia.

Privacy, Autonomy, and Liberty

We have now finished our brief survey of the first two pillars supporting the present American consensus on forgoing treatment, the two which are based in Catholic theology. The third supporting pillar is the American legal concept of privacy, autonomy, and liberty.[13] In most American jurisdictions, this concept has been interpreted to mean that patients who are capable of making decisions of this type may refuse treatment even against the advice of their physician. The patient has the right of autonomy to choose and of privacy to be left alone. Similarly, the courts in most cases have decided that patients not capable of making decisions may also refuse through surrogate decision makers. The precise relationship between this third pillar (the notion of privacy and autonomy) and the other two is not yet theoretically clear, though in most jurisdictions the practical judgments rendered have led to a growing consistency of outcomes.

Not theoretically clear is the question of what legal implications follow from the distinction between reasonable and unreasonable (or ordinary and extraordinary) treatment. The issues are complex, and we have no time to explore them in any depth here, though we will return to them when addressing the implications of the *Cruzan* case in chapter three. Remember that the *moral* obligation to use reasonable means to preserve life falls primarily on the patient him or herself. What if a patient deemed capable of making such decisions chooses to forgo a means of treatment which, in any reasonable judgment, is "ordinary," beneficial, inexpensive, and of little burden. I come to a hospital with a pain which physicians diagnose as appendicitis, but, after admission, I refuse permission for surgery. What moral obligation does this bring to the health care institution and practitioner? Should this have any bearing on the court's decisions or on the legality of forgoing treatment?

In practical terms, courts have tended to resolve such questions by upholding the right of patients to refuse for themselves with little or no insistence on the distinction between reasonable and unreasonable treatments. Of course the very fact that a person refuses a treatment which seems reasonable *might* be an indication that that person lacks capacity to decide. But it might not be, as, for example, in the case of a person who refuses treatment for religious reasons. The treatment is reasonable or "ordinary" for most of us, but most unreasonable, even repugnant, for the patient. The right to refuse has prevailed in those cases where the patient is capable of deciding. And the distinction between morally mandatory and morally optional treatment has generally not been a factor.

But in those cases where the patient is not able to choose, and the decision is made by a surrogate, the courts have required that the decision be in the best interests of the patient, that is, that reasonable treatment be given. For example, an infant with Down's Syndrome ought ethically and legally to be given basic life-saving treatment. The presence of this illness is not enough by itself to allow parents to decide to let their child die. Similarly, courts have ordered children of Jehovah's Witnesses to be transfused and have convicted Christian Science parents when medical neglect results in a child's death. But infants with truly disastrous multiple neurological disorders which would virtually eliminate any possibility of fulfilling the purposes of life need not be given life-saving treatment.

In deciding on what treatment is reasonable and what is not, the distinction between morally ordinary and morally extraordinary is helpful. But it must be remembered that the original context for that distinction presumed that the patient was the one making the decision. Certain morally extraordinary treatments might rightly be forgone by the choice of the patient and yet be wrongly forgone by decision of a surrogate. The ordinary-extraordinary distinction is, as we have noted, very flexible. It properly tells us that life need not be sustained at great burden or for little benefit. But a greater degree of unreasonableness must be shown before a surrogate can morally or legally decide to forgo a treatment than must be shown before a patient can morally decide to forgo a treatment (remember that a capable patient can *legally* decide to forgo just about any treatment). I can rightly decide for myself to withhold an expensive but quite beneficial treatment so that my children may inherit. The present legal consensus does not permit my children to make that decision for me, nor does the present ethical consensus say that it would be right for them to do so.[14]

If the patient has left an explicit order, that order should ordinarily be seen as the patient's wishes, and the surrogate should follow it, though if the order asks that eminently reasonable treatment be forgone, hospitals are properly reluctant to comply until the legality of the directive is established. In cases where the patient has made his or her wishes known, the standard to be followed is known as the substituted judgment standard. The surrogate makes the judgment which the patient would have made, since the patient's wishes are known. We will return to this question when we speak of advanced directives in chapter three. If the patient's wishes are not known, the surrogate should follow the best interests standard.[15]

In general, then, capable patients may legally refuse virtually any treatment. Surrogates may refuse only those treatments which are of little benefit or of great burden (best interests standard), or which the patient, while capable of deciding, decided against (substituted judgment standard).

Hospitals policies on forgoing treatment should be based on this emerging American consensus. That consensus is not yet perfect, but it is far enough along to allow hospitals and health care personnel to set general directions for ethical decision-making. Doubtless there will be cases, as there have been in the past, where people will differ about how the various distinctions and legal concepts apply. But there are also cases, quite probably the majority of cases, where the emerging consensus and the ethical principles on which it is based enable us to come to ethically right and legally accepted decisions about continuing or forgoing treatment.

Discussion Questions

1. What do you think the role of theology is in medical ethics? Do such notions as God's dominion over life or the redemptive meaning of suffering have any implications for health care?

2. Which of the two positions, sanctity of life or quality of life, is closer to your own? Or do you think that both are important?

3. What is the difference between "ordinary" and "extraordinary" treatment? Do we need such a distinction? Why or why not?

4. Discuss how each of the five different kinds of actions fit into the distinction between killing and allowing to die. Is active euthanasia always morally wrong? Should it be made legal?

5. What should be the legal difference between when a patient decides and when a surrogate decides? Discuss the difference between the best interests standard and the substituted judgment standard.

Endnotes

1. Medical ethics is also found with the Jewish tradition. Unlike Catholic medical ethics, however, the Jewish tradition has not generally attempted to develop the entire spectrum of issues. Nor has it tried to convince others that its position is based on reason (natural law); hence its influence has been largely limited to the Jewish community, especially to Orthodox Judaism. See Albert R. Jonsen and Stephen Toulmin, *The Abuse of Casuistry: A History of Moral Reasoning* (Berkeley: Univ. of California Press, 1988), pp. 55-58.

2. I have developed these issues further elsewhere. See *The Emergence of Roman Catholic Medical Ethics in North America* (New York: Edwin Mellen Press, 1979), pp. 436-447; "Roman Catholic Medical Ethics and the Ethos of Modern Medicine," *Ephemerides Theologicae Lovanienses*, 49 (1983), 65-67; "Individualism and Corporatism in a Personalist Ethic: An Analysis of Organ Transplants," in Joseph A. Selling, ed., *Personalist Morals: Essays in Honor of Professor Louis Janssens* (Louvain: Univ. of Louvain Press, 1988), pp. 162-164; *A Theological Basis for Health Care and Health Care Ethics*, Special Publications of the National Association of Catholic Chaplains, 1, No. 3 (NACC: 1985), pp. 57- 63.

3. For more detail and many examples see *The Emergence of Roman Catholic Medical Ethics*, pp. 232-235, and chapters four and five.

4. See *The Emergence*, pp. 436-447.

5. On the problematic nature of the term "quality of life," see Thomas A. Shannon and James J. Walter, "The PVS Patient and the Forgoing/Withdrawing of Medical Nutrition and Hydration," *Theological Studies*, 49 (1988), 623-647.

6. Alphonse Liguori argues in the 18th century that no one is obliged to use "extraordinary means," and cites previous moralists as holding the same view; the first to make the distinction may have been Banez in 1583 (see John J. Paris, "When Burdens of Feeding Outweigh Benefits," *Hastings Center Report*, 16, No. 1 (Feb., 1986), 31-32).

7. Other terms have been suggested and are in general usage, but I have not found a pair which exactly replaces the nuances of "ordinary" and "extraordinary." "Reasonable" and "unreasonable" work in some cases, but not in others. "Unreasonable" implies that the treatment is irrational. So we might want to argue that unreasonable treatment, since it is unreasonable, ought *not* be given, whereas "extraordinary" means that the patient *may* choose to reject the treatment, not that he or she should reject it. "Proportionate" and "disproportionate" suffer from the same problem, as well as from the difficulty of implying a methodology with which some Catholic theologians disagree. "Heroic" treatment might work, but "non-heroic" is awkward, and these terms suffer from the same problem as do the more traditional "ordinary" and "extraordinary," since they might imply that medical criteria determine the difference. Some wish to avoid pair-terms altogether, and speak only of the right to privacy when a patient decides, and of the best interests of the patient and of substituted judgment when surrogates decide. But this is to restrict the issue to the legal aspects and to the ethics of the law, ignoring what the Catholic tradition has properly included, the moral rightness and wrongness of the decision itself. Much of this will reappear later in this and other chapters.

8. The majority opinion now is that family and societal costs should not be considered if the decision is made by a surrogate. I have no doubt but that in the future third party payors will refuse to pay for treatment ordered by patients or by surrogates which can legitimately be called unreasonable. In addition, society may rightly decide not to fund certain classes of medical procedures; see chapter eight.

9. Attempted suicide itself occupies a strange legal status in American law. In the strict sense, it is not itself criminal; that is, no American jurisdictions list it as a crime. Yet it, along with suicide itself (the penalty was forfeiture of estate to be inherited

and ignominious burial), was criminal according to common law. Aiding and abetting suicide is still a crime by statute in most states, though not in all. See Alan Meisel, *The Right to Die* (New York: John Wiley & Sons, 1989), p. 65. To some considerable degree the old common law retains influence and makes the issue confusing. For example, police officers are bound by their job to try to stop suicide attempts if they see them, based on societal opposition as well as on the presumption that persons who attempt to kill themselves are unable to make a rational decision. In addition, persons who attempt suicide may be confined for psychiatric observation, under the presumption that their attempts at suicide prove they are mentally incompetent. In the strict sense, however, attempting suicide is no longer criminal.

10. Some further description will be given in chapter six. For a complete analysis in the context of medical ethics, see *The Emergence of Roman Catholic Medical Ethics*, esp. the first half of Chapter four.

11. Two important arguments for this position, though differing greatly between themselves, are Charles E. Curran, *Politics, Medicine, and Christian Ethics: A Dialogue with Paul Ramsey* (Philadelphia: Fortress, 1983), pp. 161-162; and Daniel C. Maguire, *Death By Choice* (Garden City, NY: Doubleday, 1973).

12. These arguments are made by Susan Wolf, "Holding the Line on Euthanasia," *Hastings Center Report*, Special Supplement, January/February, 1989, pp. 13-15. Unfortunately, the *Cruzan* decision has opened the door to precisely this kind of legislative interference. See chapter three.

13. There is much controversy over what to call this. Some argue for a "right to privacy"; others prefer to speak of a common law liberty to be free from unwanted medical treatment. I think this latter approach is preferable. We will return to the issue in the next two chapters.

14. Chapter eight will return to this issue. Note in this general context that there is a reason why the terms "reasonable" and "unreasonable" are not exact equivalents for "ordinary" and "extraordinary," at least as these latter have been developed in the Catholic tradition. The move toward eliminating them may be influenced by the fact that most hospital ethics is understandably interested in

what the hospital or the physicians may rightly do, whereas the Catholic tradition is equally interested in what the individual patient may rightly do, that is, whether or not it is morally right for the patient to forgo a life-prolonging procedure.

15. For further detail, see Ruth Macklin, *Mortal Choices* (Boston: Houghton Mifflin, 1987), pp. 99-129.

Chapter Two

Forgoing Treatment: Nutrition and Hydration

The ethical issue of withholding and withdrawing medical nutrition and hydration, whether by naso-gastric feeding, gastrostomy tube, or intra-venous lines, involves a specific application of the general principles developed in the first chapter. Because these principles are basic to the entire issue of forgoing treatment, I will begin this chapter with a review of what we have already seen.

The Basic Consensus

There are three pillars or bases for the present American consensus on forgoing treatment. The first pillar is the distinction, long applied by Roman Catholic medical ethics, between "ordinary" and "extraordinary" means of treatment. Persons are obliged to take "ordinary" or "reasonable" or "proportionate" means to preserve or prolong their lives, but not "extraordinary" or "unreasonable" or "disproportionate" means. The distinction is a moral one and not a medical one. Thus what might be a reasonable or ordinary treatment for a person who has a decent chance of recovery might well be unreasonable or extraordinary for a person whose chance of recovery is less. The obligation to use ordinary means rests with the person him or herself.

The second pillar is the distinction between killing (euthanasia) and allowing to die. Legally, killing a patient is criminal, and the Catholic tradition has held that to kill an innocent person, as for example in euthanasia, is always morally wrong. When it is appropriate to withhold treatment, the withholding may be followed by the patient's death. But it is the disease which kills the patient. Withholding is thus allowing to die, not killing. The same is true of withdrawing treatment. The two are morally equivalent, other things being equal. Finally, sedation for pain may hasten the actual moment of death, but is not considered killing when the intention is to reduce pain. Thus forgoing treatment, whether by withholding or by withdrawing, and sedation from pain are not the same as active euthanasia. They are by no means always right, but they may be right, and often are right. On the other hand, killing the patient by direct euthanasia is illegal and is considered always wrong according to traditional Catholic moral theology. "Assisting" in the patient's self-inflicted suicide is illegal in most states and is similarly forbidden by the Catholic tradition.

The third pillar is the American legal concept of privacy and autonomy, and of liberty to refuse treatment. In most American jurisdictions this concept has been held to mean that patients capable of deciding may forgo just about any treatment. Patients not capable of deciding may have this decision made by surrogates. When a surrogate makes the decision, it must be made in the patient's best interests, or as the patient would have decided if the patient were able (substituted judgment based on known wishes of the patient). The best interests standard translates in some sense back into the difference between reasonable and unreasonable treatment. Whereas a patient may him or herself forgo reasonable treatment, surrogates may choose to forgo only unreasonable or clearly "extraordinary" means of preserving life.

The Problem of Nutrition

With this very brief summary concluded, we can turn to the question of artificial nutrition and hydration.

Recently there has been a good deal of controversy over whether or not nourishment and hydration can ever be omitted or discontinued for a dying or comatose patient, or for one who is in "a persistent vegetative state."[1]

A consensus is now emerging that such treatment can be omitted, that it is a medical treatment which, like other treatments, may properly be forgone in some cases. The *Cruzan* decision of the Supreme Court has upheld this opinion. But there has been some considerable controversy along the way, and some ethicists and some jurisdictions have not agreed with the emerging consensus. A look at this issue, and in particular, at some of the cases which the courts have decided concerning it, will allow us a focus for further studying the interplay of the three pillars which form the basis of the current American consensus concerning forgoing treatment.

There are technical questions concerning the means used to give nourishment and hydration; there are ethical questions as to which means are "morally ordinary" and therefore obligatory for the patient, and which are "morally extraordinary" and therefore optional; and there are legal questions as to which means are always required in the law, which may be omitted and when, and who may make the decision. This question is one which many hospitals and chronic care facilities face often, and it is a good test case for the meaning of "ordinary" and "extraordinary" in our care of the dying.

It is important at the start to stress that the issue is medical nutrition and hydration, not ordinary food and water. Feeding the hungry and giving drink to the thirsty can never be withheld or withdrawn. Eating and drinking, food and water, have important symbolic meanings for humans. They connote dining, human relation, and, for Christians, the Eucharist. But this language is not appropriate in the context we are examining. For these reasons it is better to use the proper words, medical nutrition and hydration, than the words used for non-medical nourishment.

The *Brophy* Case

A court case which is particularly helpful in analyzing these issues is the case of Paul Brophy, a Massachusetts firefighter. Like Karen Ann Quinlan, Brophy was diagnosed as being in a "persistent vegetative state." This is technically different from a coma in that the coma victim is "asleep," that is, the eyes are closed, whereas the person in a "persistent vegetative state" has sleep-wake cycles and is therefore at times physically "awake" (the eyes are open), but is always totally unaware of anything in the environment. For most purposes, assuming the diagnosis is correct, the distinction between irreversible coma and persistent vegetative state is morally irrelevant. The word "persistent" means that this is constant and that there is virtually no hope for change.[2] Both Quinlan and Brophy were in this state.[3]

The difference between Quinlan and Brophy was that Quinlan received ventilation along with nutrition whereas Brophy received only nutrition, which was provided by a gastrostomy tube.[4] In the *Quinlan* case, the New Jersey court held that the ventilator might be removed, and also held that this should not usually be a court decision. Rather a family member was appointed guardian and was given authority, in conjunction with any ethics committee which the hospital might have, to turn off the ventilator.[5] Most ethicists have applauded the *Quinlan* decision for its conclusion, and I agree. This kind of decision ought very seldom to be a court decision,[6] and the New Jersey Supreme Court made this clear when it overturned the decision of the Superior Court which had refused to allow Karen's father Joseph Quinlan to discontinue ventilation. The State Supreme Court relied on Karen's right of privacy as a basis for her freedom from this kind of procedure.[7]

But what about Brophy? Here Judge David Kopelman of the Norfolk County Probate Court in Massachusetts refused to allow Brophy's wife Patricia to stop nourishment by the gastrostomy tube. The court made a number of judgments which many ethicists have criticized, though some have supported one or another of them.[8]

First, the court stated that even though Brophy had said over and over again that he would never want this kind of treatment, he had to have it anyway. (Brophy had actually thrown away a commendation he received for saving a man from a burning car since the man had later died, and Brophy had judged this kind of treatment to be useless. He had commented to his wife that he never wanted to be like Karen Ann Quinlan.)

Second, the court ruled that it would have been right not to insert the gastrostomy tube in the first place (in ethical terms, I suppose the judge felt that this was "extraordinary" since it was clearly invasive), but that once the stoma had been created, the nourishment is a procedure of maintenance only (in ethical terms, he might have used the term "ordinary"), and must be continued.

That is, the judge insisted on a moral and legal difference between withholding and withdrawing.

Finally, the judge stated that removing feeding is different from removing ventilation, since removing ventilation does not include necessarily the intent to terminate life, whereas removing nourishment does. In the ethical terminology we have already seen, he might have said that removing a ventilator is "allowing to die," whereas removing a gastrostomy tube is active euthanasia or "direct" killing.

Four Questions

But was the judge correct in his opinions? In my judgment and in that of most ethicists and jurists, the clear answer is no. There are four questions involved. First, is stopping different from not starting? Second, is a gastrostomy tube ethically different from a ventilator? Third, is this euthanasia, that is, is it "killing" as opposed to "allowing to die"? Fourth, who decides questions like this one?

First, is there a difference between not doing a procedure in the first place (not creating a stoma and inserting the tube) and stopping a procedure that has been started (removing the tube and stopping nourishment)? The judge clearly thought so. With few if any exceptions, ethicists do not recognize that kind of distinction as a *moral* distinction.[9]

The Roman Catholic tradition does not recognize this distinction, though some Catholics seem to think it does. Look at what would happen if we insisted on the difference. A person is brought to the emergency room, and the health care team cannot determine easily whether or not the patient can recover if resuscitation procedures are begun. So they begin them. The result is later found to be merely a prolongation of the dying process, not a treatment which will result in recovery to meaningful human living. If it is now morally wrong to stop what was started, medical professionals would be caught in an impossible ethical bind. Either they don't start treatment, and fail to cure some patients, or they start and then are required to continue useless measures for large numbers of patients. The Catholic tradition, with the distinctions we have discussed, has been able to avoid this bind. As we saw earlier, there is no moral difference between stopping and not starting. If the treatment is "extraordinary," it is right to decide not to start it; it is also right to stop it once started. The American ethical consensus has come to agree with this. So the judge was wrong.

Second, is a gastrostomy tube morally different from a ventilator? That is, is a gastrostomy tube an "ordinary means" of supplying nutrition and hydration, while a ventilator is an "extraordinary means" of supplying air? There is some controversy about this among Catholic moralists, but it is clear that the main line of the Catholic tradition has argued that this kind of nourishment, along with IV feeding and other methods of nutrition and hydration, are indeed "extraordinary" in cases like this one. As we have noted, it is important to remember that the distinction is not as such medical or technical, but moral. Medical procedures which would be quite "ordinary" in some situations, where they might be reasonably expected to help, are clearly "extraordinary," even "unreasonable" in other cases, and the example of Paul Brophy is a case of this kind. "Artificial" feeding and hydration in this kind of situation are "extraordinary." They are not the same as offering food and water to a starving or dehydrated person. Indeed, in those cases where nutrition and/or hydration are needed for patient comfort, they must always be given.

Jesuit moralist Gerald Kelly, perhaps the foremost medical ethicist of the 1950's, and accepted by all Catholic moralists as being consistent with official Church teaching (he never allowed direct sterilization or active euthanasia, for example), clearly stated that artificial feeding may be discontinued.[10] This is clearly permitted by Catholic medical ethics. And, once again, the American ethical tradition has accepted this judgment.

This gives us the answer as well to the third question, whether or not the judge was right in arguing that the intentionality of stopping feeding had to be "to kill," that is, in ethical terms, whether he was right in implying that this was "direct" euthanasia. In my judgment, and in that of most other moralists, including what I believe to be a strong majority of Catholic moral theologians,[11] this was not direct euthanasia, but was instead the stopping of an extraordinary and unreasonable means of preserving life. In cases like this, it is the disease which kills the patient, not the forgoing of treatment.[12] The Catholic position is that this is not "direct" euthanasia, and therefore forbidden, but that it is "allowing to die," that it is the non-use of morally extraordinary means, and that in cases like this one, it is permissible. Indeed, in this particular case, where Brophy had clearly stated he did not want this type of treatment, it is in my opinion morally *required* to stop it. There is still some controversy about this.[13] But I am convinced that the Catholic tradition has proposed that in cases like Brophy's medically induced nutrition and hydration may be forgone.[14] And this proposal has become, with some disagreement still remaining, part of the growing American consensus about this issue.

We can now ask the fourth and final question, the question of who decides. But first, it is interesting to note what finally happened to Paul Brophy. The decision of the Probate Court was appealed. The Massachusetts Supreme Court overturned the decision of the lower court and ruled that the gastrostomy tube might legally be removed, though it refused to compel doctors to remove it. The tube was indeed removed on October 15, 1986, and Brophy died on October 23, three and a half years after he had first lapsed into coma, and some two years after his wife had first asked that the gastrostomy nourishment be stopped.[15] Most cases have been similarly resolved, some more quickly, some not (for example, New Jersey's Nancy *Jobes* case, Danbury Connecticut's Carol *McConnell* case, Pennsylvania's *Jane Doe* case, and a large number of others). But two cases have gone against the consensus (Missouri's Nancy *Cruzan* case, which has now been decided by the U. S. Supreme Court, and New York's Mary *O'Connor* case, both of which required an explicit patient statement before treatment might be forgone).[16] We will return to the *Cruzan* case in the next chapter.

Now for the fourth question. Who is best able to make the decision? Morally, and legally, if the patient is competent the patient decides. This does not mean that the patient will always make the morally right decision. The patient may make the morally wrong decision. I may refuse a certain procedure even though it is a morally ordinary, and hence mandatory means of preserving my life. But if I am capable of making this decision, it is legally clear that no one may force me to have the treatment. The

Supreme Court's decision in *Cruzan* upheld this. And this kind of law is morally right. That is, the established common-law liberty to refuse medical treatment is based on sound moral grounds. So there is both legal and ethical precedent for saying that the patient who is capable of making this kind of decision ought to be legally able to refuse any and all treatment.[17] The adult Jehovah's Witness ought to be legally able to refuse blood transfusions even at the risk of death.[18] The question in cases like *Quinlan* and *Brophy* has to do with patients who are not able to decide. Now who makes the decision?

In the *Quinlan* case, the court said that Karen's father, together with an "ethics committee" if such existed at the hospital, should decide. I think this is correct. In the *Brophy* case, the probate court rejected the idea that Paul's wife, Patricia, could decide. The Supreme Court of Massachusetts overruled the substance of the decision, deciding that the feeding tube might be removed, but did not rule, as in *Quinlan*, that the family should be the ones to decide. And in a similar Massachusetts case, the *Saikewicz* case, the court agreed that treatment could be stopped, but explicitly rejected the New Jersey decision in *Quinlan*, and insisted that the court was the only proper place to decide such issues.[19] The same conclusion was reached by a New York court in the so-called *Brother Fox* case, but was later reversed.[20] And in some cases in New Jersey, where nursing home patients have been affected, involvement of the State Ombudsman has been mandated.[21] The implications of the *Cruzan* decision on this point are not totally clear.

Legally, therefore, the "who decides" question is controverted. There does seem to be a general movement in Massachusetts, New York, New Jersey, and other states away from this unfortunate insistence on court or government action.[22] Most ethicists, along with very many jurists, would like to see a general acceptance of the *Quinlan* decision: the decision ought, in most cases, to be left at the level of family and the health care team, with the hospital's ethics committee as a possible resource. And in most jurisdictions this is indeed the case.

Consensus on Nutrition

A growing consensus on this issue is emerging, though there is still some opposition. The consensus accepts the arguments from the Catholic tradition that medically induced nutrition and hydration may well be extraordinary means and that they may rightly be withheld or withdrawn. This withholding or withdrawal does not constitute euthanasia or direct killing. The consensus also rests on the legal concepts of liberty, autonomy, and privacy, and the courts are more and more often insisting that these decisions be made by the family and the health care team and not in the courts. This is not the legal precedent in all jurisdictions, however, and physicians must continue to be aware of differing laws in different states. Missouri, and, to a lesser extent, New York and Maine, seem the states presently out of step with the national consensus.

The consensus, as I have described it, is the approach taken by the President's Commission for the Study of Ethical Problems in Biomedical and Behavioral Research, in their *Deciding to Forego Life-Sustaining Treatment*[23] and by the Hastings Center in their recent *Guidelines.*[24] The American Medical Association now advises doctors that artificial nutrition and hydration may be removed from patients who are imminently dying and from those who are irreversibly comatose, provided the family or other surrogate concurs.[25] Similar positions have been taken by the American Academy of Neurology and the American College of Physicians.[26]

There are still some questions to be worked out. One issue which deserves attention is the question of whether or not artificial nutrition might be removed from a permanently comatose patient even against the wishes of the family or other surrogate. At the moment, it is unwise and probably illegal to do so. The consensus as it has emerged thus far in our country considers decisions like these to be *not* medical decisions in the strict sense, but value decisions or "quality of life" decisions. That is, no medical decision can be made that hydration and nutrition (and this would apply to ventilation and other similar modalities as well) is medically futile in cases like Brophy's and Quinlan's. I am in agreement with this approach which insists that such treatment cannot be called medically futile in the strict sense, such that physicians might unilaterally decide to forgo it. We will return to the issue of medical futility in the next chapter.

But even though the physician may not unilaterally decide, on the basis of medical futility, to forgo the treatment when it is keeping the patient alive, the family can make the decision that the treatment is humanly unreasonable, and thus ask that it be forgone. In my opinion, since the "treatment" is clearly futile in any meaningfully human sense, it is at least likely that the procedure will not be paid for in the future by insurance companies and federal and state agencies. But that is another topic. For now, these decisions are made by the patient or by the family, or, in some states, unfortunately, by the courts.

Discussion Questions

1. What is the difference between medical nutrition and hydration and food and water? Do you think medical nutrition is always required? Why or why not?

2. What do you think of the original court decision in the *Brophy* case?

3. Who do you think should have the legal authority to make this kind of decision?

4. What do you think of the argument that those who decide to forgo nutrition are really killing the patient, that is, that it is active euthanasia?

Endnotes

1. Legally patients capable of making the decision for themselves can refuse this treatment even if they are not dying, of course. But the usual context in which the question is raised concerns dying patients.

2. Proper diagnosis is quite possible here, when based on laboratory studies and clinical observation, especially when this is supported by positron emission tomography (PET). Recovery can be virtually ruled out. A statement to this effect has been made by the American Academy of Neurology. See "Position of the American Academy of Neurology on Certain Aspects of the Care and Man-

agement of the Persistent Vegetative State Patient," *Neurology*, 39 (1989), 125-126; "Guidelines on the Vegetative State: Commentary on the American Academy of Neurology Statement," *Neurology*, 39 (1989), 123-124. The statement suggests that clinical observation of not less than one and possibly as long as three months is needed to be sure of the PVS diagnosis. MRI and CT scanning can also help by showing structural damage. See Ronald E. Cranford, "The Persistent Vegetative State: The Medical Reality (Getting the Facts Straight), *Hastings Center Report*, 18, No. 1 (Feb/March, 1988), 30; Cranford is less positive of certain diagnosis than the later Academy of Neurology statement. The Academy statement gives quite clear support to the withdrawal of nutrition and hydration from PVS patients. The Academy is also insistent that PVS patients, despite their ability to breathe and open and move their eyes, are totally unconscious, and cannot experience pain or suffering in any way. The withdrawal of nutrition and hydration does not, therefore, cause any sensation of dehydration or starvation.

3. The court in *Quinlan* used the word "comatose" (*In re Quinlan*, in Thomas A. Shannon and Jo Ann Manfra, eds., *Law and Bioethics: Texts with Commentary on Major U.S. Court Decisions* [New York: Paulist Press, 1982], p. 170), and the two terms are often not properly distinguished.

4. Many patients with PVS can breathe without mechanical assistance, since breathing is controlled by the brain stem, which is still functioning.

5. *In re Quinlan*, in Shannon, p. 170. Quinlan actually lived for years afterwards because nutrition and hydration were continued. She never came out of her persistent vegetative state. The argument in this chapter is that nutrition might also have been removed, but this was not requested for Quinlan.

6. See Chapter three, on the *Cruzan* decision, and Chapter four, in the section on mistakes and conflicts.

7. Alan Meisel, *The Right to Die* (New York: John Wiley & Sons, 1989), p. 98.

8. On the *Brophy* case, see George J. Annas, "Do Feeding Tubes Have More Rights than Patients?" *Hastings Center Report*, 16, No. 1 (Feb., 1986), 26-28; John J. Paris, "When Burdens of Feeding Outweigh Benefits," *HCR*, 16, No. 1 (Feb., 1986), 30-32; James F. Bresna-

han and James F. Drane, "A Challenge to Examine the Meaning of Living and Dying," *Health Progress,* Dec., 1986, pp. 32-37, 98; Leslie Steven Rothenberg, "The Dissenting Opinions: Biting the Hands that Won't Feed," *Health Progress,* Dec., 1986, pp. 38-45, 99. For an opinion, given at the trial, insisting that the treatment be maintained, see Patrick G. Derr, "Why Food and Fluids Can Never Be Denied," *HCR,* 16, No. 1 (Feb., 1986), 28-30.

9. I know of no secular ethicist who insists on the moral relevance of this distinction. I have heard religious leaders insist on such a distinction, and the Orthodox Jewish tradition has claimed such a relevance (Roger C. Bone, et al., "Ethical and Moral Guidelines for the Initiation, Continuation, and Withdrawal of Intensive Care," *Chest,* 97 (1990), pp. 952-953, 955). For a different interpretation of the Jewish position, see David F. Feldman, *Health and Medicine in the Jewish Tradition* (New York: Crossroad, 1986), esp. pp. 91-96.

10. Gerald Kelly, "The Duty of Using Artificial Means of Preserving Life," *Theological Studies,* 11 (1950), 203-220. For citation in context by contemporary authors who are arguing the issue, see John J. Paris, "When Burdens of Feeding Outweigh Benefits," *Hastings Center Report,* 16, No. 1 (Feb., 1986), 30-32; Eileen P. Flynn, *Hard Decisions: Forgoing and Withdrawing Artificial Nutrition and Hydration* (Kansas City, MO: Sheed & Ward, 1990), p. 79; Richard A. McCormick and John J. Paris, "The Catholic Tradition on the Use of Nutrition and Fluids," *America,* 156 (1987), 358. Kelly says that artificial means such as oxygen and intravenous feeding "not only need not but should not be used, once the coma is reasonably diagnosed as terminal" (p. 220). Some argument might remain about what is meant here by "terminal," but it is most likely, given the rest of Kelly's argument about benefit and burden, that what we now call "irreversible coma" and "persistent vegetative state" would fit. In this article Kelly argues that these means are "ordinary" but "useless" and therefore optional, thus adding a confusing distinction which is not necessary if "ordinary" and "extraordinary" are considered as moral rather than medical terms, as I have proposed, and as is more in consonance with the development of the distinction in Catholic medical ethics. Kelly's later use of these terms clears up his confusion here (*Medico-Moral Problems,* 1958 ed. [St.

Louis, MO: Catholic Hospital Assoc. of the United States and Canada, 1958], p. 129.

11. Those who disagree do not correctly understand the Catholic tradition on this question. The question of intentionality is complex, and often quite confusing. For a detailed technical treatment, see *The Emergence of Roman Catholic Medical Ethics*, pp. 247-258. The principle of double effect correctly insists that the agent not intend the evil effect. Thus the agent may not rightly intend the death of the patient in the moral sense, that is, as an end desired and wished maliciously. The agent inevitably intends to permit the patient to die, but not as an effect delighted in from bad motives. The best and simplest test to tell the difference is simply to ask whether or not the agent would have allowed the patient to die had there been an "ordinary" alternative which would have permitted meaningful recovery. If the answer is "no," as it almost always is, the agent cannot be said to have intended the patient's death in the sense forbidden by the principle of double effect. Rather death must be said to be a foreseen and permitted, but unintended side effect. On the unfortunate tendency of some Catholic moralists to conflate the intention of the agent into the physical intention of the act (physicalism), often stated as "the agent may not intend the bad effect either as means or as end", see *The Emergence*, p. 255, pp. 421-429.

12. There is often confusion here. A patient in a "persistent vegetative state" is often said not to be terminal, or not to be dying. By this is meant that with medically induced nutrition and hydration the patient may live many years. But this is an incorrect analysis which confuses the issue. PVS patients are indeed dying; they are dying from the brain injury which makes it impossible for them to eat and drink, just as patients with end-stage lung disease are dying because their disease makes it impossible for them to breathe. Medically induced ventilation can keep breathing for them, but they are still said to be dying patients, and if the ventilator is withdrawn, as is quite proper in many cases, they die from the disease, not from the withdrawing of the ventilator. The same is true for patients in irreversible comas or PVS. They are dying of a disease which will kill them unless these morally extraordinary means are employed to keep them alive. As another example, the cause of death in patients with end-stage heart disease is the disease, not the forgoing of a heart transplant. If this analysis were not true, forgo-

ing extraordinary means of treatment would always be the cause of death, and thus would be a direct killing. But, as we have seen over and over again, this is not the case, either according to American law or according to Catholic medical ethics.

13. For example, in New Jersey, the state Conference of Catholic Bishops argued in the *Jobes* case that artificial nutrition must be maintained. Yet in a similar case, in Rhode Island, Bishop Gelineau agreed that artificial nutrition could be stopped for a patient, Marsha Gray, in a persistent vegetative state. In Pennsylvania, too, there has been some opposition by bishops to certain "Living Will" bills which do not include restrictions about forgoing hydration and nutrition. Opponents of the position I have been advocating include James McHugh, "Artificially Assisted Nutrition and Hydration," *Origins*, 19, No. 19 (Oct. 12, 1989), 314-316; and William E. May, et al., "Feeding and Hydrating the Permanently Unconscious and Other Vulnerable Persons," *Issues in Law and Medicine*, 3, No. 3 (1987), 204-211. A particularly interesting document is that of the Pope John XXIII Medical-Moral Research and Education Center, "Feeding and Hydrating the Permanently Unconscious and Other Vulnerable Persons: A Report to the Congregation for the Faith," unpublished typescript distributed to dioceses (Braintree, MA: Pope John XIII Center, 1988). The main report is the longer document of which the article by William E. May, et al., just cited, was the summary statement. Yet this report includes criticisms, some of them rather scathing, by a number of Catholic moral theologians. Among these are rejections of the main conclusions by two "conservative" Catholic moral theologians. On theological grounds Benedict Ashley correctly rejects the document's central argument that physical life can never be a burden, and argues that the fight against euthanasia is better made by staying with the Catholic tradition which permits the cessation of unwarranted treatment than by rejecting that tradition. Albert S. Moraczewsky, of the Pope John XXIII Center, whose illness prevented him from chairing the drafting group, makes a series of interventions which, on the basis of traditional Catholic moral theology, convincingly refute the main arguments of the document. Unfortunately, American bishops, as well as the Vatican Congregation for the Faith, for whom the document was written, may well be swayed more by the report itself than by the appended refutations. In the next chapter we will look at Catholic reaction to the *Cruzan* case.

14. A particularly helpful brief review of the issues from the Catholic perspective is Kevin O'Rourke, "Father Kevin O'Rourke on Hydration and Nutrition: Open Letter to Bishop McHugh," *Origins*, 19, No. 21 (Oct. 26, 1989), 351-352. Another source, often cited, is the doctoral dissertation by Daniel A. Cronin (now Bishop of Fall River, MA), "The Moral Law in Regard to the Ordinary and Extraordinary Means of Conserving Life" (Rome: Pontifical Gregorian Univ., 1958). A list of key citations from Catholic authors recognized as orthodox is given by James J. McCartney, "Catholic Positions on Withholding Sustenance for the Terminally Ill," *Health Progress*, Oct., 1986, pp. 38-40.

15. "The Last Word," *Hastings Center Report*, 16, No. 5 (Oct., 1986), 47; also "The Last Word," *HCR*, 16, No. 6 (Dec., 1986), 32.

16. For a critique of the *O'Connor* case, see George J. Annas, "Precatory Prediction and Mindless Mimicry: The Case of Mary O'Connor," *Hastings Center Report*, 18, No. 6 (Dec., 1988), 31-33.

17. I find it helpful in this context to distinguish three levels of moral judgment: 1) the moral rightness or wrongness of the action (the decision to forgo); 2) the legal status of the action; 3) the moral rightnesss and wrongness of the law establishing the legal status. In the case where I choose to reject a morally "ordinary" means of preserving my life, the answer to 1) is that I act wrongly, though I may or may not sin in doing so—that depends on "subjective" factors like knowledge and consent; the answer to 2) is that the law says no one can force me to have the treatment; and the answer to 3) is that that law is a morally right law.

18. A theoretically interesting point is whether or not, from the perspective of Catholic moral methodology, the Jehovah's Witness patient: 1) makes a decision which is objectively wrong, because the transfusion is in fact "ordinary" and thus mandatory, though he or she does not sin since the decision is made from invincible ignorance; or 2) makes a decision which is objectively right, since, given the repugnance the patient feels toward "eating blood," for this patient the blood transfusion is indeed objectively "extraordinary." The latter approach seems more irenic, but risks relativism. The former is probably technically preferable. For a Catholic defense of the right of Jehovah's Witnesses to refuse blood, see Richard J. Devine, "Save the Body, Lose the Soul," *Health Progress*, June, 1989, pp. 68-72.

19. Alan Meisel, *The Right to Die*, pp. 236-248.

20. *In re Eichner*; see Meisel, p. 244. On this issue see also President's Commission for the Study of Ethical Problems in Medicine and Biomedical Research, *Deciding to Forego Life Sustaining Treatment*, (Washington: GPO, 1983), pp. 154-160; also John T. Rago, "An Intrusive Judiciary Obscures the Right-to-Die Question," *Juris, The Duquesne Law School Newsmagazine*, 19A, No. 3 (Spring, 1986), 10-13.

21. Meisel, *The Right to Die*, pp. 252-254.

22. Meisel, *The Right to Die*, pp. 238-248.

23. Pp. 196, 159-160.

24. The Hastings Center, *Guidelines on the Termination of Life-Sustaining Treatment and the Care of the Dying* (Briarcliff Manor, NY:.The Hastings Center, 1987).

25. American Medical Association, *Current Opinions* (Chicago: American Medical Assoc., 1986), 2.

26. "Position of the American Academy of Neurology on Certain Aspects of the Care and Management of the Persistent Vegetative State Patient," *Neurology*, 39 (1989), 125-126; "Life, Death, and the American College of Physicians: The *Cruzan* Case," *Annals of Internal Medicine*, 112 (1990), 802-804.

Chapter Three

The Cruzan Decision and Advanced Directives

Part One
The *Cruzan* Decision

There is one potentially major cloud on the horizon concerning the emerging consensus about forgoing treatment. It is the case of Nancy Cruzan, appealed from Missouri to the United States Supreme Court. The Court has now decided its first case concerning the forgoing of life-sustaining medical treatment.

Nancy Cruzan was in her early thirties. For more than six years at the time the case was heard, she had been in a persistent vegetative state as a result of an automobile accident in 1983. She was cared for in a state hospital in Mount Vernon, MO, hooked up to a feeding tube which kept her alive. Her parents asked for permission to remove the tube. In many states, as we have seen, this could have been done at the bedside without court order. But in Missouri disagreement resulted in a court hearing.

The Circuit Court granted the parents' request. But the state of Missouri appealed to the Missouri Supreme Court, which in a 4-3 split decision overturned the lower court and ruled that because Missouri was a right-to-life state Nancy Cruzan could not be taken off the feeding treatment. Her parents, with the support of many *amicus curiae* briefs, appealed to the United States Supreme Court. The case was decided on June 25, 1990.

What Might Have Happened

When the case was appealed to the Supreme Court, there were a number of possible directions the Court might have taken. One helpful way to show the importance of this case is to speculate on what the Court might have decided, and to assess the implications of those possible rulings.

The worst outcome would have occurred had the Court connected this case with the abortion issue and used it as a way to establish an extreme constitutional interest in defense of life by misapplying to this issue a right-to-life interpretation of the constitution. To do this the Court might have insisted that no life-sustaining treatment could ever be forgone. Or it might have allowed this only for competent persons, and have refused it for all others. This move toward a more vitalistic posture would have been possible in *Cruzan* without directly overturning *Roe v. Wade*, the 1973 abortion decision, with which the *Cruzan* case is often unfortunately linked. Courts are usually slow to overturn their prior decisions directly, and this might have offered the Court a chance to move in this direction without a direct repudiation of its earlier ruling.

As we have noted, Missouri decided as it did in *Cruzan* because of its stand as a right-to-life state, and it is Missouri which sent the Supreme Court the *Webster* case, where the Supreme Court *did* move in a more conservative direction away from some previous interpretations of *Roe v. Wade*. In addition, some among the "right-to-life" movement, though by no means all, have tied the two issues together, insisting that states have an absolute interest in preserving life, an interest which requires them to have laws against all or almost all abortion and against all or almost all cessation of life-sustaining medical treatment.

That the Court did not choose this disastrous direction is probably due to a number of reasons. First, the abortion controversy concerns two beings, the pregnant woman and the fetus. All recognize the woman to be a human person and many claim personhood for the fetus. In *Cruzan* there was no question of a second person being harmed. Second, Nancy Cruzan, like all patients with her condition, would never be conscious; in most cases the fetus, if not aborted, would grow to live a sapient, sentient, meaningful human life. Third, and perhaps most importantly from the Catholic perspective, the tradition of the Roman Catholic Church is, as we have seen, best understood as permitting the forgoing of Cruzan's treatment. The official position of Catholic moral theology should thus have been in favor of overturning *Cruzan* and permitting withdrawal of treatment, though some bishops and theologians, misinterpreting their tradition, disagree. In the abortion issue the official teaching of the Church is quite clear that all "direct" abortions are morally wrong, though many Catholics, including a number of Catholic moral theologians, hold that this judgment cannot be absolute.

The difference between these two judgments in Catholic ethics is based on the distinction between killing and allowing to die. Abortion, when it is a "killing," that is, when it is a "direct" abortion, is always wrong, according to traditional Catholic moral theology. It is considered the direct killing of an innocent person and, like direct euthanasia, is always forbidden. But when abortion is an "allowing to die," as in so-called "indirect abortions," for example in hysterectomies as cure for uterine cancer of pregnant women, or in salpingectomies as treatment of ectopic pregnancy, it is permitted. In the *Cruzan* case, since there was no question of killing, forgoing treatment is not contrary to Catholic tradition.

For all these reasons, and doubtless for its own reasons as well, the Supreme Court did not choose to rule that life-sustaining medical treatment must always be maintained in cases like Cruzan's.

A second possible outcome, one with equally disastrous potential, was that the Court might have taken the opportunity to throw the issue completely back to the states and require state-by-state regulation. States might then have ruled that nutrition and hydration might never be forgone, even by competent patients; or that no life-sustaining treatment at all might be forgone; or that surrogates might never choose to forgo such treatment; or that though such treatment might be withheld, it might not be withdrawn; or states might have passed other similarly absurd restrictions. As we have already noted, most states have decided that there is no need for laws on this issue, that decisions can be made by the patient or the surrogate; state legislatures need not design detailed legislation. The Supreme Court has not opened the door to the chaos which that decision might well have brought.

The best decision would have been for the Court to overturn the Missouri decision and with it the Missouri law, and thus uphold the right of surrogates to refuse unreasonable treatment. Unfortunately, the Court rejected this direction as well. But, though it did not decide as it ought to have, it did avoid the worst of its possible options.

The Actual Decision

The actual *Cruzan* decision is a complicated one, and all its implications are not yet clear. There is both good and bad news. This doubtless accounts for the varied reaction the decision has received in the media and from ethicists, jurists, and health care professionals. Those who feared a disaster were pleased; those who hoped for the right decision were disappointed.

First, the good news. The Supreme Court decision was not the disaster it might have been. The Court upheld the right of competent persons to refuse medical treatment and based this on the liberty guarantee of the fourteenth amendment to the U. S. Constitution. The court ruled that medical nutrition and hydration are indeed medical treatment, and may rightly be forgone. It ruled that withdrawing does not differ from withholding. It pointed to the right of competent persons to write living wills, and implied that these directives must be followed when they provide clear and convincing evidence of a patient's wishes. And it suggested the importance of durable power of attorney laws, such that a competent person might hand over decision-making authority to another (we will return to these advanced directives later in this chapter).

In thus ruling, the Court has established for the first time a nation-wide legal right to forgo treatment. Eight of the nine justices, with the exception of Antonin Scalia, concurred in this, establishing the likelihood that this will not be overturned by a later decision. This is in keeping with the emerging consensus described and supported in this book. It is good law and good ethics. Those who feared a disastrous decision by an arguably conservative court are rightly relieved that this did not happen.

But there is bad news as well. Those who had hoped that the sadly mistaken Missouri decision and its unethical law would be overturned were disappointed. In a splintered 5-4 decision, the Court ruled that states may require clear and convincing evidence that patients had wished life-sustaining treatment to be forgone before surrogates may choose to forgo it. On this basis the Supreme Court upheld the Missouri decision refusing to allow Cruzan's nutrition to be stopped and upheld as well the Missouri law requiring clear and convincing evidence of a patient's wishes.

This part of the decision is badly misguided. The dissenting opinions of Justices Brennan and Stevens accurately demonstrate the potential for harm which this decision can bring if other states now begin to join Missouri, New York, and Maine in requiring clear and convincing evidence of patient wishes. In this the majority opinion, written by Rehnquist, is seriously flawed. And the opinion of Justice Scalia, which would have had our nation reverse the emerging consensus in radical ways, is quite simply outrageous.

But what is so problematic about allowing states to require "clear and convincing evidence"? It certainly seems reasonable. As Justice Rehnquist points out, decisions to forgo treatment are not reversible. If the requirement for clear and convincing evidence can be met by advanced directives like living wills and durable powers of attorney, why all the fuss?

The problem is twofold. First, "clear and convincing evidence" is the highest standard of evidence which the law can require in civil matters. To the degree that states may now move toward restrictive laws requiring irrational levels of clear and convincing evidence, most of us may never be able to meet the criteria. Most persons who write living wills cannot accurately foresee which precise sets of treatments they want forgone in which medical circumstances. Few of us know what diseases we will catch. We can write general directives, but these might not meet the requirements of clear and convincing evidence.

Second, the poor and uneducated among us, and possibly the young as well, could be disenfranchised from the right guaranteed to the rest of us. Poor people will not hire lawyers to help them through the potential maze. Medicare and Medicaid do not reimburse physicians for counselling patients on this question. On this issue the five justices of the majority have been remote from real people in real situations. Clinical experience demonstrates that most people do not have living wills or durable powers of attorney. Loving relatives make the decisions for them. If states now rush to require clear and convincing evidence, many Americans will be forced to endure useless and costly medical treatment. And though Justice Rehnquist is right when he says that decisions to forgo are not reversible, state requirements of evidentiary hurdles are not reversible either. Patients like Nancy Cruzan may be forced irreversibly into useless death-prolonging treatments, becoming pawns of technology.

We have noted a number of times the disadvantages of having decisions like these made by the judicial system. A recent article by Steven Miles and Allison August lends further support to the position that these decisions are best made by patient, family, and health care team in the clinical setting. Miles and August present evidence of sexist bias in judges' decisions concerning patient choices to forgo treatment. Courts are far more likely to accept such choices when men make them than when women do.[1] In twelve of fourteen cases involving women, courts decided there was insufficient evidence of their choice, whereas only two out of eight men failed similar evidenciary requirements. Requirements of clear and convincing evidence will exacerbate this sexism, since they will necessitate constant involvement of state legislatures and courts to determine whether or not the precise requirements have been met.

The majority of the Court feared that relatives might not always act in the patient's best interests or follow established standards of substituted judgment. But this fear is an empty one, based more on theory than on actual clinical reality. As we have discussed at length, physicians may not forgo treatment based simply on a surrogate's decision. Unless there is evidence that the patient, while capable of deciding, wished the treatment forgone (substituted judgment standard), the best interests of the patient must be served. Thus it must be clear that the treatment is "morally extraordinary," indeed, that it is unreasonable. The treatment must be of little benefit or impose significant burden. These quite proper restrictions, coupled with civil and criminal laws which can be brought to bear in cases where surrogates decide to forgo out of malice or greed, are already quite sufficient to prevent an outbreak of the criminal behavior which the justices fear.

Nor is there any evidence that this kind of crime occurs with any regularity. As we will note in the next chapter, conflicts today arise more often when physicians want to stop and family members want to continue than the other way around. There is simply no reason to require the kind of evidence of the patient's own wishes which the Court has allowed states to require. To this extent, the Court decision is a bad one indeed. It may cause great harm.

This harm is only potential, however. The decision need not be catastrophic. Indeed, it need have no effect at all on the consensus we have been describing. At present, only New York, Missouri, and Maine have developed law or legal precedent which requires this kind of evidence. And, as we have already noted, there is movement even in these states to come more in line with the general American agreement not to require such hurdles.

Hospitals need not alter their procedures. The Supreme Court merely upheld an existing Missouri law. It did not require such a law on the federal level or insist that states pass similar laws. With proper understanding on the part of state legislatures, unnecessary and harmful laws requiring "clear and convincing evidence" of prior patient wishes will not be enacted. States need only recognize durable powers of attorney for health care decisions.

What would have happened to Nancy Cruzan had the Circuit Court not accepted new evidence? She would have continued to be degraded by useless and costly treatment until: a) the Supreme Court reversed its decision; b) Missouri enacted humane laws; c) her parents moved her to another state; or d) the forced feeding finally failed, and she died despite it.

Catholic Controversy over *Cruzan*

During the course of the *Cruzan* appeal, Catholic pastoral leaders and Catholic theologians took widely divergent positions. An exploration of these positions may be helpful in furthering our understanding of the issues at stake in *Cruzan*, and will serve as well as a final review of the relationship between Catholic moral theology and American law, and thus as a study of the relationship among the three pillars which support the present American consensus on forging treatment.

a) *The Problem.*

I argued in the last chapter that Catholic tradition judges the forgoing of artificial nutrition in cases like that of Nancy Cruzan to be morally right. Despite this fact, there has been considerable controversy in the American Catholic Church over this case. The reason for this controversy is best understood by looking once again at the three pillars on which the currently emerging American consensus concerning forgoing treatment has been based. The disagreement is based on the fact that there is a good deal of theoretical controversy concerning the relationship between the first two pillars, the "moral" ones, and the third, the "legal" one, that is, between the two pillars which come from Catholic moral theology (the ordinary/extraordinary distinction and the killing/allowing to die distinction) and the pillar which comes from Anglo-Saxon common law and/or from American constitutional law (the concepts of liberty, privacy, and autonomy).

As we noted in the first chapter, this theoretical controversy has never really been resolved, despite the fact that courts have been moving toward a practical resolution of this relationship in cases concerned with forgoing treatment. In addition, there is considerable debate among legal scholars over whether or not a legal right to privacy exists in the constitution, and over how far it, or similar legal rights and freedoms, ought to extend.[2]

These debates are basic to the Catholic controversy over *Cruzan*.

b) *Two Catholic briefs in the* Cruzan *case.*

Among the *amicus curiae* or "friend of the court" briefs submitted to the Supreme Court in the *Cruzan* case were two by official Catholic organizations.

One Catholic position is presented in the brief submitted by the United States Catholic Conference.[3] The USCC is the educational and research wing of the National Conference of Catholic Bishops. Its brief argues against the request to withdraw the gastrostomy tube. In my judgment it is not a good brief.

In the brief, the bishops cannot, and do not, appeal to their own tradition to argue that it is morally wrong for Cruzan's treatment to be stopped. They seem to be aware that their own tradition would not allow them to say that withdrawal is immoral, though they never explicitly state what they think the morality of withdrawal in this case would be. Nonetheless they argue that it ought to be illegal. They do so mostly because they oppose the understanding of the right to privacy and autonomy on which the legal submission by Cruzan's family was based. This, in turn, is at least partly because they fear that the support of such a right to privacy will sustain the so-called right-to-abortion, which the Church officially opposes. This is clear in the brief itself, where reference is made to abortion on demand as a result of such a right to privacy.

The bishops fear, properly I think, that an absolute stress on the right to privacy and autonomy to the detriment of the state's interest in support of life would create an imbalance not intended in the Constitution, which would support an unrestricted right to abortion, and which would also open the door to euthanasia. They fear that the right to privacy will support a legal right to assistance in suicide. Therefore they opposed the Cruzans' petition to remove the feeding tube.

But this means they argue that it ought to be illegal to do what their own tradition says it is morally right to do. And this is incoherent. It is also dangerous. If the decision in *Cruzan* had rejected patients' and surrogates' rights to refuse useless treatment—indeed, if as a result of the actual decision states begin to impose silly regulatory hurdles before surrogates can forgo treatment—a very likely result will be a backlash, both on the basis of economic impossibility and on the basis of human cruelty to patient and family. The backlash is very likely to lead directly to what the bishops most fear, legislative action to permit euthanasia. Indeed, there is already some evidence that the *Cruzan* decision has furthered the euthanasia movement.

The confusion posed here results from the lack of theoretical clarity noted earlier about the relationship between the legal notions of liberty, privacy, and autonomy which have developed within Anglo-Saxon and American jurisprudence and the Catholic insistence that persons are obliged to use morally ordinary means of treatment to preserve their lives but are not obliged to use morally extraordinary ones. As we have already seen, the courts have tended to give patients with decision-making capacity the right to decide to refuse just about any treatment at all. The bishops fear, I think, that this will lead to the right to euthanasia on request. That is, since persons can legally refuse even beneficial and generally available medical treatment, and they can, then it will be a short step to suggesting that persons can demand the right to be killed or to be assisted in killing themselves.

But the Bishops cannot claim that their own tradition rejects the right to refuse morally extraordinary treatment, treatment which is of little benefit or which, while of benefit, is of considerable burden. Nor can they claim that the continued treatment of Nancy Cruzan offered her sufficient benefit to have made it an ordinary means and therefore obligatory. Nor can they claim that there was no burden involved, certainly to the family and to society, and, in terms of useless infliction, and thus of degradation, though not of actual suffering, to Nancy Cruzan herself. Nor can they claim that their own tradition holds that the forgoing of morally extraordinary treatment is euthanasia, that is, is killing. Rather, the Catholic tradition says it is allowing-to-die, and is morally right in cases like Cruzan's. Nor do they claim that they would want the law to make it illegal for surrogates to choose to forgo other morally extraordinary means, such as ventilation; yet they make no coherent attempt to distinguish medical nutrition from medical ventilation. The end result, then, is that the USCC, in its wish to oppose abortion and euthanasia, has ended up arguing that what their own tradition says is morally right ought to be illegal.

But a second Roman Catholic brief was submitted in the *Cruzan* case, this one by SSM Health Care System, a St. Louis-based corporation of the Franciscan Sisters of Mary, representing 130 Catholic health care facilities nation-wide.[4] This brief makes all the proper distinctions and comes up with the right answer, true to Catholic tradition. Like the USCC, the SSM brief argues against the absolutizing of the right to privacy such that euthanasia might become a legal right. For the SSM, as for the USCC, sanctity of life is essential.

It is quite clear that the Constitution does not propose an absolute right to privacy or autonomy. This argument was rejected when, for only one example, states and the federal government imposed taxes. I have no absolute right to keep all my earnings and do with them what I want. The common good requires sharing, even a sharing legally enacted by government. Humanly as well as legally there is no such thing as perfect privacy or perfect autonomy. Privacy and autonomy are unhappy terms if they are taken to imply a reductionist isolated individualism. Informed consent, a medical ethical process based on the notion of patient autonomy, does not presuppose that the patient, or anybody else for that matter, makes decisions free from all sources of social influence.[5] This notion of privacy and autonomy is neither possible nor desirable. In arguing against absolutistic interpretations of the right to privacy and autonomy, the USCC and the SSM briefs are in agreement.

But, unlike the USCC brief, the SSM brief properly points out that in the *Cruzan* case the withdrawal of treatment was the withdrawal of extraordinary means, and was not euthanasia. It insists that beneficial (or "morally ordinary") treatment may not legally or morally be withheld by surrogate decision-makers, a position with which the courts have generally agreed. It insists on the importance of the benefit-burden analysis. It argues against the two extremes mentioned in the first chapter, the extreme of insisting that everything be done to preserve biological life and the extreme of disregarding the importance of physical life altogether. It is, in sum, well-written, properly reflective of the Catholic tradition, and the basis for good law.

There remains the question of what to do about persons who are capable of making decisions and who reject morally "ordinary" treatment. Should this decision on their part be made illegal? Should they be forced to have the treatment? As I have already stated, I think the present agreement of the courts that persons capable of making these decisions be allowed to refuse any and all medical treatment (that adult Jehovah's Witnesses, for example, be allowed to refuse blood transfusions) is morally correct. But I recognize that this is an area where Catholic tradition and American law may be seen, in some interpretations, to disagree. In the *Cruzan* case, however, there was no such point of contention. Catholic tradition is clear that Cruzan's treatment could rightly be forgone, since it was the forgoing of morally extraordinary means, which is ethically right, and since it was allowing to die and not euthanasia.

c) Summary.

A few points of summary will conclude this section.

First, the Catholic tradition is quite clear that medically induced nutrition and hydration may rightly be forgone when this treatment can legitimately be called morally extraordinary, that is, optional. It is clearly such when its benefits are outweighed by its burdens, as is the case for those in persistent vegetative state, and for similar patients. Catholic tradition does not hold that this is killing. Rather is it allowing to die, and is morally right in this kind of case.

Second, there is some theoretical confusion remaining about the extent of the so-called right to privacy. Does this right mean that people should be allowed to commit suicide with no interference, or that physicians should be able to assist in suicide, or actually to kill their patients? So far, American law has rejected these options, at least in most jurisdictions.[6] Also, thus far the courts have agreed that some sort of best interests or substituted judgment standard must be added to the right of privacy or the liberty to refuse treatment when surrogates decide that treatment should be forgone. Though the exact parameters of this issue are not yet totally clear, the general agreement on what constitutes the best interests of incompetent patients is quite sufficient to avoid most serious abuses and deviations.[7]

Third, the Catholic community is concerned, and I agree with this concern, about the erosion of the state's interest in preserving life. Though I personally disagree with the Catholic position that all direct euthanasia and assisted suicide is morally wrong, I find myself opposed to its legalization or decriminalization, largely because of the great difficulty we will have in writing laws which will protect the poor and the handicapped.

Fourth, some Catholic leaders and theologians have decided that they ought to stem the erosion of the legal right to life by arguing against the legal right to forgo treatment. I believe this to be a mistaken position. It is likely to lead to a furthering of the movement toward the legalization of euthanasia. Nancy Cruzan's parents should have been allowed to withdraw her treatment. Such a decision would have been proper according to the developing American legal consensus. It would also have been proper according to the centuries-old tradition of Catholic moral theology.

Part Two
Advanced Directives

The Supreme Court has ruled in *Cruzan* that states may require clear and convincing evidence of a now incompetent patient's wishes before surrogates may choose to have treatment withheld or withdrawn. For reasons which should by now be apparent, states ought not pass such legislation. But even if they do, there are ways in which persons may make their wishes about treatment known in advance in case of the very likely event that at some time they will need to have treatment decisions made for them by surrogates. Advanced directives are not new to the *Cruzan* decision. As the consensus concerning forgoing treatment has emerged, one of the problems it has encountered is this very one. What is the legal status of decisions to forgo treatment, and how can we be sure that these decisions are the ones a patient actually wants?

When a sick person is competent to make decisions, there is usually no legal problem. As we have already seen, it is clear in common law, and it has been decided on constitutional grounds as well, as interpreted by American courts, and now by the Supreme Court, that we have the right to refuse any and all medical treatment for virtually any reason, as long as we are competent to make this kind of decision. The question of competence itself is a complicated one, of course, and there is always the temptation to assume mental incompetence when the decision to refuse treatment conflicts with some generally held value. But legally, the right of persons capable of deciding has now been established. They may choose to forgo medical treatment.

The problem addressed by advanced directives is not that of the competent adult. It is the problem of a patient who, though alive and not dead, cannot make these decisions. It is the patient whose situation is addressed in the *Cruzan* ruling.

Durable Power of Attorney

Two general approaches to this question have been suggested. The first is simpler, and, in my judgment, has a number of advantages. One ethicist has called it the "Committee of the Person,"[8] and it is what we usually mean when, in this context, we speak of Durable Power of Attorney. During one's life, one may appoint another person or a group of persons to make decisions concerning the treatment to be given in case of inability to make such decisions for oneself. The advantages of this approach are its flexibility and its stress on human friendship and love. One person expresses a trust in another to do the best possible. No one can ever predict completely the circumstances of a particular process of dying. This approach simply says to a friend or to a group of friends: "I trust you; do what you think is right, what you *feel* I would want. I trust your motives. If you make a mistake, so be it. It is better for me to put this trust in you than in my physicians, or the courts, or even (possibly) my family."

This approach is admittedly not perfect. There are some aspects of it which might possibly be called disadvantages. What of possible conflict of interest? The person I appoint might turn out later on to hate me, or want my money. What of the burden this might impose on the friend or committee of the person? In this approach, as indeed in aspects of this whole question generally, what one thinks one will want when one is healthy and watching people dying on TV can be quite different from what one actually feels and wants when one is dying oneself. Despite these difficulties, there is much which is humanly attractive in this idea. Assuming the actions taken by the friend or committee do not include active euthanasia, there would be no reason for the tradition of Catholic moral theology to reject such an approach.

Legally, this approach is best done through a durable power of attorney. Durable powers of attorney are unlike the usual kind in that they endure even when the person is no longer competent. An ordinary power of attorney, which, for example, a person might give a broker to make stock trades, ceases when the person is no longer able to revoke it. But a durable power of attorney is made precisely for situations when the person cannot act for herself or himself. Power of attorney can be granted to apply in areas of medical treatment. It is generally not necessary to have a lawyer draw one up, but it is probably a good idea. There are simple forms to sign.

The *Cruzan* decision has clearly increased the importance of the durable power of attorney. The exact implications of the majority opinion are not yet clear, but in her concurring opinion Justice O'Connor suggested the possibility of a future Court ruling that surrogates appointed by such power of attorney might have exactly the same right to decide as the patient would have if capable. If it did so rule, this would go beyond the general consensus by allowing such surrogates to withhold humanly beneficial treatment based on substituted judgment, and would not require that such decisions be in the best interests of the patient.

Whatever the precise meaning of this opinion may be, it is quite clear that the Court intended explicitly to suggest the durable power of attorney as one of the ways in which states might acknowledge that patients have given clear and convincing evidence of their wishes. In the wake of *Cruzan*, especially in those states with unfortunately strict evidence requirements like New York and Missouri, durable powers of attorney may be the citizens' best bet.

Living Wills

The second kind of advanced directive is an instruction directive, made through a document often called a Living Will. This is a document drawn up or a form filled out by a person in good health giving instructions concerning the kind of treatment he or she wishes if and when he or she is seriously ill and not competent to make personal judgments. There is a semi-standard form of this living will, though there are a number of variations of it. The operative paragraph in the form suggested by "Concern for Dying" is this:

> If at such a time the situation should arise in which there is no expectation of my recovery from extreme physical or mental disability, I direct that I be allowed to die and not be kept alive by medications, artificial means, or "heroic measures." I do, however, ask that medication be mercifully administered to me to alleviate suffering even though this may shorten my remaining life.

It is clear that in this document there is no question of active euthanasia. Though the document is vague, it enables us to express our general desires concerning treatment. It gives the physician at least a rough sense of our wishes. It says, in effect: "Don't do stupid stuff to me!" The living will is morally acceptable for those who find comfort in signing one, and is in keeping with the Catholic tradition.

The issue becomes far more complex, however, when the question of statutory change in state laws is introduced. These "Natural Death Acts" generally make legally binding, or at least legally recognize documents similar to, but often more specific than, the living will. So far few ethicists have given complete approval to the actual natural death acts which have been passed or which are now under consideration. Reasons vary, but a few are common.

First, some natural death acts imply the legalization of active euthanasia (a bill introduced into the Idaho legislature, but not passed, falls into this category;[9] in the past year or two, a number of initiatives have been introduced to make active euthanasia or assisted suicide legal; these will doubtless increase in the wake of the *Cruzan* decision). Moralists who oppose active euthanasia oppose those statutes which allow this or are even potentially open to that possibility.

Second, some natural death acts are quite vague. It is hard to know what exactly they mean. Third, and this is paradoxical but quite important, some natural death acts are so specific that they imply that *only in this specific case* can treatment be refused or terminated. These bills tend to reduce the flexibility now given the families of dying incompetent patients, at least implicitly. In some states, for example, natural death acts specifically rule out the inclusion of nutrition and hydration as treatments which a person may request be forgone. It is likely that the *Cruzan* decision has now eliminated this particular restriction. Yet with this kind of legislation, living wills may actually and paradoxically increase the likelihood that treatment will be continued, either because the law forbids including the permission to forgo this or that treatment, or because the document which the person indeed signs does not explicitly include a particular treatment or a particular circumstance in the general permission granted to withhold or withdraw treatment.

Fourth, in a similar way, there is the danger that those who have not signed such a document will find more and more that invasive and useless medical measures are taken to prolong life simply because they do not have such a document. And physicians, and possibly courts, may assume that because they never signed such a document they did not want treatment withheld under any circumstance. The passing of a statute to enact a right which people already have can reduce that right by implying that the state grants it, whereas in fact it is a "natural" right, recognized as such by common law, and, as we have already noted, by the courts in many states. States should not accept the opening given them by the Supreme Court in the *Cruzan* decision to legislate on these matters.

This problem is increased in those bills which require that the document be periodically renewed, as does the California Natural Death Act, the first to be passed. What if the person fails to renew it? Does this imply that he or she wants no cessation of heroic treatment even when such treatment would be ordinarily easily forgone with the family's agreement? Does this imply that there is no clear evidence of the patient's wishes?

Now these difficulties may not be enough to lead to the conclusion that all such legislation is harmful. The symbolic value of living wills is important. It is clear, however, that caution must be taken in the way these statutes are written and in the way in which they are interpreted and enforced. It may well be the case that in this issue no law is better than the statutes which are likely to be written by our legislators.

For example, the legislation now being debated in Pennsylvania is such that if one of the bills under consideration is passed, citizens of that state will be apt to lose the morally correct flexibility which is currently available to them. In other states, restrictive living will legislation has been the reason why courts have refused to allow morally proper forgoing of treatment which legislators have ruled cannot be rejected in living wills.

It is important to point out something often overlooked. Even in the absence of statutory legislation, living wills have legal value. There does not have to be a state statute affirming advanced directives like living wills to make them legal. As long as there is no law against them, they remain perfectly legal documents which give directives to physicians. They make it easier for health care professionals to know that the patient had thought about these issues and what decisions the patient had come to. They relieve the minds and consciences of the family, who often worry what to do. They may help resolve disputes between family members who disagree about what the patient would have wanted. For all these reasons, living wills are a good idea, even if specific legislation is fraught with danger.

Of the two approaches, the better is some sort of "committee of the person," which, when made legal by the granting of a durable power of attorney, allows greater flexibility than is possible with a living will. Now a trusted friend will decide rather than a physician or the court. And this approach offers as well what I consider theologically essential: an enhancement of human trust and of trust in God. When the "committee of the person" is made legal by a durable power of attorney, the person has ensured as much as is possible that flexible and humanly meaningful decisions about treatment will be carried out. Signing a general living will document is also helpful, as it adds another indication of what the person wants.

Implications for Hospitals

For health care providers, advanced directives are helpful ways of learning what a patient would say if she or he could tell them what to do. They are legally and morally required to consider them as important indications of patient consent or lack of consent to treatment. Early review of these documents is an important part of proper health care.

In some cases, living wills can go beyond the usual general set of instructions and inform the physician exactly what to do and what not to do as a specific illness, which a competent patient knows will render him or her unable to decide, progresses through medically anticipated stages. In these cases, physicians should accept the living will as the equivalent of a present decision by a capable patient.

A further point is important. The absence of a living will or of a durable power of attorney is not an indication that a patient wants heroic measures or morally extraordinary means of treatment. Often a patient will have said something to the personal physician.

Physicians ought to discuss this with patients, and get a sense of the patient's wishes. This type of discussion can be begun in a very nonthreatening way while the patient is still quite healthy. Indeed, family members often discuss issues of this kind among themselves. Physicians and nurses should ask them if their sick relative has talked about this. Finally, in the absence of a durable power of attorney, decisions about treatment are made by the surrogate, who is ordinarily the next of kin. The lack of documents and of power of attorney can never be construed as an indication that a patient would have refused to allow the forgoing of treatment.

One final point is also important, one further caution, a caution which applies to any statute whose purpose is to enable the legal allowing of death. Laws governing the question must ensure that such policies are not carried out in order to rid society of individuals it considers burdensome or expensive to maintain. The wealthy have better access to medical care facilities and scarce resources. This results in earlier deaths for the poor and powerless. There is always a temptation to eliminate the poor as a way of eliminating poverty. Whatever laws are enacted, controls are essential to make sure this does not happen.

Discussion Questions

1. What is your opinion on the *Cruzan* decision? Is it too restrictive, too permissive, proper?

2. Of the alternative possible rulings, which is closest to your own position?

3. What do you think states should do in the wake of the decision?

4. Discuss your own experience with advanced directives. Which of the two approaches have you found most helpful? What provisions have you made for yourself and your family?

Endnotes

1. Steven H. Miles and Allison August, "Courts, Gender and 'The Right to Die'," *Law, Medicine and Health Care*, 18, Nos. 1-2 (Spring-Summer, 1990), 85-95.

2. I am myself persuaded that the best legal grounding for the right to forgo treatment is not the claimed constitutional right to privacy, first articulated in *Griswold v. Connecticut*, the case which struck down a statute forbidding contraception, and repeated in *Roe v. Wade*, the decision legalizing abortion, and then in the Quinlan case and often since then, but the long-recognized common law liberty to refuse unwanted medical intervention. An excellent review of this is found in an unpublished paper by David S. Pollock and Todd M. Begg, "The Constitutional Right to Die" (Pittsburgh: Pollock and Adams, 1990). The Cruzan decision did indeed base itself on this sort of liberty rather than on the right to privacy, and in this the decision was correct. The liberty was claimed on the basis of the fourteenth amendment.

3. "USCC Brief in Nancy Cruzan Case," *Origins*, 19, No. 21 (Oct. 26, 1989), 345-351.

4. "Continuing or Discontinuing Treatment: Ethical Criteria: Catholic Health-Care System's Brief," *Origins*, 19, No. 17 (Sept. 28, 1989), 279-286.

5. See Richard M. Zaner, *Ethics and the Clinical Encounter* (Englewood Cliffs, NJ: Prentice Hall, 1988). Zaner argues persuasively that the clinical context demonstrates how the notion of autonomy is seldom if ever perfectly realized. Zaner is probably too pessimistic about the usefulness and importance of informed consent, but his work is quite helpful in showing the importance of social context. No one is ever totally autonomous.

6. In some jurisdictions assisting in suicide may not be illegal. This is the claim made with respect to Dr. Jack Kevorkian's macabre suicide machine in Michigan. Actually killing the patient is, however, criminal homicide in all states. See Meisel, *The Right to Die*, p. 62. As we have already noted, though attempting suicide is not itself a crime, the state can take certain measures to prevent it.

7. The next chapter will return to this question when we ask about mistakes in treatment decisions. The most interesting at-

attempt thus far to establish legal guidelines for what constitutes substituted judgment and best interests is found in New Jersey's *Conroy* case. Here the court suggested criteria for a "pure-objective standard" when the patient's wishes are unknown, and a "limited-objective standard" when the patient's wishes in general can be ascertained. The former is a best-interests standard and the latter a combination of best interests and substituted judgment. See Meisel, *The Right to Die*, pp. 280- 284; also the section on the Conroy Case in Joanne Lynn, ed., *By No Extraordinary Means: The Choice to Forgo Life-Sustaining Food and Water* (Bloomington: Indiana Univ. Press, 1989), pp. 227-307. But these general guidelines are problematic (see Marvin S. Fish, "Euthanasia: Where Are We? Where Are We Going?" *Scalpel and Quill: The Bulletin of the Pittsburgh Institute of Legal Medicine*, 23, No. 4 (Dec., 1989), 2-13.

8. Daniel C. Maguire, *Death by Choice* (Garden City, NY: Doubleday, 1974).

9. Robert M. Veatch, *Death, Dying, and the Biological Revolution* (New Haven: Yale Univ. Press, 1976), p. 193.

Chapter Four

Forgoing Treatment: Some Specific Questions

Three issues will occupy us in this chapter. The first section will look at the issue of medical futility, when the physician makes unilateral decisions to forgo treatment based entirely on medical expertise. Part two will look at the problem of mistakes in diagnosis and prognosis and at the difficult question of what to do in cases of conflict. The final section will address the question of brain death.

Part One
Medical Futility

We have alluded to the concept of futility in earlier chapters and can now develop it in greater detail. This notion has important implications for the problem of forgoing treatment and will doubtless be discussed more and more in the years to come.

We are all aware of the change that has occurred in the last twenty years or so toward a greater emphasis on informed consent and other issues of patients' rights. Certain decisions about treatment are made by the patient when he or she is able to decide, or by the patient's surrogate when the patient cannot decide. These decisions are not to be made unilaterally by the physician or the health care team. One reason for this change in approach was the general acceptance of a criticism made against the older paternalistic approach. Robert Veatch is one of the strongest critics of medical paternalism. In 1973 he wrote an important article attacking what he called the "generalization of expertise."[1] By this he meant the tendency of health care professionals, especially physicians, to assume that their considerable expertise in medicine gave them expertise as well in ethics and in determining correct human values for their patients. Physicians are professionally trained to make medical decisions, he said, but not necessarily to make decisions about what patients ought to do in other areas of their lives. To assume they could was a fallacy, the fallacy of generalization of expertise.

We will return to some of the theoretical considerations of this issue in the next chapter. For now I want simply to stress that while I agree with Veatch's position attacking the generalization of expertise, this criticism does not mean that health care professionals have no expertise whatsoever. It does not mean that physicians are reduced to giving their patients a list of options, a bibliography of articles in the *New England Journal* and the *Annals of Internal Medicine,* and telling them to go home, read up on it, and come back with a choice of treatment. Physicians, nurses, physicians' assistants and other health care professionals are still the experts in medicine and health care, and unilateral decisions can be made, even without consulting the patient or the patient's surrogate.

I like to use a silly case to make that clear. If you are a physician, and I go to your dialysis center with a head cold and demand dialysis as treatment, offer $1000 in cash, insist that I am an autonomous person, quote to you from the literature against paternalism and the generalization of expertise, and threaten to sue you if you don't do what I want, you are still required ethically and legally to refuse my request. I don't have any idea of what I am talking about. Your medical expertise must override my stupid desire. You must unilaterally reject my demand, regardless of how autonomous I make it sound. My demand contradicts the standard of care. You do not need to try to refer me to another physician or nurse who might (illegally and unethically) do it. You must simply tell me that dialysis is no treatment for my cold and send me away (unless you have reason to suspect I might be crazy and self-destructive, I suppose, and then you would try to get me committed for psychiatric observation).

Similarly, physicians have no obligation to give medically futile treatment to any patient. If the treatment is *medically* futile, doctors simply do not give it. They are not obliged to inform the patient or ask the patient's permission or that of the family. This applies to CPR, antibiotics, and all sorts of treatment which in other circumstances might be warranted, if in this case they are medically futile.

It should be clear by now that the way in which futility, especially medical futility, is defined will be crucial. If a treatment is medically futile, the health care professional, usually the attending physician, unilaterally decides not to do it. In some cases, where the family might be expected to wonder why a treatment is being stopped, or not started, it is a very good idea to inform them as to why the treatment is not being used. In other cases, where the family or the patient would be unlikely to wonder about it, the physician might not inform them. In neither case is it necessary to get their consent. The expertise required to know what treatments are *medically* futile is the health care professional's, not the patient's, and the decision can be made unilaterally and should be maintained despite the patient's demand for the treatment.

Now what exactly is meant by medical futility? There is some recent controversy about this, but the best attempt at definition or description is, in my judgment, that given by Stuart J. Youngner.[2] He suggests that there are many different ways in which futility might be defined. A treatment is clearly futile if it will fail in strictly physiological terms. The dialysis will not clear the blood; the vasopressor will not better the blood pressure; electric cardioversion will not start the heart; arrhythmia control will not stop the fibrillation. Or a treatment might be called futile if, while it works in the direct or local physiological sense, it does not postpone death by even a few minutes. The cardioversion does start the heart, but the heart stops again almost immediately, and this continues each time it is done. The dialysis does clear the blood, but since the patient is immediately moribund from cardiac arrest, the dialysis is not postponing imminent death from another cause.

It is clear to me that if either of the above criteria of futility are met, the futility is indeed medical futility, and the treatment must be forgone by the physician. No consent is needed by the patient.

The treatment is useless in the very strictly medical sense. The decision about its uselessness is made by the medical expert.

But there are other possible uses of the concept of futility. What if the treatment does indeed prolong physical life for a day or so, but cannot lead to the patient's recovery? The patient cannot survive until discharge but does survive for many hours, or a few days or weeks in the hospital. What about the patient in a persistent vegetative state maintained for many years on medical nutrition and hydration? Or what if the treatment does result in discharge from the hospital, but the patient's level of living (quality of life is the term most often used, but it can be misused and misunderstood) is such that the patient cannot continue to carry out the basic purposes of life? And what about the problem of probability? What if the best a physician can do is know that a treatment is 75% likely not to postpone dying, but 25% likely to do so, though not until discharge from the hospital? In these cases who makes the decision? Is this still the kind of futility which can properly be called medical futility so that the physician may make a unilateral decision to forgo treatment?

There is considerable controversy in the literature on this question, and the issue has received serious study only in the last few years or so.[3] The more common question, the one we have been reviewing through the first three chapters, is that of whether or not treatment may be forgone when the patient or surrogate requests it be forgone. This present issue differs in that here we are speaking of whether or not the physician may stop treatment against the wishes of or without consulting the patient or surrogate.

I myself am quite clear as to what the correct answer is. At least I am sure as to what the answer is which best fits into the emerging American consensus on forgoing treatment. The health care professional, usually the attending physician, may decide unilaterally to forgo treatment when it is medically futile, and medical futility means a NO answer to either the first or the second of these two questions:

First, will the treatment do, in the immediate local physiological sense, what it is intended to do? If the answer is no, it is medically futile and must not be given.

Second, assuming the answer to the first question is yes, will the treatment and its resulting local physiological effect cause a postponement of physical death? Here, of course, we are assuming that the patient is dying. Treatments against acne may be quite effective and not have any life-prolonging results. But if the patient is imminently dying and the treatment does not postpone physical death, even though it does accomplish in the local physiological sense what it is intended to do (it does purify the blood or balance the electrolytes), the fact that physical death is not postponed by even a very short time means that the treatment is medically futile and should not be given.

There is, of course, one exception to this. Treatment which relieves pain or other patient discomfort is not futile just because it does not postpone physical death. With this exception, however, these two questions can serve to define medical futility. Treatment which is futile for other reasons is not medically futile in this sense, and the decision to forgo it must be made only after consultation with and with the agreement of the patient or surrogate. Perhaps I want to be kept alive to see the Red Sox beat the Yankees even though I know I will never leave the hospital. This reason may appeal only to someone from Massachusetts, but I am, and it does appeal to me. Or perhaps a patient wants to live until after the marriage of a son or daughter; this reason would, I think, appeal to most of us as a valid reason for resuscitation, even if the patient is virtually certain to die before leaving the hospital. Or perhaps a surrogate wants to continue hydration and nutrition for a patient in a persistent vegetative state, like Karen Ann Quinlan or Nancy Cruzan. They do this for religious reasons, or even out of fear or guilt or simply ignorance. Now the reason does not appeal to me at all. But the consensus in our nation is that this cannot be called *medically* futile treatment, and the decision to forgo cannot be made unilaterally by the physician or by the health care team or by the hospital.

This consensus may not hold for the future. Other sets of criteria for medical futility are being proposed. Some argue that, in addition to the quite restrictive criteria I have been supporting, medical futility can be determined as well on the basis of small probability of success and/or on the basis of society's agreement that even a medically successful outcome is not humanly beneficial.[4]

The "and/or" in the last paragraph is important. These two criteria could be conjunctive or disjunctive. That is, both could be required or either one could suffice. There is a major difference. If both are required before a treatment can be said to be medically futile, then, though the notion of medical futility is extended somewhat from the restrictive definition I have suggested as the present consensus, it is not expanded anywhere nearly as much as it would be if the proposed criteria were to be disjunctive. For example, if the criteria are conjunctive (if both are required), nutrition and hydration for most patients in persistent vegetative states would not meet the criteria for medical futility. The treatment might be said to yield an outcome which society (but how decide this—take a vote?) would consider to be humanly undesirable. But the odds of reaching this medically successful outcome are great. With this conjunctive use of the proposed criteria, surrogates would still get to decide, not the physicians. But if the criteria are disjunctive, that is, if either would suffice as a basis for determining the medical futility of a proposed treatment, then physicians could unilaterally choose to end nutrition for patients like Nancy Cruzan, since "society" would have decided that the outcome was not truly beneficial. Under this disjunctive use of these criteria, I might not get to see the Red Sox play.

Criteria based on probability of success and societal determination of benefit are not yet generally accepted as reasons for declaring a treatment to be medically futile. Despite the literature which recommends this, physicians should not make unilateral decisions to forgo treatment on this basis. Patients and families get to decide whether or not to forgo a treatment with small probability of success and/or with poor quality of life as a result of success. I think this is ethically correct. I do not want to see the criteria for medical futility widened to include probability and quality of life judgments. Patients and surrogates, not physicians, should make these decisions. But if this present tentative consensus should change in the future, I would argue for the conjunctive rather than the disjunctive use of the proposed criteria. This would reduce, though it would not eliminate, the problem of determining which outcomes society thinks to be beneficial.

There is a second area, however, where change is likely to be made in the future. Pressures for cost-containment will, I think, be likely to lead to refusal by third party payors to pay for some treatments which have low probability of success or where the outcome is one which "society" thinks to be of little if any benefit. As a nation we may decide that certain treatments of this kind will be available only for those who choose to pay for them personally. But that is another issue. It is not as such a question of medical futility; it is a question of allocation of resources.

One more point will be helpful here. The way in which a physician or a nurse present data about treatment is crucial in how the patient or family decides. Suppose a case where CPR would probably start the heart and result in a few more days of dying from cancer. The doctor might say: "If his heart stops, we have a machine which will start it again and keep him alive. You want us to keep him alive, don't you?" Or the physician might say: "As you know, your husband is dying. We've done all we can to help him get better, and there is nothing more we can do to help him recover. We do have a technique which can start his heart up again if it stops, but it can cause damage, and we know the heart will just stop again in a few days or so. In the meantime he won't be able to do anything except lie in bed with all these machines. What would you like us to do?"

Part Two
Mistakes and Conflicts

It is a normal, but sometimes unfortunate characteristic of our society and its media that we learn more about the bad than the good. Every day hundreds of thousands of blacks and whites go off to work and school and play together; we tend to hear most about racist attacks and riots. Similarly, in medical ethics, every day patients and families and health care professionals make difficult decisions to maintain or to forgo treatment. We hear about them mostly when those concerned disagree with one another and take the decision to court, or when a decision is later shown to be the wrong one, made on the basis of a mistaken diagnosis or prognosis. Talk shows introduce us to people who recovered from "irreversible" comas and "persistent" vegetative states. Or, on the obverse side of the coin, we meet those whose recovery was unwanted, and who now sue for having been treated. Though analysis of particular cases is impossible here, some general remarks may be helpful.

Mistakes

In one sense, mistakes in diagnosis and prognosis are inevitable. Medicine is at least as much an art as a science; it depends on empirical investigation, clinical insight, proper history, and other such aspects which by definition demand interpretation and human interaction, and which thus can never achieve perfect accuracy. Even those laboratory tests and other procedures which are at least theoretically perfectible are, of course, subject to the human error of the tired analyst and the breakdown of the machine that does them.

Medical ethics has insisted all along that health care professionals must do their human best to try to reduce the number and scope of their mistakes. They are responsible for keeping up with their field, for asking for consultations from specialists, for trying to reduce the probability of error as much as possible. But as long as medicine is practiced by humans on humans, mistakes will continue.

From another perspective, some of what we might call mistakes are better seen as inevitable uncertainties. Except in some medical situations, where the diagnosis and prognosis do indeed approach or even reach 100%, physicians are almost always slow to claim certainty. We have spoken of the problem of probability when speaking of medical futility. Physicians often will tell patients or surrogates that there may be a very slight chance that a certain treatment will help for a short time, or that there is a very slight chance that it may even lead to recovery, but that the side effects are likely to be severe. This kind of situation, which is more common than cases where prognosis is certain, does not indicate that anyone has made a mistake.

From the ethical perspective, one can speak of mistakes of undertreatment and mistakes of overtreatment. These may result from actual mistakes in prognosis, or they may be cases where the "very slight" chance in fact came true, where the treatment worked against the odds, or failed against the odds. With our delight in demanding perfection where none is possible, and our insistence on seeing death as someone's fault (the doctor's or the patient's), we are likely to hear about these "mistakes," and to want to pass a law forbidding them or recover damages when they happen.

It is, of course, perfectly possible, at least in the very short haul, to eliminate all mistakes of overtreatment *or* to eliminate all mistakes of undertreatment! We simply decide to treat nothing at all (and thus avoid all overtreatment) or we force medical invasion on everyone up until the very last instant, when the fifty-second attempt at CPR finally fails to start the heart even for a few seconds (and thus avoid all undertreatment). Mistakes of overtreatment can be avoided, but only at the risk to our health which would result from the virtual elimination of all treatment for the seriously ill. Mistakes of undertreatment can be avoided, but only at the risk of denying us our right to refuse unwanted and unneeded treatment and at the cost of massively overtreating large numbers of people.

This means simply that such "mistakes" will always be with us. Attempts to eliminate them by legislating in detail which treatments are legally mandated for which illnesses would be both futile and dangerous. Similarly wasteful and futile would be attempts to require court action for every case where a surrogate suggests that a treatment be forgone.[5] As we have noted, states should resist the invitation of the Supreme Court in *Cruzan* to legislate such hurdles.

Conflicts

Conflicts over which treatments to use and which to forgo occur often in the practical hospital situation. The literature of past decades tended to stress cases where physicians insisted on heroic, even humanly irrational treatments, often over family objections. In cases like these, the principles we have been speaking of thus far come into play rather directly.

But I have discovered in my own work in hospitals that the real cases of conflict now tend to arise as often, and possibly even more often, when physicians are convinced that a treatment is of great burden and/or of little benefit, and want it forgone, but the family insists on doing everything possible. I think this shift is due largely to the laudable increased sensitivity of physicians and other health care personnel to medical ethical issues of patient autonomy and informed consent. It may also be due to our growing awareness of the need for cost containment, and to the fact that hospitals will often take serious losses by continuing this kind of treatment. Payment schemes like Diagnostic Related Groupings (DRG's) have resulted in major hospital losses in some cases of this type. Physicians naturally defend the fiscal viability of the hospitals they work in, even when they are themselves able to bill for the service they render. And hospitals and HMO's put pressure on physicians not to treat needlessly, since now the hospital, or the HMO, will take a loss if treatment exceeds repayment.

Whatever the reason, conflict situations are very likely to arise when families insist on treating, and physicians, with their medical expertise, think it inappropriate. And, of course, the other type of conflict situation still often arises, when the physician wants to treat and the family wants to stop. There are a number of suggestions which can help in this kind of conflict.

First, the importance of early communication cannot be overstressed. Advanced directives are often very helpful in this regard. Hospital education programs and patient education literature are excellent ways of insuring that patients will consider their options before they lose the ability to decide for themselves. A patient education brochure is included as an appendix to this book.

Second, we have already spoken about medical futility. If the treatment is medically futile in the strict sense, the physician must not use it, despite what the family (or even the patient) says.

Third, the physician may well help resolve the problem by trying to communicate with the family. As we have already noted, the way a physician presents the medical and human aspects of the diagnosis, prognosis, and treatment options often determines how the patient or family will respond. In many cases, nurses, social workers, clergy, and friends of the family can help. Some people are naturally better at this than others.

Fourth, time-limited trials are often very helpful. The family may need time before being ready to accept the inevitability of death. All may agree on maintaining aggressive treatment for a limited time to see if it is helpful, and then on forgoing it if, as appears likely, it turns out not to be of real benefit to the patient.

This method should not be used in cases of strict medical futility, of course, and if the attending physician is convinced that any further aggressive treatment is burdensome to the patient, he or she will naturally resist this approach. The physician is obliged not to harm the patient. But in many cases there is at least some chance the treatment may be of help, if only for a short while, and a time-limited trial can ease the family's burden and alleviate the conflict.

Fifth, the physician may want to call a consult by the hospital's ethics committee. Chapter eight will return to the role of these committees.

Sixth, in some cases the physician may simply be unable in conscience to follow the family's wishes. My own opinion here is that this will rarely happen; usually it will be a question of medical futility or of failed communication. But it can happen, and the physician has not only the right, but the duty to withdraw from the case, assuming, of course, that he or she has been able to get another qualified doctor to accept the patient. When this is not possible, the physician must continue to care for the patient, trying to apply the principles we have presented as they seem best to fit the specific case.

Seventh, there are times when the physician is certain that the family is insisting on useless and terribly burdensome treatment which does not quite fit into the strict definition of medical futility I have proposed. In these cases, the physician may want to go to court to ask for a court-appointed guardian who will be authorized to forgo the aggressive procedures. Hospital attorneys will help in this. In most cases, physicians and hospitals will want to avoid this approach, but in some cases it will be the only ethically responsible path.

There is, of course, one final possibility, but I do not offer it as a suggestion. The physician can simply choose to override the wishes of the surrogate and stop treatment, even though the treatment is not really medically futile. No physician has yet been convicted of criminal charges for forgoing treatment in this kind of situation. But it is a dangerous and ethically dubious decision. In virtually all cases of conflict, one of the above-suggested approaches will prove successful.

Part Three
Brain Death

Treatment is not "forgone" for the dead. No treatment can be given to the dead body of what once was a human person. Only the respect owed to corpses is proper.

"Brain death" is not different from any other kind of death. It is death pure and simple. It is arguably unfortunate that the term is used, because so many think it means a different kind of death, or an earlier death, or even a preventable death. "Brain death" refers to criteria used to determine that a person has indeed died when the usual criteria for determining this event (cessation of breathing and heart beat) are not available because heart and lung function are being forced by machines. But no one who is declared "brain-dead" would have been thought to be alive before the criteria and the machines which necessitated them were invented. Total brain death means virtually instant cessation of cardiac and pulmonary function in the absence of machines. Both the higher brain, the neo-cortex, and the lower brain and brain stem are dead. The person is dead. Heart and lungs may be forced to work, but this does not mean that human life of any sort continues.

This is now almost universally accepted.[6] Some jurisdictions do not yet have laws which explicitly accept neurological criteria for determining that death has occurred, and this may cause some hesitation in these jurisdictions, but it is at least arguable that since these are medical criteria, the lack of explicit state acceptance should not be a problem. Continued treatment would be medically futile in the strict sense we have already proposed.

Some controversy remains about how to respond to persons who, from religious bases, reject the notion of brain death and insist that the hearts and lungs of such persons be forced to continue to function in the body, arguing that the person is alive. The most common judgment made here is that religion cannot legitimately reject a medical fact, and that this is indeed a medical fact and not a question of faith or of philosophy. Persons who are dead cannot properly be claimed to be alive. No medical treatment may be given to the dead. A dissenting opinion is made by those who believe that patient and family autonomy should always prevail in such cases and by those who reject brain-death criteria. The former opinion, that this is a medical determination which cannot be denied on other bases, is held by a majority of ethicists and physicians, and is most in keeping with the central argument of this book. At the very least, anyone insisting on ongoing treatment for brain-dead, that is, for dead persons, should be asked to bear the total cost of such treatment.

A second controversial issue concerns the determination of the status of persons in irreversible comas and persistent vegetative states. These patients are not brain-dead, since their brain stems continue to function. But they have irreversibly lost all higher brain function. They are "vegetative" and will remain so, but their hearts and lungs will continue to function, often without medical intervention. We have already discussed the ethical and legal issues concerned with forgoing medical nutrition and hydration in such cases. But such issues would be moot if we were to declare these persons dead. Some argue that this is precisely what we should do.

I believe that there is a legitimate theological argument for this approach, though I am not totally sure that it is completely convincing.[7] It is clear, however, that society is not yet ready to claim that breathing bodies may be dead. In addition, there is a serious danger of backlash against organ transplantation, especially since it is mainly the transplant specialists who are proposing that partial brain death be sufficient for declaring a person to have died. This context, of harvesting cadaver organs, is a bad one for making this kind of decision. This is also true of the proposal to declare anencephalic infants to be brain-absent, and therefore dead. Finally, there is a danger that this change, like the proposed change in the law against active euthanasia, would cause a backlash against the present American consensus on forgoing treatment.

It is possible that this may change in the future. But for now only total brain death, including death of the brain stem, should be considered to mean that the patient has died. Total brain death simply introduces a new set of criteria for determining the same moment of death. But neocortical criteria, according to which the irreversibly comatose would be declared to have died, would indeed push death earlier: patients who would, decades ago, have been thought to be alive would now be said to have died. Physicians would have to do things to their bodies to get the hearts and lungs to stop. Society is not ready for this, and probably need never accept it. With the sensitive forgoing of treatment, persons in irreversible comas can be allowed to die. They need not be declared already dead.

One final argument supports this position. Decisions to forgo medical treatment for the living need not be traumatic, but they should not be automatic either. Declaring a person to have died allows an easy escape from what should be a decision requiring some serious thought. Ethics should offer comfort and relief from false guilt and fear, but it should not adopt ethical or legal short cuts to turn important decisions into thoughtless ones. Comatose persons should not be declared dead. Brain-dead persons have indeed died.

Discussion Questions

1. Do you agree with the definition of medical futility proposed here? What do you think medical futility means?

2. Do you think physicians should be able to decide on their own to forgo treatment which has some, but very little chance of success? Should doctors be allowed to turn off nutrition and hydration for comatose or PVS patients without the approval of the surrogate?

3. What is your own experience in dealing with conflicts in this context? Do you have any additional suggestions for dealing with this problem?

4. Discuss the difference between total brain death and higher brain death. Do you accept the idea that comatose patients should be declared to have died?

5. What do you think should be done when families claim that brain-dead patients are still alive?

Endnotes

1. Robert M. Veatch, "Generalization of Expertise," *Hastings Center Studies*, 1, No. 2 (1973), 29-40.

2. Stuart J. Youngner, "Who Defines Futility?" *JAMA,* 260 (1988), 2094-2095.

3. In addition to Youngner's article, already cited, articles include Leslie J. Blackhall, "Must We Always Use CPR?" *NEJM,* 317 (1987), 1281-1285—Blackhall gives more latitude to physicians' unilateral decisions than I believe is appropriate; Tom Tomlinson and Howard Brody, "Ethics and Communication in Do-Not-Resuscitate Orders," *NEJM,* 318 (1988), 43-46—these authors make very helpful distinctions between medical futility and quality-of-life futility; Donald J. Murphy, "Do-Not-Resuscitate Orders: Time for Reappraisal in Long-Term-Care Institutions," *JAMA,* 260 (1988), 2098-2101—Murphy argues that physicians may unilaterally write a DNR order when the future quality of life is low (p. 2100), a position I do not accept; Troyen A. Brennan, "Incompetent Patients with Limited Care in the Absence of Family Consent," *Annals of Internal Medicine,* Nov. 15, 1988, pp. 819-825; Philip J. Boyle, "DNR and the Elderly," *Issues in Health Care,* St. Louis Univ. Medical Center for Health Care Ethics, Dec., 1988; John J. Paris, Robert K. Crone, and Frank Reardon, "Physicians' Refusal of Requested Treatment: The Case of Baby L," *NEJM,* 322 (1990), 1012-1015.

4. These criteria are proposed by Lawrence J. Schneiderman, Nancy S. Jecker, and Albert R. Jonsen, "Medical Futility: Its Meaning and Ethical Implications," *Annals of Internal Medicine,* 112 (1990), 949-954. They argue that either a very small probability of medical success (less than one to three percent—no successes in the last 100 cases) or an outcome which does not offer benefit to the patient as a whole (it only prolongs the life of an unconscious patient or it maintains life dependent on intensive medical care) is a sufficient warrant for declaring a treatment medically futile. They wish these criteria to be independent—either one is enough. They propose explicitly that nutritional support for a patient in a persistence vegetative state be considered medically futile and that physicians forgo it regardless of the wishes of the patient or the family (p. 950). If medical care does not offer patients the opportunity to achieve any of life's goals, it must be refused by physicians regardless of the wishes of patients or surrogates (pp. 949, 952-953).

5. As chapter nine will suggest, our society will have to limit medical expenditures, and this limitation will probaby include al-

location based on medical treatment and condition. This will require our nation to make enormously difficult decisions as to which treatments national health insurance will fund for which conditions. Thus, to some extent, society will be forced into legislation of the kind I am arguing against. But the contexts are different. In the present context, legislation would mandate the treatment itself or allow it to be forgone. These are decisions best made in the clinical context, by the patient, surrogate, and health care team. In the future context of funding by national health insurance, legislation would not mandate that a treatment be used or forgone, but would simply decide whether or not national health insurance would pay for it. This is something third party payors already do. As we will see when we deal with this issue, individual persons could still ask for the treatment, and pay for it from other than government sources. The enormous difficulty of making allocation decisions, to which we will return in the last two chapters, is reason to avoid such legislation if we can. I believe that from the perspective of funding and allocation and cost containment we will not be able to avoid it. But in the present context we can and we should avoid it. These decisions are best made at the bedside, not in the legislature or the courts.

6. See the Hastings Center *Guidelines on the Termination of Life-Sustaining Treatment and the Care of the Dying,* pp. 86-90. See also the objection of Robert Veatch, p. 159.

7. See Louis Janssens, "Transplantation d'organes," *Foi et Temps,* 4 (1983), 308-324. For my analysis of this argument, see "Individualism and Corporatism in a Personalist Ethic: an Analysis of Organ Transplants," in Joseph A. Selling, ed., *Personalist Morals: Essays in Honor of Louis Janssens* (Louvain: Univ. of Louvain Press, 1988), pp. 159-161.

Chapter Five

Whatever Happened to the Good Old Medical Ethics?

The title of this chapter requires some explanation. By it I mean that I will describe the move away from the kind of "medical ethics" which was proposed in the nineteenth and early twentieth centuries in the codes of professional medical associations, particularly the American Medical Association, and in books classified as works in medical ethics which expanded on the codes and which claimed to speak to doctors about what was "ethical." I am going to argue that this approach to "medical ethics" was never really ethical, though it did include a number of valid ethical insights. I am going to argue that we are better off without it. It was paternalistic, condescending, elitist in the bad sense of that word, and intraprofessionally relativistic. Ridding ourselves of it is good, not bad.

But I am also going to argue that getting rid of this inadequate basis for health care ethics is no help at all if it means that we eliminate a bad ethic in order to replace it with a worse one. It is no help to move from paternalism to an isolated individualism (paternalism: "I'm the father-doctor and you're the patient-child, so you do what I tell you"; isolated individualism: "I've given you three articles from the *New England Journal*—you're your own boss, you figure it out.") Nor is it any help if we move from condescension to indifference (condescension: "There there dear, how are we feeling this morning, doctor will make it go away"; indifference: "Look, lady, I don't really care how you feel; there are plenty of people sicker than you.") It is no help to move from elitism to an egalitarian camouflage for uncaring autonomy

Examples

73

(elitism: "I went to Johns Hopkins and studied medical ethics at Harvard, so I know what's medically and morally right for you"; uncaring autonomy: "We're both equal parties to the doctor-patient contract, so you decide and sign the proper form on the places checked and give it to my receptionist.")

Finally, it is no help if we move from intraprofessional relativism, which had a bad basis for verifying ethical judgments, to general ethical relativism, which has no basis at all (intra-professional relativism: the basis for verifying moral principles and judgments is what the medical profession decides, on the basis of what is good for doctors and for the profession; general ethical relativism: there is no basis at all for verification of moral principles and judgments; one person's moral opinions are as good as another's, so if one physician wants to sacrifice some money for the care of patients and another wants to sacrifice some patients for the care of money, it's all relative anyway and who's to say what's right and wrong). Ridding ourselves of paternalism, condescension, arrogant elitism, and intraprofessional relativism is good, not bad. But replacing them with isolated individualism, indifference, uncaring autonomy, and general ethical relativism is bad, not good.[1]

Thus far we have devoted four chapters to the issue of forgoing treatment. This chapter and the next will emphasize theory. The present chapter will tackle two sets of issues. First, I will speak about why most ethicists feel we are well rid of the old medical ethics of the doctors' associations and medical schools as well as the old nursing ethics or professional adjustments of nursing associations and nursing schools. Second, I will speak to the entire issue of the basis for ethical judgment, the rarified question of epistemology and metaethics. How can we know anything ethical? Can we verify judgments of right and wrong? Does ethics have any meaning at all, or should ethicists, and that includes physicians who study ethics, all simply go away, leaving hospitals to more useful pursuits free from idle and futile speculation?

Part One
Intraprofessional Medical and Nursing Ethics

We have already seen that until very recently, at least very recently from an historical perspective, that is, until somewhere in the 1960's, only Roman Catholics and, to a lesser degree, Jews, were doing what might with any real validity be called medical *ethics* or health care *ethics* or bio-*ethics*. Secular philosophers and theologians other than Roman Catholics were involved in theoretical discussions of morality and in practical applications of morality to issues in sexuality and in social justice. But in the Western world only Catholics and, to a lesser extent, Jews, attempted systematically to apply moral principles or laws to medical practice.

Within the medical profession itself there was a field known as "medical ethics," but this was not truly ethics in the sense of an investigation of the morality or ethics of medical practice. It did indeed include at times some dimensions of moral philosophy, but its greatest emphasis was on questions of intra-professional etiquette. It was a field of discussion practiced by physicians among themselves which consisted of an intra-professional dialogue on issues largely of "etiquette" and included the formulation and interpretation of intra-professional codes of "medical ethics."[2]

Medical moralists (philosophers, theologians, and those physicians who did approach the discipline from a philosophical and/or theological background) often disassociated themselves from the "medical ethics" of the professional associations. They often explicitly rejected the rubric "medical ethics."

There are two basic reasons for this disassociation. First, much of the content of the codes lies in the field of etiquette rather than ethics in our current meaning of the term. The kind of horse one owned, the size of letters used on billboards, the restrictions placed on criticizing other physicians, insistence on giving free service to other physicians, opposition to medical insurance, politeness to colleagues, proper speech and dress were some of the topics discussed.

Criticism of this kind of "medical ethics" was common. In his 1927 edition of Percival's 1803 code of medical ethics, Chauncey Leake states of that code and of others written under its influence:

"the chief difficulty . . . is that no clear distinction is drawn between the incidental etiquette of medical practice, and the fundamental ethical problems of the profession. . . . [There is] considerable emphasis on medical etiquette. This phase of the matter has since remained in a position of exaggerated importance."[3]

My own research into this kind of "medical ethics" has substantiated this charge. Very little study is made in the books and articles of intraprofessional "medical ethics" of those issues which we would consider to be essential: informed consent, forgoing treatment, patients' rights, health care delivery, abortion, allocation of resources, etc. I remember finding at last, in a late nineteenth century book by Daniel Webster Cathell, a section on abortion. Thinking that I might discover here some analysis of the morality of abortion, I found instead Dr. Cathell's advice that the physician should avoid bringing notoriety on himself and should be sure to get paid in advance by "unmarried negresses, ladies of easy virtue, and other low females" who might try to get off without paying when they discover he will not abort.[4] The same book includes the advice that a physician should get "a good looking horse and a genteel carriage . . . getting it indicates your practice is growing. . . . If you unfortunately have a bony horse and a seedy-looking, pre-Adamite . . . buggy, do not let them habitually stand in front of your office."[5] In other words, show off the Mercedes but keep the Pinto in the garage.

The second reason why this kind of "medical ethics" was criticized as not being in any real sense a study of the morality of health care was that the approach was all too often one of professional self-interest. The codes of ethics seemed designed to protect physicians from scrutiny more than to better their practice. In technical terms, this kind of medical ethics used a reductionist intra-professional metaethical relativism as a basis for verification of its moral judgments. We will come back to this later on. In simple language, this means that the medical profession *posited* right and wrong, decided what it should be, based largely, though not entirely, on what would be good for the medical profession.

This aspect of the codes was similarly criticized. George Bernard Shaw is cited as saying that, "Professional etiquette has for its object not the health of the patient or of the community, but the protection of the doctor's livelihood and the concealment of errors."[6] Writing in 1934, a physician claims that to patients "ethics would seem to mean a fraternal conspiracy to dissemble and cloak our manifold sins and wickedness and to thwart patients in their divine right to hire and fire doctors as they please. . . . they are mystified by the tender care with which doctors avoid speaking ill of each other, by our reluctance or refusal on occasion to accept each other's patients for treatment, by our aversion to advertising and, in short, by our ethics."[7]

The picture is not entirely grim, however, and there have been defenders of the codes and of their interpretations. Surely many, probably most physicians have been women and men of the highest moral standards. And the very fact that there was such a thing as "medical ethics" at all indicated the interest physicians had in *something* ethical. This professional ethic was part of the development of professional medicine. The medical vocation became one worthy of special ethical attention. Even if the theoretical approach for the ethics of the professional associations was not based on a perspective of general ethics, but rather on a perspective of professional self-interest, the associations were nonetheless doing something called ethics. And some of the conclusions they reached, even though often based on the wrong motivation, were the right conclusions, and medicine and the health of the nation is better off for their having been reached than we would have been had there been no "medical ethics" to reach them.

It is perhaps important that I now correct any impression I might seem to be giving that I think physicians are, by and large, egoistic creeps. I don't, any more than I think ethicists are, by and large, egoistic creeps. Some of us are. Some doctors are. Some nurses are. A moral theologian once asked me if I found that I could work with doctors, if they were open to moral issues, if they had moral concerns about their practice. I said yes, that indeed I had been edified by many of the physicians I work with, since they were not only open to moral discussion, but recognized how essential moral sensitivity is to good medicine.

Some ethicists, especially those who reject the very concept of professional medicine, argue that physicians are, by their very professional status, part of the problem rather than part of the solution. I am convinced this is false. The health care ethics now being studied in some (but not in nearly enough) medical schools, and now being debated and written about in the pages of the major medical journals, is far removed from the self-serving pompous brand of pap which characterized much of the older approach. Health care ethics is now an ecumenical cross-disciplinary field involving philosophers, physicians, nurses, theologians, and legal scholars. The field can draw on the insights and the moral sensitivity of the different professions, and this very mix of interested persons has made possible the important advances in health care ethics which have taken place in the last thirty years.

Within the nursing profession, parallel to the "medical ethics" of the medical associations, but different in many ways, was intraprofessional "nursing ethics," which included nursing association codes, as well as books, articles, and courses in "professional adjustments." The very term "professional adjustments" is indicative of the tenor of what this was. The nurse was to "adjust" to her profession (in this time, virtually all nurses were women). Unfortunately most of the adjusting was that of properly deferring to her superiors, who were the mostly male physicians. "Nursing ethics" in the period we are talking about consisted largely in the discussion of nursing etiquette. Issues included discipline, the religious life of the good nurse, her personal appearance, conversation, her social life, budget, job applications, and the like. Just as "medical ethics" has now changed toward a much more valid moral discipline, so has "nursing ethics." Works in health care ethics for nurses now tackle the same issues as do those written for physicians, and the active role of nurses in the theoretical and the practical advance of proper health care cannot be overemphasized.[8]

We can now turn to the second part of the chapter, the issue of metaethics, and in doing so we will continue our basic theme of "whatever happened to the good old medical ethics?" We are studying the basis of health care ethics.

Part Two
Metaethics

The technical term "metaethics" means "beyond ethics," and refers to that area of ethics which deals with the possibility of meaning and knowledge of ethics. It is the epistemology of ethics.

Epistemology is the science of knowledge, the branch of philosophy which asks about human knowing. Maybe we make everything up. Maybe all human knowledge is groundless. Perhaps nothing and no one exists except me, and I imagine everything I think I know! Maybe not. Epistemology can be strange stuff.

Yet health care has certain epistemological presuppositions.[9] It presumes a certain epistemological realism, that is, that its knowledge is based on reality. Health care professionals presume that there are patterns in human nature, ordered ways in which the body will react to disease and to its treatment. If there were no patterns, scientific medicine would be impossible. All of us claim that we know something about these patterns, and that they actually exist, despite the fact that they are very complex and are not identical from patient to patient. We claim that we know ahead of time, at least with a decent degree of certitude, how bodies will act and react. We do not have to start absolutely brand-new with each new patient. We have a body of knowledge, which we know to be true, about biological processes, about treatments, about diagnoses and prognoses.

We know enough, I hope, to be humble about all of this. Sometimes we make mistakes. Some diseases have no cures. Our ignorance is great. But our knowledge is great, too. If we could not claim some certain knowledge about the human body, we would have to abandon the attempt to study and to practice scientific medicine. We make certain epistemological presuppositions without which we could not practice medicine.

The same is true in ethics. But ethics is different from the more immediately empirical and experimental areas of human knowledge. Very few people would want to argue that it is just a baseless opinion that appendectomies help in the treatment of appendicitis. Many want to argue that ethics is a matter of baseless opinion. And so we have metaethics, the epistemology of ethics. Does ethics have any meaning, and if it does, how do we verify it?

Three Theories

There are three major answers to that question.[10]

1. Non-cognitivism.

The first answer is called non-cognitivism, or emotivism. I will here describe it in its most radical form, a form which I think is easily dismissed. Later, after I have dealt with the other approaches, I will return to a more sophisticated form of non-cognitivism. Radical non-cognitivism, or radical emotivism, says that ethics has no meaning whatsoever. There is nothing to be known, no cognitive content. It is all an emotional outburst. To say that the Nazi genocide was wrong is merely to show forth an emotional revulsion to it, much as one might react in revulsion to stepping in deep doodoo. Yuch! But maybe the Nazis were right. It's all meaningless.

2. Relativism.

The second answer to the metaethical question is relativism. In my judgment, it is not any better. Relativism eliminates any possibility of verifying ethical judgments of right and wrong. We can, of course, verify that people do in fact make this kind of judgment. And we can describe the judgments made. Most South African Blacks claim that Apartheid is morally wrong. Many South African Whites claim it is morally right. They all have a right to their opinion, since nothing can be verified about whether it is right or wrong beyond stating that opinions vary. Some think abortion is wrong, some think it is right, and some aren't sure. It's all a matter of opinion. Some think socialism is right, some think capitalism is right, some work for war and some for peace, some for self and some for others. It doesn't matter, really, because it's all relative. It's all a matter of opinion.

Relativism, which I reject, has to be distinguished from situationalism or contextualism. I also reject radical situationalism, but I accept the fact that situational differences do make for important differences in moral judgment. It is right, I claim, to forgo CPR in a patient with bony metastases who asks that CPR be forgone. It is not right to forgo it for a child who has spent five minutes in a frozen pond. The situation, the medical reality, is different. To recognize the morally relevant difference is not relativism. Relativism rejects all moral judgments, all ethical conclusions, because none of them can be verified. Morality is merely a matter of opinion.

Now we have what we need to look again at the charge I made earlier against much of the "good old medical ethics." I said it was intraprofessionally relativistic. That is not the same as the more general relativism we have just defined, but it is often its practical result. If there is no objective basis for ethical principles and ethical judgments, it is easy to create such a basis in individual or group self-interest. If ethics is merely a matter of opinion, it is easy to claim that my opinion or our opinion is the right one. Though those who designed the codes and wrote the books about medical ethics and medical etiquette from this perspective would have denied it, they in fact most often based their conclusions on what was good for their own profession. It was relative to themselves and their profession that they judged, not on the basis of a wider objective standard.

I have already stated, and state again, that this basis was often far better than no basis at all, and that it often led to quite proper ethical judgments. I think, for example, that the ethical judgment rejecting advertisements by physicians and by health care institutions was a good judgment. I wish we did not have hospitals competing for patients by trying to outdo each other in hyping one or another service claimed to be unique. But I have to say that the reason the older codes forbad advertising was the fear that this could cause people to wonder about the perfection of doctors. The AMA wanted a kind of professional sanctity. I am convinced that the motivation for opposing advertising was similar to the one which protected physicians from any kind of outside regulation and which urged them never to criticize each other. For similar reasons, the AMA has opposed national health insurance. Physicians' associations have not had a particularly good record of disciplining and removing those of their own members who have proved incompetent or even dangerous; yet they have often tried to prevent the growth of alternative approaches to health care, such as homeopathy and chiropractic. The basic motivation for this was the promotion of the profession and its members. That, I think, was the primary motive for opposing competitive advertising. Yet the judgment was right. The decision of the Supreme Court in 1975 properly interpreted the AMA's motive for prohibiting advertising, but the Court's insistence that physicians be free to advertise has had deleterious effects on the nation's health care system.[11]

3. Metaethical Absolutism and the Natural Law.

I return now to metaethics. In addition to the two theories we have seen, non-cognitivism and relativism, both of which deny that ethical judgments have any basis for verification, is a third theory which says they do. This theory is sometimes called metaethical absolutism. The word is problematic if it is taken to imply dogmatism or legalism, but we will use it. Metaethical absolutists claim that ethical judgments do have meaning and can be verified. There are a number of types, depending on what source is used for verification. Some say that God gives us direct and immediate knowledge of right and wrong by means of direct, supernatural revelation. This might be in the Bible, or in a vision, or in a revelation to a religious leader. Supernatural metaethical absolutism thus rejects non-cognitivism and relativism, but it also rejects the idea that human reason can discover right and wrong. God must tell us, and God must tell us directly.

Other metaethical absolutists claim that ethical judgments are verifiable on the basis of moral intuition. This is known as intuitionism or intuitional metaethical absolutism.

Finally, some claim that ethical judgments are verifiable by human reason examining reality. This is sometimes called empirical metaethical absolutism, sometimes foundationalism, and sometimes the natural law. This is, in my judgment, the best of the options. Though I cannot prove it to be true, I am convinced that norms of right and wrong are discoverable in the patterns of reality, that God's creation, as God creates it, reveals to us the divine will.

This is very Catholic. God does not create chaos, but order. God does not allow original sin to destroy our reason and our freedom, but graces us with the ability to learn and to discover. God helps that discovery through the Bible and the leaders of the Church, who, enlightened with the knowledge of Christ's revelation, offer insights based on that enlightenment. But the primary source of moral knowledge is the very creation which God creates. We will return to this issue in the next chapter. For now, we can note the compatibility this approach has to the epistemological presuppositions of scientific medicine we mentioned earlier. Natural law theory, like scientific medicine, assumes there are patterns to creation and to human nature, patterns which can be discovered, patterns which are not rigid or immutable but which are nonetheless stable enough to serve as a basis of valid knowledge. In my judgment, this is the best approach to a solution for the metaethical question.

Rational Positivism

I stated earlier that I would come back to emotivism. I wanted to give a simple definition of emotivism, identifying it with radical non-cognitivism. Under this simple definition of emotivism, ethical judgments and principles have no basis whatsoever. They are simply emotional outbursts. There is a far more sophisticated kind of metaethic, one which arises from the same epistemological skepticism which gives rise to non-cognitivism, but which allows us to do ethics and to reach ethical judgments. I myself think it is flawed in serious ways. But it is the position of many philosophers today. I want to call it rational positivism. It is that variation of, or descendent of, non-cognitivism which argues that ethical judgments of right and wrong are decreed, or posited, by rational persons thinking reasonably.

Now there is a major difference between this and natural law. That is, there is a difference between insisting that only that judgment can be verified which reasonable persons do come to agree upon, on the one hand, and, on the other hand, insisting that those judgments can be verified which reasonable persons can discover to be reasonable. In the first case, the judgment is posited, decided upon, decreed, by the persons who make it without any claim that it can be shown to be itself the right judgment. Even those who make it admit that it may be the wrong judgment. There is, in the last event, no way to know what the right judgment is. And this is not only true of judgments in areas of great complexity, but true of all judgments. Recall the difference we have seen between situationalism or contextualism and relativism. The same difference applies between situationalism or contextualism and rational positivism.

I do think, of course, that the fact that reasonable people make an ethical judgment does give it a considerable degree of valid support. And I also recognize that the judgments actually made by those philosophers who hold to this kind of a metaethic are very much apt to be similar to those judgments actually made by philosophers who claim a stronger basis for verification, as natural law thinkers do. Nonetheless there is a difference. And that difference, though very theoretical in itself, does have practical results in that gradually it seeps through the society that even that society's wisest persons have no basis for judging, and that they think no-one else has such a basis either.

I myself believe that the final result of this approach is the very kind of egotistic type of relativism with examples of which I began this chapter. If the difference between right and wrong is no more than what persons decree it to be or posit it to be, even if the decreeing persons are said to be reasonable, then perhaps after all I may be content with doing what I want for myself. There is no real basis for moral judgment.

If, on the other hand, we accept the idea that, even though it is often very hard to know exactly what is right to do in some complicated questions, and even though persons of reason and good will often disagree about these questions, and even though bad persons will transgress the right and do what they and others know to be wrong—if, despite this, we continue to claim and to believe that there *is* a difference between right and wrong, then society in general, and the professions of health care in particular, will better avoid the swamp of relativism and its almost inevitable practical concomitant: individualistic or sectarian egoism, the practical judgment that what is beneficial, or pleasurable, or profitable for me, or for my sect, group, or profession, is indeed what is right.

Conclusion

So, then, we have three major answers to the metaethical question about meaning and verification. Non-cognitivism says ethics has no meaning; it is a pure emotional outburst; no ethical judgments can be verified. Relativism says we cannot verify ethical judgments; we cannot prescribe; all we can do is be aware that people make such judgments, and describe how they differ from person to person and from group to group. Metaethical absolutism claims that judgments can be verified. Supernatural metaethical absolutists claim that God tells us in some specifically definable, supposedly supernatural source of revelation, such as the Bible, or the teaching of a Church leader. Intuitionists claim that we know right and wrong based on a valid built-in moral sense. Natural law theorists claim that we discover right and wrong by studying the patterns of the world and of ourselves.

The Roman Catholic moral tradition, to which we will turn in the next chapter, has traditionally claimed a natural law approach. It has not claimed that it will always be easy for us to arrive at the correct answer, especially in difficult questions. Indeed, Thomas Aquinas, who is largely responsible for introducing natural law theory into Catholic thought, based on the work of the Greek philosopher Aristotle, stated clearly that the more specific judgments of the natural law, the so-called secondary and tertiary precepts of the natural law, were not perfectly clear, and that there would be a good deal of disagreement about them. He nonetheless claimed that they, too, were discoverable by human reason. It may be hard for us to reach right conclusions in complex matters, but the task is a worthy one because, in principle, the right judgment can be reached.

I will end now with my own definition of natural law theory, a definition which I think to be accurate in describing the best of Catholic moral theology in this context.

Natural law theory is the claim that human persons discover right and wrong by their God-given reason and life experience, examining individually and collectively the patterns of creation as God is creating it. We will continue to examine this approach in the next chapter when we take a closer look at what has been happening in Catholic medical ethics over the past half-century.

Discussion Questions

1. Do you agree with the criticisms against the "good old medical ethics"? What were its positive aspects? What about nursing ethics?

2. Discuss the kind of confidence you have in medical ("scientific") knowledge. Compare this to the confidence you have in ethical knowledge.

3. Of the three general approaches to metaethics, which is closest to your own? Why?

Endnotes

1. For possible reading in this context, I suggest Larry Churchill's article on "Reviving a Distinctive Medical Ethic," *Hastings Center Report*, 19, No. 3 (May-June 1989), 28-34. Alan Bloom's book *The Closing of the American Mind* is also relevant, though I agree with Churchill's characterization of that book as reactionary. A book which brilliantly suggests models of virtue for physicians is William F. May, *The Physician's Covenant* (Philadelphia: Westminster, 1988). Similar in intent is James F. Drane, *Becoming a Good Doctor: The Place of Virtue and Character in Medical Ethics* (Kansas City, Mo: Sheed & Ward, 1988).

2. For more detail on this topic, and for reference to sources, see David F. Kelly, *The Emergence of Roman Catholic Medical Ethics in North America* (New York: Edwin Mellen Press, 1979), pp. 81-94.

3. Chauncey D. Leake, ed., *Percival's Medical Ethics* (Baltimore: Williams and Wilkins, 1927), p. 37.

4. Daniel Webster Cathell, *Book on the Physician Himself and Things that Concern His Reputation and Success*, 10th ed. (Philadelphia: F. A. Davis, 1898), p. 79.

5. *Ibid.* page 27.

6. Burton J. Hendrick, "New Medical Ethics," *McClure*, 42 (Jan., 1914), 117-118.

7. Park J. White, "Doctor's Ethics," *Hygeia (Today's Health)*, 12 (1934), 498.

8. It is interesting to note that a number of the Roman Catholic medical ethics texts of the first half of this century were written for nurses. These works were indeed works in health care ethics, similar to Catholic texts written for physicians and priests.

9. See Albert R. Jonsen and Stephen Toulmin, *The Abuse of Casuistry: A History of Moral Reasoning* (Berkeley: Univ. of Califor-

nia Press, 1988), pp. 23-46; Edmund D. Pellegrino and David C. Thomasma, *A Philosophical Basis of Medical Practice: Toward a Philosophy and Ethic of the Healing Professions* (New York: Oxford Univ. Press, 1981), esp. pp. 82-169.

10. This typology is taken from Robert M. Veatch, "Does Ethics Have an Empirical Basis?," *Hastings Center Studies*, 1, No. 2 (1973), 29-40. I have found this technical usage of the term "metaethics" to be the most useful, though some authors use it in a wider sense.

11. In *Goldfarb v. Virginia State Bar*, the Court applied the Sherman Antitrust Act to the medical profession (Charles J. Dougherty, *American Health Care: Realities, Rights, and Reforms* [New York: Oxford Univ. Press, 1988], p. 138).

Chapter Six

Catholic Medical Ethics

The previous chapter addressed the topic of "Whatever Happened to the Good Old Medical Ethics." We looked at the development over the past three decades away from the kind of intraprofessional medical ethics of the medical associations which had typified much of the field until the 1960's. I was critical of that older approach, first because much of it concerned etiquette and not ethics, and second because the basis for its judgments was what was good for the profession of medicine. It was less the ethical or moral investigation of health care practice than the development and interpretation of codes of medical ethics which were largely, though not totally, intended to enhance the prestige of medicine. We also found parallel problems with the older nursing ethics or professional adjustments of the nursing associations. Some of the conclusions reached in the codes of ethics were quite correct, but the method was inadequate.

From there we proceeded to talk about the problem of the basis for ethical judgment, the problem of metaethics. I argued against relativism and emotivism and what I called rational positivism, and I argued in favor of some kind of natural law theory. I ended the chapter by defining natural law theory as the claim that human persons discover right and wrong by their God-given reason and life experience, examining individually and collectively the patterns of creation as God is creating it. I suggested that this approach to metaethics is harmonious with the epistemological presuppositions that all of us in health care make all the time, that is, that there are patterns in the way God creates, that we can learn about these patterns, however imperfect our knowledge remains, and that we can act on this knowledge for human benefit.

This natural law approach has been the approach claimed by the Roman Catholic tradition.[1] But it has taken a number of twists over the centuries. It is clear that the last 30 years have seen quite a shake-up within Catholic moral theology, and in medical ethics in particular. Since the 1960's, when the Church called the Second Vatican Council, there has been much debate and dispute within Catholic circles as to the proper method to be used and the proper conclusions to be reached in medical ethics. The most public of these debates has concerned contraception, but other issues have been questioned as well, including active euthanasia and abortion. Similarly, in sexual ethics, discussions have been widespread about issues previously assumed to be settled, such as divorce, homosexuality, pre-marital relations, and so on. What has happened? That is the topic of this chapter: "Whatever Happened to the Good Old Catholic Morality?"

We will begin with a brief history of Catholic medical ethics. Then we will take a look at its material definition, that is, at the topics it dealt with and now deals with. The third section will speak to the question of method. How did Catholic medical ethics tend to reach its judgments prior to the Second Vatican Council, and what has changed since then? Finally, we will turn briefly to the issue of authority. Who judges, and how has that changed since Vatican II? Clearly this is a large task.[2] But the notion of the natural law will serve as a thread which we can trace when we speak of method and authority. First, then, a brief history of Catholic medical ethics.

Part One
History

Over the centuries there have been a series of variations in the relationship of medicine and the Christian religion. Catholic medical ethics developed in response to these variations.[3] During some centuries medicine was practiced largely by priests and monks, and during other centuries it has been practiced largely or only by physicians who have not been members of the clergy or of religious orders. Before Hippocrates in Greece, what there was of medicine was done by "holy-men" and "holy-women." This was and is common in other cultures as well. After Hippocrates, Greek medicine became a relatively "lay" profession rather than a specifically "religious" one. This process shifted back and forth several times until the 18th century, when Enlightenment ideology declared science to be the future road for humankind and religion to be useful only to the extent that it could support scientific, and thus human, progress.

The rift between religion and medicine begun in the Enlightenment called for some sort of dialogue, and a field of study known as "Pastoral Medicine" developed in Europe to bridge the gap. Pastoral medicine spoke to clerics and theologians about what they might need to know of medicine, especially about hygiene and first aid, so that country pastors might be of some use to their parishioners. It spoke also to physicians about what they might need to know of religion, spirituality, and morality. What we call medical ethics was thus only one part of pastoral medicine.

Medical ethics, as that discipline emerged within Roman Catholicism, developed out of this pastoral medicine tradition, with some connection as well to the medical ethics of the medical associations of which we spoke in the last chapter. Much of what pastoral medicine had investigated was dropped by medical ethics. Catholic medical ethics, whatever name it called itself, gradually became the moral or ethical investigation of the daily professional practice of medical personnel. It differed from the intraprofessional medical ethics of the medical associations in that it argued not on the basis of what was beneficial to the profession but on the basis of what was right and wrong according to natural law.

Up until the 1960's, Catholic theologians, philosophers, and pastors were almost the only ones doing what can legitimately be called health care ethics. The Jewish Community also has a tradition of medical ethics, but it has been based on Rabbinic interpretation of Jewish Law with little attempt to claim either basis in reason or universal application. The medical associations labored under the problems we have already discussed at some length. Thus, prior to the last thirty years or so, medical ethics was almost entirely a Catholic field of study. Clearly this has changed since the 1960's. Perhaps the most obvious characteristic of Roman Catholic medical ethics from the mid 1960's to the present is that it is no longer the only source or even the single most important source of medical ethical scholarship. The field is now essentially ecumenical.

Part Two
Material Definition

Now we can turn to the material definition of Catholic medical ethics, that is, at the topics it has considered and does consider to belong to its scope.[4]

Catholic medical ethics grew out of pastoral medicine. Unlike pastoral medicine, medical ethics focussed only on areas of ethical importance. Since the field developed to bridge the gap between religion and morality on the one hand and medicine on the other, it naturally came to emphasize what physicians were actually doing in their medical practice. Thus medical ethics became the moral investigation of the actual daily practice of health care professionals.

The topics chosen for inclusion were those procedures which nurses and physicians encountered in their professional practice. These tended to be mostly physical interventions to cure physical ailments. Thus Catholic medical ethics naturally began to analyze this kind of procedure more than the wider spiritual, psychological, and structural questions connected with health care. Structural issues in particular, though not entirely neglected, were underemphasized. Too little attention was paid to issues of the health care system and to questions of allocation of resources, while great attention was paid to individual surgical and other procedures, especially to those connected with sex and reproduction. Euthanasia, abortion, contraception, sterilization, organ transplantation, and, later on, genetic interventions, received much attention in the literature prior to Vatican II. Catholic medical ethics thus came to be "physicalist" and "individualist." It was interested in a moral analysis of the medical procedures actually done by health care professionals.

These issues are by no means unimportant. Indeed, I confess that when I turn to the more exasperatingly complex questions of structures of health care delivery, as I will do in chapters nine and ten, I often long for the relative calm of the traditional questions.

Much of this book has focused on forgoing treatment, which remains an issue of the utmost importance. But health care ethics must be more than analysis of individual procedures within the patient-nurse-physician relationship. These larger questions of allocation, complex as they are, are also ethical issues which demand attention.

In contrast to this individual professional approach which prevailed up until the 1960's and Vatican II, today's medical ethics has extended its topical array to include the entire sphere of individual and structural, microethical and macroethical issues connected directly or indirectly to medicine and biology. Political, social, psychological, national and international concerns now constitute an important part of medical ethics. Catholic medical ethics, no longer alone in the field, contributes along with other traditions and perspectives to these wider issues as well as to the more immediate issues which it had earlier emphasized. The change is a good one. We can hope that with good will, and perhaps some good luck as well, our nation will be able to converse about, and then to develop, a better and more just health care delivery system than it now has.

Part Three
Method

The area of methodology is, of course, of far greater complexity than the general history and definition of the field which we have been tracing thus far. It also inevitably enters into issues of debate and controversy, since it is questions of method, and of the judgments reached in accordance with the method, which are now so much in dispute within Catholic health care ethics. This section will be an overview of the basic methodological approaches taken by the discipline.[5]

Prior to the Second Vatican Council in the 1960's, Catholic health care ethics developed a methodology intended to enable it to arrive at universally applicable solutions to medical ethical questions. The method was based on a kind of cause-and-effect analysis which ethicists found quite appropriate when applied to the kinds of topics we have already seen emphasized in the discipline, physical interventions (operations and medications) for physical ailments, i.e., the actual procedures done by health care professionals. Indeed, I am convinced that the very compatibility of this ethical method with the supposed "scientific" method of cause-and-effect analysis (diagnosis and prescription) of modern medicine made it even more attractive to Catholic moralists who were called upon to offer specific answers to the moral questions medicine posed. Catholic moralists wanted to come up with the same kinds of scientifically accurate, absolutely clear and precise answers to moral dilemmas that doctors were (supposedly) arriving at in their scientific approach to medicine.[6] And the methodological approaches developed by Catholic ethicists enabled them to claim to do that.

Physicalism

Critics of this method have called it "physicalism," and I agree with this critique. "Physicalism" is an emphasis in moral analysis on the physical and biological aspects of the action being questioned. The ethical judgment which results—whether the action is right or wrong—is applied whenever the physical act is the same. In Catholic medical ethics prior to Vatican II, this emphasis was dominant to the relative neglect of other aspects of human behavior, such as the social, psychological, relational, and spiritual aspects.

It is time to return to the notion of natural law. Natural law theory, we recall, claims that people can use their reason and their life experience to reach ethical conclusions by examining the patterns of God's creation. But this leaves open the question of what kind of patterns to emphasize. The physicalist method emphasizes only the physical and the biological patterns of creation to the neglect of other significant aspects of human nature. If only physical and biological aspects are considered, it becomes possible to conclude, for example, that all homosexual acts are morally wrong since they cannot lead to biological procreation. For the same reason, all contraception is wrong if it gets in the way of the physical and biological integrity of the individual sexual act, which is said to have as its goal the physical procreation of the species.

Thus condoms are absolutely forbidden as a method of birth control while "natural family planning" is permitted. Condoms keep sperm physically away from eggs, and thus are said to violate the integrity of the sex act. Refraining from sex during the fertile period does not violate any individual sex act, and thus is not forbidden. The fact that many couples find modern methods of determining the fertile period to be more intrusive and more disruptive than the use of a condom or of the anovulant pill is not given proper significance in the moral analysis. These methods of contraception (condoms, pills, and so on) achieve the same result as does natural family planning: sex without children, a result which, it is interesting to note, Catholic authors prior to this century would have considered immoral. Yet these methods are forbidden while NFP is permitted. The difference is the act of sex itself. The difference is the biological and physical cause-and-effect process within the contraceptive method.

This critique of physicalism does not mean that biology has no importance. Nor does it mean that there is no moral relevance to the means used. Nor does it mean that a good end justifies an immoral means. But it does mean that physical or biological cause-and-effect relationships ought not by themselves determine the rightness or wrongness of human actions. Biological and physical aspects are humanly significant. That human significance must be considered when making moral judgments. But the biological fact alone does not enable us to reach moral judgments. To claim that it does is "physicalism." Unfortunately, this approach was characteristic of pre-Vatican II Catholic medical ethics.

Physicalist method was applied to a wide variety of medical ethics topics. The core principle was the principle of double effect. We will not go into detail about the principle here, though a grasp of it is necessary for a complete understanding of many of the conclusions reached in Catholic medical ethics.[7] By applying the four conditions of the double effect principle, Catholic moralists were able to distinguish direct sterilization, always forbidden, from indirect sterilization, sometimes permitted; direct abortion, always forbidden, from indirect abortion, sometimes permitted; direct euthanasia, always forbidden, from allowing to die, sometimes permitted; direct cooperation in an evil act, always forbidden, from indirect cooperation, sometimes permitted; and even direct lies, always forbidden, from indirect falsehoods called mental reservations, sometimes permitted.

Some of the conclusions reached by the principle of double effect are arguably valid. For example, the distinction between active killing and allowing to die, which has been rehearsed at great length in earlier chapters, and on which current American law is based, is clearly important, even if one might argue that it ought not be as absolute as Catholic tradition requires. But some of the conclusions reached are silly. Double effect physicalism forbids the use of condoms to gather semen for fertility analysis unless the semen is gathered in a condom with holes in it during sexual intercourse, since the sex act cannot be violated and enough semen must be able to get to the egg to allow for fertilization, despite the fact that the semen is being gathered because there has been no fertilization. So husbands and wives are required to have sex while technicians wait to grab a condom and hope there is enough semen in the condom with holes in it to find out whether the sperm count is sufficient. There have been arguments about what constitutes enough holes of sufficient size, and some have insisted that if even one sperm is deliberately kept from getting to the egg, the act is immoral.

Similarly, the principle of double effect has been used to allow salpingectomy while rejecting salpingostomy in cases of ectopic pregnancy. The fallopian tube can be removed with the fetus inside, but the fetus can never be directly removed from the tube. In some rare cases this means that surgery which might preserve fertility is forbidden in favor of surgery which must destroy it. One final example of such silliness is the notion of mental reservation, where physicians were told it is permissible in some cases to tell a patient dying of sepsis that his or her temperature is normal, and reserve the words "normal for someone dying of infection"!

Though I am very critical of this approach, and though I must say that physicalism was the dominant method for much of pre-Vatican II medical ethics, I do not intend to give the impression that Catholic medical ethics during this period was worthless, any more than I intended in the last chapter to say that the medical ethics of the medical associations was without value. Pre-Vatican II Catholic medical ethics did attempt to propose and to develop a legitimate rational basis for medical ethical judgment. Quite properly, it kept before the medical community the essential fact that health care is at its core a moral undertaking, subject to ethical principles, and that health care professionals ought be good, ought develop the virtues of their calling and live them out. Despite the physicalist method it used in analyzing many individual procedures, Catholic medical ethics was and is anti-physicalist in its insistence on including the ethical and not just the technological aspects of medicine and health care.

And Catholic medical ethics developed certain principles and distinctions which have made significant contributions to the emergence of medical ethical judgments in important areas. Our detailed examination of the issue of forgoing treatment pointed some of these out, especially the distinction between ordinary and extraordinary means of preserving life and the distinction between killing and allowing to die. I myself am convinced that had these distinctions not existed in the tradition received from Catholic scholarship, such common practices as properly sedating dying patients from pain might not have been accepted.

The method I have called physicalism has come under much criticism in recent years. The debate continues today, of course, and the issue is not settled. Many Catholic scholars have rejected the older approach. Others claim that it is really not valid to label it physicalist, and they continue to defend the conclusions reached by the principle of double effect.[8]

We have noted the natural affinity between the topics emphasized in pre-Vatican II Catholic medical ethics and the physicalist method it used. Since the wider issues of social justice, health care delivery, allocation of resources, and so on, are less easily resolved by this kind of method, these issues have demanded a different approach. And many of today's Catholic scholars have noted the deficiencies in the older approach even when they are applied to individual issues of physical treatment.

Personalism

There is no one name for the method proposed as a corrective for physicalism. A name most commonly used is "personalism." As long as this is not taken as meaning the individual person alone or isolated from community, but is taken to assume that the person is inherently social, the term is acceptable. Personalism rejects the physicalist emphasis of much of the older tradition. It insists on emphasizing those wider aspects of the patterns of creation, especially of human nature, which double effect physicalism often neglected. Thus personal, social, psychological, economic, familial, and similar factors are given consideration in making medical ethical judgments. Less emphasis is placed on the act itself, on the physical chain of cause and effect within the act which was stressed so much in the principle of double effect. Consequences are stressed along with rules. The method is often called proportionalism, or even consequentialism, pointing to the movement away from clear absolutes based on acts, and toward judgments made in a wider context where humanly significant results need to be stressed and where the proportion of good results and bad results is more important than it is when the act itself is sufficient to make the judgment.

This is not the place to go into detail trying to distinguish all the various forms of utilitarianism, consequentialism, and proportionalism, or to distinguish them from all the competing schools of deontology, where rules and obligations are stressed, sometimes to the neglect of effects or consequences.[9] It is enough to say that over the last 30 years or so Catholic medical ethics has moved away from a more strict rule-based method, where judgments are applied to acts in a way which often ignores situational flavor. Now human goals in the human context are more important.

One result of this, of course, is that Catholic moralists differ among themselves about the precise moral judgment to make in certain cases. Some of us argue that this or that action is clearly wrong; others say it is clearly right; others not quite so sure what the right answer is. But this does not mean that Catholic scholars have become relativists. No Catholic moralist, to my knowledge, would hold that this is simply a matter of opinion. Some issues are hard to resolve. The principle of double effect led to solutions which many now think to be inadequate. But the shift in Catholic medical ethics away from physicalism has been an advance. It frees the discipline to use its theological and philosophical inheritance in a manner more in keeping with the richness of human nature as God is creating it.

Theological Principles

In the introduction to chapter one, I pointed out the importance of two theological principles for the issue of forgoing treatment.

These are the theological principles of divine sovereignty and of redemptive suffering.[10] I showed how these principles were sometimes used as a kind of proof text, where their theological richness and complexity could be ignored.

It is precisely the shift away from physicalism which has challenged us to pay proper attention to the complex and multicolored symbolic meaning of these principles. They help us understand ourselves in relationship to God. Though they do not provide easy answers, they set our questions in proper context and thus contribute to a theologically and humanly excellent health care ethics.

Part Four
Authority

The issue of authority is as complex as that of method, but I will not attempt any lengthy analysis.[11] Who is said in Catholic moral theology to have the authority to make moral judgments?

The Problem

Once again, the best place to start is with the notion of natural law. Remember that natural law theory is the claim that persons can use their reason and life experience to discover right and wrong from the patterns of God's creation. In the last chapter, when dealing with metaethics, we saw a number of competing theories. One of these is supernatural metaethical absolutism. This is the theory that we can base our ethical rules and judgments on God's will. We know our judgments are right because God tells us, and God tells us in some specific source of supposedly supernatural revelation. We have also seen that natural law theory, as the Catholic tradition proposes it, also holds that God's will can be known as the basis for moral judgment. But the source of our knowledge is different. According to natural law theory we learn God's will by examining the patterns of creation. Supernatural absolutists hold that we learn God's will more directly, in some definable place like the Bible or the teaching of a particular Church leader. And this is where the controversy comes in within Catholic medical ethics. What is the specific role of the Church, and in particular of the pastoral leaders of the Church, of the magisterium of bishops with the Pope?

There was a time in the history of Catholic medical ethics when this was really not too much of a problem. Major Catholic scholars could claim quite specifically a purely natural law approach to the question. Popes and bishops had not made many pronouncements on medical ethical questions. Only Catholics were doing medical ethics in any great depth, and the claim could be made that this scholarship gave the theologians the expertise necessary to uncover the natural law. Catholic scholars were the only real investigators of the patterns of creation in this area; they alone did medical ethics. They thus knew the natural law from purely natural sources. Since it was not based on Christian supernatural revelation, it did not depend on the teaching of the Church; and it was binding on everyone, including non-Catholics.

Still, there were problems. The major problems arose from two factors. First, Pope Pius XII in the 1940's and 1950's made a large number of statements on medical ethical questions, and, though these were claimed to be natural law judgments, in some cases Catholic scholars changed their own opinions as expert scholars to be in agreement with the statements of the Pope. Why would they do that if they were the experts? Second, scholars from outside the Catholic tradition began to study medical ethics and to propose alternate principles, alternate methods, and alternate judgments. Their criticism was part of the process which led to a critique of physicalism, though this critique had begun as well within Catholic theological scholarship. Their criticism also led to a defense of prior Catholic positions, and often this defense in effect retreated from natural law theory and used the argument that these conclusions are known to be right because the Church makes them rather than the proper natural law argument that the conclusions are known to be right because we can discover them in the patterns of creation.

All of this surfaced in most visible form in the birth control debate, when Pope Paul VI first established a commission of experts to look into the question (this would be in keeping with natural law theory) and then overrode their findings in issuing *Humanae Vitae*, an encyclical letter which had as much to do with authority as it had to do with sexuality and contraception.

I will not try to unravel this controversy here. Threads which need to be unravelled, and which have received much discussion in the literature, include the difference between infallible and non-infallible magisterial teaching, the *locus* of teaching authority in the Church as a whole and in the bishops and in the Pope, the difference between private and public dissent, the importance of reception (the importance that the Church as a whole receive a teaching), the problem of sin, and the whole question of the relationship of nature and grace, reason and revelation.[12] No depth is possible here.

Some Clarifications

We can, however, clarify a few points. The Catholic tradition is well based in natural law theory. This theory holds that ethical judgments can be discovered by reason and life experience. Clearly the hierarchical magisterium—the world's bishops together with the Pope—have an important role in discovering the natural law. Indeed, as the Church's leaders, they have a role which the rest of us cannot duplicate. But theirs is not and cannot be the only role. If what I have called a kind of ecclesiastical positivism takes over, Catholic medical ethics will lose its tradition and will lose its credibility.

In the previous chapter I noted the intraprofessional relativism of the "good old medical ethics," according to which ethical judgments were often made by the medical profession on the basis of its own interests rather than on the basis of the wider common good. I also spoke of a kind of "rational positivism," according to which ethical judgments are decided upon by rational persons, but do not have any basis in the patterns of creation. In both of these approaches, ethics is posited, not uncovered. The same problem arises from ecclesiastical positivism. Even though it is not intended, what is often perceived is that Church leaders make up moral right and wrong. Since they claim it is based on natural law, discoverable in the patterns of creation, why cannot the rest of us discover the same rules and judgments? All persons have access to the patterns of creation. Catholic medical ethics is better served by an honest cooperation among the various members of the Church, including the communities of the hierarchy, of theologians, and of the faithful.

Conclusion

The basis of medical ethics which prevailed in the codes and commentaries of the medical profession—that is morally right which the profession claims to be right—and the basis which can sometimes be found in Catholic medical ethics—that is morally right which the Church hierarchy claims to be right—are both no longer representative of the field. There are those within Church and profession who would have us return to these positivistic bases, of course, and we should hope that they do not succeed. Even if they do, it is likely that they will succeed only in isolating Church and professional society from the doing of health care ethics, thus effectively silencing the voices of the Church and of the medical associations.

Despite what I consider to be the serious shortcomings of the restrictive approaches typical of Catholic medical ethics prior to Vatican II, Catholic theologians and Catholic pastors of that time accomplished something of true significance. Catholic medical ethics played an important role in the creation of the contemporary multifaceted discipline which health care ethics has become. In a number of areas Catholic medical ethics laid a base for analyses and conclusions which are now becoming standard medical ethics procedure in the United States and elsewhere. Its restrictive approaches were never really true to the message of Jesus Christ or to the best of Catholic theology. If Catholic health care ethics remains true to its theological heritage, it can continue to be an essential component in American health care as it continues to serve the revelation of God.

This chapter and the last one have examined the basis of health care ethics. The proper basis can be found by studying human nature, as human persons are, in ourselves and in our society. This is what theologians and philosophers ought to mean when they talk about natural law. Ethical principles and conclusions are not posited; they are not created out of thin air; they do not depend on what this professional association or that Church leader or that philosopher happen to claim. They are rather derived from, discovered in the patterns of God's creation. We get at them by knowing who we are. That is the proper basis for health care ethics.

Discussion Questions

1. Discuss the relationship of medicine and religion. Do they have anything to say to each other?

2. What do you think of the difference between "physicalism" and "personalism" as alternative approaches to Catholic medical ethics?

3. Some say that Catholic morality has become too uncertain, that we ought to return to the stability we used to have. What are your ideas on this?

4. Choose one or two of the specific questions to which the double effect principle gives clear answers. What is your moral analysis of these issues?

5. Discuss the problem of authority in Catholic moral theology. What directions would you suggest?

Endnotes

1. The word "law" in this traditional term is problematic. It implies externally imposed rules of a possibly rigid sort. Yet natural law theory, as we are discussing it, is based on the patterns of God's creating power and grace as these are inherent within, not imposed upon, human nature. The definition of natural law that I give here emphasizes patterns of human and created order, rather than externally ordained hierarchies. It is probable that the term "law" was partly responsible for the physicalist understanding of natural law theory to which we will return later in this chapter. See *The Emergence*, p. 245, n. 4, pp. 449-454. The word "natural" is also problematic in light of the contemporary theology of nature and grace. We will note this again later.

2. This chapter draws heavily on my *The Emergence of Roman Catholic Medical Ethics*. Notes will reference pages in this book for more detail. Briefer versions of material found in the book are "Roman Catholic Medical Ethics and the Ethos of Modern Medicine," *Ephemerides Theologicae Lovanienses*, 59 (1983), 46-47; and "The History of American Catholic Medical Ethics," in *Perspectives on American Catholicism*, 1789-1989, ed. Virginia Geiger and Stephen Vicchio (Westminster, Md.: Christian Classics, 1989), pp. 253-274.

3. See *The Emergence,* pp. 13-81.

4. See *The Emergence,* pp. 102-228, 407-416.

5. See *The Emergence,* pp. 229-310, 416-429.

6. The fact is, of course, that medicine is not and has never been a "theoretical" science in this sense. Nor is ethics. That is the problem with this kind of approach. For a detailed analysis of the issues here, see Albert R. Jonsen and Stephen Toulmin, *The Abuse of Casuistry: A History of Moral Reasoning* (Berkeley: Univ. of California Press, 1988), esp. pp. 23-46.

7. See *The Emergence,* pp. 244-274, 421-429.

8. The monthly publication of the Pope John XXIII Medical/Moral Research and Education Center in Brighton, MA, *Ethics and Medics,* often typifies and defends this approach. The best and most complete source for the official Catholic teaching in medical ethics, which defends the traditional positions, but which includes as well much helpful methodological analysis and critique, is Benedict M. Ashley and Kevin D. O'Rourke, *Health Care Ethics: A Theological Analysis,* 3rd ed. (St. Louis, MO: Catholic Health Association, 1989).

9. The literature on this is vast. See, among many other sources, Richard M. Gula, *What Are They Saying about Moral Norms?* (New York: Paulist Press, 1982); Lisa Sowle Cahill, "Teleology, Utilitarianism, and Christian Ethics," *Theological Studies,* 42 (1981), 601-629; John R. Connery, "The Teleology of Proportionate Reason," *Theological Studies,* 44 (1983), 489-496; Kelly, *The Emergence,* pp. 421-429; and any of the many articles on the topic by Charles E. Curran.

10. See *The Emergence,* pp. 232-235, 436-447.

11. See *The Emergence,* pp. 311-401, 429-436.

12. This last is probably the most i mportant theological issue to be considered. It asks if we can legitimately claim that there are two different levels to the way God makes known His/Her will to us, natural and supernatural. It is probably better theology to deny that any knowledge we have is either purely natural *or* purely supernatural, since *we,* as humans, are both "natural" and "supernatural," and thus we think and learn in this "mixed" fashion. The "natural law" is thus not "natural" in the strict sense. But

neither does it depend on specific revelation, in the sense that such revelation would be available only to believing Christians and subject to a special supernatural authority of the Pope and bishops. I think we have just begun to work our way through this question, due largely to the theological anthropology of Karl Rahner.

Chapter Seven

Pain and Pain Management

Introduction

The spiritual and ethical issues of pain and pain management are many. In this chapter, I will first review in an introductory fashion some of the Christian approaches to the meaning of pain and give my opinion of them. This should be of help to health care personnel in dealing with patients. Many health care professionals often ask these questions. But even those who do not, perhaps because they do not themselves believe in a God, will care for patients who struggle with these difficult problems. Later sections of the chapter turn to some of the practical ethical questions of pain management and to the role of the clergy in hospital ethics.

The meaning of the word "patient" is instructive. The word comes from the Latin *pati*, which means to undergo. The patient is the undergoer, the sufferer, the one put-upon. A number of sociological and psychological studies have been done about the patient's "role," and these studies have been partially responsible for the insistence over the last two decades on patient autonomy, informed consent, and patient participation in treatment decisions and implementation. Medical evidence supports the claim that patients who actively participate in their own recovery do better than those who do not. Still, the patient is more the done-to than the doer. The patient is poked and prodded, dressed and undressed, looked at and talked about, often by hordes of strange people who "round." That poking and prodding and looking at and talking about is all part of good medical care, though there are better and worse ways of doing it. But it symbolizes and reminds the *patiens* daily that she or he is the sufferer, the one in pain.

A second easy point to make is to distinguish, as is often done, between pain and suffering. Pain is largely physical. Suffering is largely spiritual and mental. People often insist that the pain itself is not the worst of it, and good pain management can effectively reduce and often eliminate pain in the strict physical sense. But we need to remember that even in the absence of "pain," real human suffering may remain to the *patiens*, to the one who undergoes.

I often wonder if health care professionals realize what the hospital environment does to patients. The professional is in control. It is where he or she works. For the patient, the experience is totally different. Every noise is a sign that something is wrong. As a patient in the ICU, I fear that the beeps and the buzzes are *my* beeps and buzzes, that the nurses and the doctors are talking about *me*. In teaching hospitals, I am talked about by all sorts of strange people, usually in the morning, who come in large groups. What is so awful about me that all these smart women and men want to find out about my body? The doctors must all be lying when they tell me I'm getting better. They tell me to relax, but I'm bathed in light and surrounded by noise.

There is clear evidence that the attitude of the patient has a considerable effect on the success of medical treatment. Trust is one of the most important aspects of the patient-doctor relationship. Human illnesses are never purely physical, since the human person is always psyche and spirit as well as body. The more a patient is actively and confidently involved in the healing process, the more likely it is to work.

Doctors and nurses might try an experiment. They might try to stay for one 24-hour period in an ICU bed. We professionals all too seldom have a real idea, from actual experience, of what it is to undergo a stay in a hospital.

The Problem of God and Suffering

The principle theological problem with pain and suffering is why God permits it. The question of why God causes or permits evil is known in theology and philosophy as the problem of "theodicy." That is, it is the problem of the justification or justice of God. It is a very difficult problem.

In simple terms the problem can be described as a dilemma arising from three factors. First, God is said to be all-good. That is, God wants us to be happy; God loves us; He sent His Son Jesus to save us. God's purpose in creation is to extend the divine love to us, God's people. Second, God is said to be all-powerful. That is, She can do anything She wants. God is God, after all. Third, the world we live in includes an enormous amount of evil. If God is all-good and all-powerful, why all the pain and suffering? If God is a loving God who is omnipotent, then why does God not eliminate all the suffering and agony and pain we experience and see around us in our world?

For many people, the problem of theodicy is and has been a reason for concluding that there is no God. God cannot be justified. Theodicy is impossible. It is easy to see why this answer is appealing. For some atheists, human experience demonstrates clearly that there is no way a real "God" could have created or tolerated a world like this one. But if human life and the universe itself are seen as an accident, a fortunate (or unfortunate, depending on where you stand) mixing of atoms with no plan behind it, then pain and suffering are simply part of that great accident. It's the way it is. Many major thinkers have made this judgment, and I do not think it is wise of those who believe in God simply to dismiss it. This kind of "atheism" comes from great insight and from a grappling at some considerable depth with a real human and religious issue. It is sometimes closer to real religion and to real Christianity than what often passes for more normal forms and expressions of Christian living. Probably many of us, at one time or another, have asked the question. Maybe on alternate Tuesdays we think this answer has some merit. Why, after all, does God cause, or permit, all this agony?

There are three general sets of answers possible. First, we can conclude that God is not really good, or at least not all-good. Perhaps God is really a big computer in the sky. He has his control groups, who don't get cancer as children, and his experimental subjects, who do. God is simply interested in figuring out what happens to the different groups. This answer is not too different from denying God altogether. God started the universe and now sits back and watches the experiment, with some interest but with no real desire for one outcome rather than another. God is an "objective" research scientist. Let's try everything and see what happens.

Or maybe God is even worse than that. Maybe God is a sadist. God delights in pain and suffering. The only reason God permits some good and pleasure and happiness is so that people can know what they are missing when they are in pain.

A second answer is that God, while all-good, is not all-powerful. She would if She could but She can't. This is, to me, a far more attractive answer, and, with nuance, I accept some aspects of it.

There are a number of possible ways in which this answer is made. Some have believed that there are two gods, or two sources for creation. One of these is good, but the other is evil. The evil god keeps the good god from eliminating pain and suffering. The evil god inflicts it, and the good god reduces it. Since each is as powerful as the other, neither is omnipotent. Clearly Christianity has rejected this answer. But remnants of it remain in the notion of a devil. The devil made me do it. It wasn't God and it wasn't me. It was this other powerful being. Blame him. Still, in Christianity it is clear that the devil, whatever this myth really means, is supposed to be a fallen angel, that is, a creature of the one God. Theoretically God should be able to get rid of the devil. So why doesn't He?

Another approach to this idea that God is not all-powerful is more sophisticated. Some Christians, among them those who follow "process theology," hold that God is growing along with creation. God as God transcends creation, that is, is above and beyond it, but God is also within creation, and in that sense is struggling with the rest of creation to work towards the good, to eliminate pain and suffering and death. But this answer, too, questions or at least is in tension with one of the basic doctrines of traditional Christianity, that God is indeed all-powerful, and most Christians have not accepted it. So the question remains.

Christian Answers

The third set of answers to our question accepts the doctrine that God is all-good and all-powerful. There are a number of approaches Christians use within this set of answers, and as we mention these it will become clear how this is important to health care workers and to patients.

The most widespread traditional answer is that God is not really responsible for evil. We are. God's original plan for creation did not include the presence of evil, but humans sinned and thus introduced evil into the world. To some extent this answer works for the evil caused by sin, but it is at least partially problematic when applied to physical evils like pain and illness and death. It is true that the story of Adam and Eve in Eden, if accepted literally as an historical document, can be interpreted as reporting this kind of event. Eden is claimed by some to be an historically existing place where disease, accident, sin, and death were in fact non-existent. Mosquitoes and lions did not bite; stones did not fall on anyone and there were no storms; no one caught cold. But today we know that this is inaccurate. Pains and disease exist apart from people's sins.

Despite the problematic nature of the answer, however, it contains important theological and ethical truth. Many physical evils are indeed the result of human sin and error, ecological mismanagement, greed, violence, and so on, and this attempt at an answer does have the important advantage of urging us to live more virtuous lives and thus reduce the pain our actions cause.

Even the reality of death as we know it is made humanly traumatic by the fears and lack of trust which sin causes and exacerbates. Death, as this human reality can rightly be said to be "caused by original sin," is not the simple passage from this life envisioned and desired by God, but is rather a wrenching and often fearful experience, dreaded by most of us. In some cases, a morally wrong act causes it directly (homicide, for example); in other cases structural moral evils cause death (poverty, injustice, racism, sexism, the lack of a just health care system, etc.). In still other cases, which nurses and doctors are all too familiar with, family conflicts caused by greed, envy, intra-familial rivalry, and even hatred greatly increase the human suffering which goes along with a patient's death. These even affect treatment decisions. So human sin does indeed inflict pain and suffering. Yet it is not possible to conclude that all physical evils—all pain, disease, and accident—are caused by human sin.

This answer, that people's sins cause pain and suffering, can even be destructive. It is one thing to think of Adam and Eve and blame it on them. It is another to blame it on ourselves. Sometimes, of course, as we have just seen, we are right to do so. But this can be very dangerous indeed, and the danger shows another important problem with this answer to the theodicy question. Maybe "bed 18" has cancer because she smoked. Maybe "bed 12" has AIDS because he used drugs. Empirically this might be true. But why does *God* cause this result for this kind of behavior? Does God create the HIV to punish homosexuals and drug users? Does God create cancerous lung cells to punish smokers? And what about the child with leukemia? Such an answer returns us to God the sadist. Those who propose this explicitly, for example, those who preach that AIDS is God's punishment for sexual sin, are in fact blaspheming the God of Jesus Christ.

Still, many of our patients may think that their illness is God's punishment for sins real or imagined. And this may get in the way of recovery or of pain management. If one really believes, for example, that a disease is God's punishment for sin, what right do we have to try to take away God's punishment? What right to we have to undo what God wants done? We should let everybody die. So the idea that disease is God's punishment for sin can be a major problem for health care.

Another theologically and humanly distorted notion is the idea that God uses pain and suffering to test us. A remarkably large percentage of college students, in my experience, like this answer. Pain and suffering are tests from God to see if we pass. Maybe college students are so often being tested, by me and others, that this appeals. The introduction to the Job story, where God agrees with Satan to test Job, leans in this direction, though Job's final answer does not.

This, too, looks too much like the sadist God or the experimenter God. Lovers don't inflict pain on their loved ones to see if they can remain steadfast. God is not like this. But if patients believe this about God and about their pain, they may be ambivalent about pain management. They may feel guilty about analgesics, since it might seem that they are avoiding the test. In fact, of course, it is much more likely that pain, at least too much of it, will get in the way of spiritual peace and will make it harder for the dying patient to prepare for death.

Persons who see pain as a punishment from God or as a test from God have an answer of sorts to the question we began with, but it is not a sufficient answer. It makes it very hard for those who believe this way to love the God who is constantly punishing and testing them.

Helpful Ideas

Well, what is left? Not any easy answer. Not any answer which will solve this very difficult issue of theodicy. But I think there are three ideas which help. First, in creating, God could not create perfection. That is because only God is totally perfect, and God cannot be created or God would be a creature and not God. This means there must be some sort of limitation in creation. And God chose to create a physical universe, where all sorts of physical wonders exist. A necessarily limited physical creation means union and separation, growth and decay, death and new life. In some sense, then, if God were to create a wondrous, yet necessarily limited, physical universe where people are embodied and not just angels, God had no choice but to include the limits of physical reality. This doesn't answer the question of why children get leukemia, but it sets it into perspective. A loving God creates a universe which of necessity offers both beauty and rot, life and death, pleasure and pain. God might have created something entirely different, but the wonders of *this kind* of creation would have been lost had God done so.

A second idea which may help here is the notion of human freedom. The Adam and Eve story tells us this. God chose to create people free. This freedom is our glory and our woe. In order to give us the glory, God needed as well to give us the possibility of the woe. Of course this helps us understand only those evils and sufferings which result from human action, and is dangerous when we think it means that all pain and suffering is God's punishment for human sin. But it correctly reminds us that much human agony does result from our sin, and it urges us to try to do better.

A third help is to remember that by suffering we learn better how to relate to others and help carry their burden. This does not mean that we choose suffering for its own sake. Christianity is not supposed to be masochistic. But it is clear that the experience of human hardship and suffering makes it possible for us to understand what others are enduring, to be less judgmental of them and of their behavior, and to join them in empathy and sympathy. This is the principle reason why suffering can truly be an ennobling part of human living. It is central to the theological concept of redemptive suffering. In this sense suffering helps us to mature. Sensitive persons are better care givers than those who lack this virtue.

Does any of this solve the problem of evil? No. The theodicy question remains a mystery. That is the final answer of the Book of Job. Only God can really know why there is pain. Yet God remains a loving God—not a punishing God, not a testing God, but a loving God who must permit and in some sense even cause pain in a physical universe where people are free.[1]

Anger

Now that we have looked at, but not solved, the theodicy question, we can ask about anger. In our study thus far, we have arrived at no complete answer to the theodicy question. I have rejected the punishment and test answers, at least in their crude form. I think the nature of a physical creation where people are free helps set a context for the right answer, but I am aware that this context does not solve the question of the presence of pain. Innocent persons suffer. So we often get angry at God. "Good God," we always say, "Good God." Really? Good God, why does the baby have spina bifida? Whom do we blame? The theoretically right answer is that we blame no one. As people of faith we try to remember that God does not delight in this, that somehow it is part of God's plan . . . somehow. And for some of us, some of the time, the belief that God takes the dying baby to heaven is of help. But often this is not enough, and so some of the time there is anger at God. That's all right. God is big enough to take our anger. It proves we care.

The Ethics of Pain Management

Previous chapters have addressed the question of sedating a dying patient even though sedation may hasten the moment of death. We have concluded that this is morally right and legally proper. I will now add a few remarks on the ethics of pain management outside of the context of the dying patient.

Some questions come to mind. First, what about the patient who asks not to be sedated? This may be for a good reason—he wants to be alert to talk with his visiting relatives, or for a reason we might think is a bad one—he wants to suffer more for his sins and thus get out of purgatory quicker. The answer to this question, of course, is that if the patient is capable of making decisions about this kind of treatment, that decision must be followed. Clearly the idea of slipping a sedative in the orange juice is out. This applies even when the lack of sedation causes problems to the health care team. Of course, if the lack of sedation makes it impossible to treat, the patient must be informed of this, and there might be cases where doctors and hospitals would be justified in telling such a patient that they could no longer offer care, though this would happen rarely if ever. Surrogates may never reject proper pain management for patients who are not capable of deciding for themselves. This would be against the best interests of the patient.

Second, what about the problem of addiction? This is a complex issue, of course, but it ought to be possible to avoid two extremes. The first extreme is the theory that addictive drugs ought never be used in physically addictive amounts. It is clear that physical addiction is not a major problem for a dying patient, but that pain is. Morphine dosages which would be criminal apart from the patient's condition may well be quite proper as sedatives for the patient with terminal cancer.

The second extreme is the theory that addiction is impossible for old people, or irrelevant. This is the "quick fix" theory, and is in use at times in nursing homes and other institutions where the staff want quiet patients. When addiction to drugs is likely to prove harmful to the patient, which may well be the case when the patient is not dying, then clearly the possibility of addiction must be considered, and reduced or eliminated if possible.

The Role of the Clergy and the Chaplain

Clergy and chaplains can be of great help to patients as they struggle with their illness. In this last section of this chapter, I want to explore briefly their role, not only in relationship to pain, but also in the larger context of the focus of the whole book. What is the role of the clergy/chaplain in critical care ethics? I will use the terms "clergy" and "chaplain" interchangeably here, even though all Churches have clergy who are not trained as chaplains, and most have chaplains who are not ordained.

I am going to focus first on what I think the role of the clergy to be even if they do not have any real knowledge of medical ethics, and then what I think to be their role if they do.

All clergy and chaplains have a major role to play regardless of whether or not they have any specific knowledge about, much less expertise in, health care ethics. The first thing they need to know is that they do not have such an expertise, if they don't. Clergy who are unfamiliar with medical ethics are not helpful when they try to make judgments based on their own personal opinions and force these on patients and their families. For Catholics, this sometimes happens when priests who have not kept up with their own tradition insist that the Church's teaching is what it is not.

The second thing sensitive clergy and chaplains know is not to impose themselves on patients and families who don't want them. Clergy should not take such rejection personally (except in the rare case in which it is indeed their own fault), and should make it clear that they are available if the patient or family should want to speak with them.

On the positive side, all clergy, including those who have little or no knowledge of medical ethics, can be tremendously helpful in three areas.

First, patients and families want clergy and chaplains to help them deal with the spiritual aspects of illness and of dying. Different traditions have different ways of doing this, but whatever the mix of personal praying and sacramental symbol, the presence of this help as part of the process of dealing with illness and of preparing to make treatment decisions can be quite helpful.

Second, clergy and chaplains can help mitigate false guilt and fear. I do not mean by this that they should always help do away with guilt and fear. Guilt can be real. Fear can be salutary. But very often patients worry that their illness is a punishment from God. They may fear that this same God is preparing them for eternal punishment. The Christian belief in an afterlife ought to serve as a sweet consolation for the dying patient and his or her family. Christians ought to believe that the God of Jesus Christ is a merciful and forgiving God, a God who wants all persons to live eternally with God in Jesus, in this life and after death. Christians ought to believe that the God of Jesus Christ offers them, and all human persons, the grace which makes this happiness possible.

Yet fear of hell or of purgatory often overwhelms the trusting confidence God asks of us and offers to us. Dying patients may fear meeting God. Sensitive clergy can be of great help in talking through these issues with the patient and with the family. This is an important part of the spiritual preparation for death; it is indeed an important part of the spiritual dimension of any illness. Good chaplains can offer important help to patient and family during this difficult time.

Another aspect of the problem of guilt and fear arises when families worry needlessly that their decision to continue or to forgo treatment means that they are not doing the loving thing for the dying patient. This is especially true when they decide to forgo life-sustaining treatment. Clergy, even those not familiar in any depth with the tradition of medical ethics, can be very helpful in supporting families who obviously love the dying patient and are trying hard to make the right decision. They can help the family understand the difference between relief at the end of an ordeal and malicious desire for the death of their loved one. They can help them recognize the difference between intending to kill and finally resigning themselves to the inevitability of death.

Third, chaplains can help facilitate communication among family members. Families need help in coping with illness and death and in making difficult treatment decisions with some degree of equanimity. Clinical experience demonstrates that families with strong religious backgrounds are often those most easily able to make difficult decisions about forgoing treatment. Such families are more apt to have spoken about death, and to share common values about which kinds of treatments they feel to be humanly reasonable. They may share a belief in a loving God who will welcome them to heaven. They may share a sense that purely biological life is not of ultimate value, and thus share a degree of resignation when medical treatment can no longer be of real help. Such families will agree that "death was a blessing," even as they mourn their loss. Clergy and chaplains will support this. Indeed, chaplains and other clergy will very often find their own faith enhanced and their fears of death reduced by working with and listening to such families.

But this is not always the case. The anticipated death of a family member can also cause rancor within the family. Some relatives will insist on treating; others will want to stop. This can pose a major problem for physicians and for hospitals and nursing homes. The presence of a chaplain or clergyperson can help in getting the various viewpoints expressed with less acrimony, and may help in resolving the crisis.

All of this can be done by clergy and chaplains, whether or not they are knowledgeable in medical ethics. Clergy who do know something about medical ethics can do all this and more. The minister may be the only one present who understands the basic consensus which has developed about the moral and legal rightness of forgoing treatment. If he or she does know this (but the "if" is important—it cannot be presumed), then he or she can serve to help articulate the issues involved. Physicians and nurses are often unaware of what the difference is between substituted judgment and best interests, or of how to determine the difference between medical futility where the doctor decides, and other kinds of value decisions where the patient or family decide, or what the law allows and forbids. Often hospitals have literally no one who is aware of these issues in any depth. The hospital counsel may be a good contract lawyer, but may not have done any research into the laws and cases about who decides to forgo treatment and on what bases. The hospital may not have an ethics committee or a resident or consulting ethicist. Often the rabbi, priest, minister, or hospital chaplain is the only one there who knows what the general consensus is on these questions.

In addition to knowing the general American consensus, knowledgeable clergy know their own religious tradition. This is less easy than it sounds, as any good theologian will testify. Within religions and within denominations, some differences remain as to specific issues. Clergy should not force this tradition on a family, but are certainly able to help the family come to an informed decision based at least in part on the religious tradition family and minister may share.

Roman Catholic clergy and chaplains, *if* they understand their tradition (my teaching experience in Catholic seminaries has shown me that some do and some don't), can be of significant support by explaining to families how flexible the Catholic tradition is in this area. Catholic tradition rejects direct euthanasia, but it has been very much aware that not all medical treatment is mandatory, even if it will prolong life. Treatments which are of little or no real human benefit to patients, or whose burdens outweigh those benefits, are not mandatory in the Catholic tradition. The American consensus has come to agree with this long-standing tradition. Similarly, the American consensus has come to agree that there is no moral difference between withholding and withdrawing treatment. Catholic clergy and chaplains who know their tradition can thus give moral support to families faced with this difficult decision.

Discussion Questions

1. What experience of pain or other suffering have you had? What is it really like to be a patient in a modern hospital?

2. Of the three general answers to the theodicy question, which is closest to your own? Has this changed during your life?

3. Are the "helpful ideas" suggested in this chapter of any help to you? What other ideas do you suggest?

4. Discuss the role of the clergy and of hospital chaplains. What has been your own experience?

Endnotes

1. The notion of God actually being in some sense responsible for evil, or causing it, comes from Karl Rahner's notion of transcendental causality. God does not cause pain as its efficient

cause. But because God could have prevented evil by not creating a physical universe with free and transcendent human creatures, God can in some sense be said to be the transcendental cause of evil.

Chapter Eight

Ethics Committees

Over the last two or three decades, from 1960 to the present, there has been a significant increase in the importance of medical ethics in the United States. The literature is now enormous. Whereas only *Hospital Progress* and *Linacre Quarterly*, two Roman Catholic publications, had been devoted to the study of health care ethics prior to the 1960's, such periodicals now abound, led by the prominent *Hastings Center Report*, which began publication in 1971. Medical ethics think tanks have grown up all over the country; the federal government and state governments have commissions and task forces focussed on bioethical issues and policies; law courts hear cases; hospitals and medical schools hire ethicists; medical journals publish articles on ethics. And hospitals have ethics committees. Indeed, there are now associations of ethics committees, and there are consultants hired to help them get started. The latest estimate I have seen says there are now ethics committees at about half of the nation's 6,000 hospitals.

This chapter will look at Ethics Committees (Institutional Ethics Committees, or IEC's, also called Hospital Ethics Committees, or HEC's), and at how to get one started. The fact is, of course, that there is no one right way for such a committee to be set up or to function within a hospital. There is a general consensus, which I support both from theoretical bases and from my own practical experience, that such committees are, on the whole, helpful within hospitals. But an ethics committee is, after all, just one more committee, and, like all other committees, it will have no intrinsic value. Ethics committees do not make hospitals ethical. They do not have automatic expertise about ethics just because they have the title. Some of them are excellent, some good, some fair, some

119

worthless, and some meddlesome. That is not specific to ethics committees; it's the way committees are.

The chapter is divided into two parts, preceded by a brief introduction. The two parts will be, first, what ethics committees usually look like, their situation within hospitals and their makeup, and, second, what they do.

Introduction

Many interesting historical and theoretical questions come to mind when we ask why the enormous growth in medical ethics has occurred in recent years. Why are ethics committees so common now? There were so very few of them twenty years ago. Other chapters suggest reasons: the increase in medical technology, prolongation of the dying process, increased costs, insistence on patient autonomy and criticism of physician paternalism, the consumer movement, various legal decisions.

On the more practical level, we can recall that the immediate impetus for institutional ethics committees were court cases and federal guidelines in the United States which referred to them. In the *Quinlan* case, the court suggested that an ethics committee, if the hospital had one, might be consulted in cases of forgoing treatment, and that the courts were not the proper place for making decisions of this kind. I think this is right. In the now revised so-called "Baby-Doe Regulations," the Federal Government issued guidelines about treatment for handicapped infants, and suggested that all hospitals have Infant Care Review Committees. Other court cases and other government documents have also suggested the presence of IEC's.

It is a perfectly good idea to have ethics committees, but this government context needs to be looked at with some hesitation. Legislation is now pending in Washington which would mandate IEC's in virtually all hospitals. While the intent is good—these committees could be of considerable help—hesitation is in order before we change the basic ethos of IEC's. Hospital ethics committees are internal to hospitals, and ought to be voluntary. Were government to mandate their existence, it might also mandate their role. Especially in the light of the *Cruzan* decision, with the danger that states will impose regulations making it difficult for surrogates to choose to forgo treatment, IEC's might become the arm of the state for imposing and administering such restrictions. The context for infant care review committees, under the original "Baby Doe Regs," was one of investigation of possible criminal activity, which does not set the proper context for ethics committees. IEC's are internal organs within health care institutions which serve as one resource among many for enhancing the hospital's purpose: the health care of its patients.

A further introductory remark may seem all too obvious, but is important nonetheless. The hospital ethics committee is not the only, or even the most important source of ethical reflection or of ethical decision-making within the hospital. It does only a very small part of the ethics which hospitals must do. If the various constituencies in any institution get the idea that they can pass off ethics onto this committee, much as decisions about patient competency are handed over to a consulting psychiatrist, or pulmonary diagnoses to a pulmonary specialist, or follow-up care to a social worker, then the hospital will lose, not gain, by the presence of such a committee.

Medicine has become specialized. Health care ethics must not become one more specialization. It is true, of course, that ethics committees ought to develop certain skills that perhaps other members of the hospital community have not developed in the same theoretical or even practical way. That's why we have them. But ethics is not a specialization in the same sense that other specializations are. All members of the hospital community need to make ethical decisions, and indeed are faced with these issues all the time. The ethics committee, if it is a good one, will help in this. But it must not be seen as a dumping ground for ethical decisions. The ethics committee, as one speaker put it in a talk I attended, is but one community of wisdom and concern within the hospital.[1]

Part One
Makeup

We will begin with what the ethics committee is not, then speak of how it might be structured within the hospital, then turn to the makeup of the committee itself.

1. What the Institutional Ethics Committee Is Not.

First, the Institutional Ethics Committee is not an Institutional Review Board. The IRB is required by law to serve as a kind of screening and approval committee for any experimental protocol where research is to be done using human subjects and where federal funds are involved. The IRB has decision-making authority within the institution and serves as a gatekeeper and a regulator of experimental research. The IRB clearly has functions which are of ethical import. It is wise to have a member of the IRB on the ethics committee, or some other way of maintaining contact. But the IEC is not an IRB.

Second, the IEC is not a "Medical Morals Committee." This is of no importance for most hospitals, but it is in some Catholic hospitals. The medical morals committee was often the body charged with enforcing official Catholic teaching in the hospital. Some of these, I am sure, did function validly as ethics committees. Other were merely watchdogs and censors. The ethics committee is not this.

Third, the IEC is not a Quality Review Board. Nor is it a Risk Management Committee. These serve valid functions in the hospital, and proper risk management and quality review are part of good ethics. But the function is quite different.

Fourth, and very clearly, the IEC is not a Prognosis Confirmation Committee. This is legally important, as well as logically apparent. At times, courts have tended to confuse the two, asking ethics committees to comment on the patient's prognosis. And hospitals sometimes do the same thing, especially if a court case is anticipated. Prognosis is clearly an essential datum for making the ethically right decision about treatment. But physicians, not ethics committees, make prognoses.

Fifth, the IEC is not an Infant Care Review Committee. As we have noted, federal guidelines suggest such a committee. Actually, this is a bad name for it, since its proper function is not to review diagnoses and prognoses but to review the ethical and legal rightness and wrongness of treatment decisions for infants. It is really an Infant Bioethics Review Committee or a Pediatric Ethics Committee. I myself see no reason why this should not be a sub-committee of the institutional ethics committee, but in many hospitals it was established first, and such a subordination, while logical, might be politically difficult.

2. The Institutional Structure of the Ethics Committee.

There are four possible ways the IEC can fit into an already established hospital structure.

First, it can be a Medical Staff Committee. The advantage of this is that physicians may accept it better, since it is one of their own committees. Sometimes the claim is made that this also reduces liability problems, but this is doubtful. The disadvantages are that it becomes a physicians' committee and the input of other members may be reduced, that it tends to get split up into specialized fields in the manner of most medical staff committees, and that the areas which it treats may be reduced to those of immediate practical importance to physicians, who constitute an essential part of any hospital, but who are not the whole of it.

Second, it can be a Committee of the Administration. This has the advantage of theoretically widening the input, and opening it up to the whole hospital. But in some institutions it has the disadvantage of having the committee look like one more imposition onto the health-care side by the money-and-regulation side of the institution.

Third, it can be a Committee of the Board of Trustees. This is probably helpful if the health-care side sees the administration side as more bothersome than supportive, but the disadvantage is that the Committee might be seen as even more "outside" than an administrative committee would be.

Fourth, it could be a Nursing Committee. This is not as silly as it may seem to some at first hearing, since the nursing staff is usually in the middle of all ethical issues. It is not really any different from making it a medical staff committee. Indeed, a recent editorial in *Hospital Ethics* suggests that a nursing ethics group be established in addition to the IEC to deal with ethical issues specific to nurses.[2] But if the IEC itself were to be a nursing committee, this would carry with it the disadvantage that it would be seen as representing a part of the hospital rather than the whole. Physicians would be unlikely to participate.

Fifth, it could be a committee of some other area of the institution. This is generally not a good idea. For example, it could be a Pastoral Care Committee. But ethics is not the same as pastoral care. As we noted in the last chapter, some chaplains may be expert in ethics, but there is no reason to assume this. The pastoral care division must be represented on the IEC, of course. Similar objections can be made against making it a committee within social work, psychiatry, etc.

Well then, where should it fit? It should fit wherever it will work best within the individual hospital. Idiosyncratic features of each institution will be more important here than wider theoretical considerations. Theoretically, the most logical structure is probably an administration committee. But if there are reasons in a hospital why a medical staff committee or a board committee would be better, these reasons should prevail.

3. Membership.

We can now take a look at the internal makeup of the committee. Who gets to be on it? Here there is a general consensus about the overall look of the committee. It should probably have 15 to 25 members, though some are smaller and some larger—some of its work will be done by subcommittees, so it should not be too small—and approximately one-third should be physicians, one-third nurses, and one-third others. The membership should be balanced as to gender and race if possible; committees should try to avoid having all the physicians male and all the nurses female.

a) Non-physician, non-nurse "others."

If possible, the IEC should have an ethicist with some theoretical background about the state of the art of ethics. She or he should be acquainted with the general consensus about many of the major ethical issues in the health care community. Some hospitals may want to hire a full-time ethicist. Two or more hospitals might consider a joint appointment. Full-time ethicists have to know, or be willing to learn, their way around inside the hospital, doing rounds, visiting patients, etc. The ethicist on the committee probably does not need to have that background, though those who do can offer more immediately practical advice in some situations. But the committee ethicist does need to know his or her way around the methodological and practical issues of health care ethics.

There is always a danger that the ethicist will dominate the committee. Ethicists are usually, though not always, experienced at teaching and at public speaking. They know their field and think that their own distinctions are always helpful. Committees should try not to let them dominate and should insist that they always distinguish consensus from personal judgment. Ethicists can be very helpful in pointing out the issues to be considered and in presenting the majority and minority opinions. But they also have made their own judgments, sometimes strongly, about certain issues. It is important that they are explicit in distinguishing these judgments from what most think to be true, or what some think to be true. The ethicist should probably not chair the committee, though he or she can, of course, chair a meeting now and then and may be called on to give formal lectures to the committee.

Should the hospital lawyer be on the committee? Here opinion differs. Some say absolutely yes, some say absolutely no, and others have no strong opinion one way or the other. Those insisting that the lawyer be a member argue that the ethics committee may unwittingly enter into illegal or legally unwise decisions and that there are liability and malpractice issues the lawyer will spot before it's too late. Those resolutely opposed to a lawyer's presence argue that this is an *ethics* committee, and that the committee will stop doing ethics the minute a lawyer says what the law is. Also, they argue, and this is quite true, that many hospital lawyers don't know the law on these issues.

My own opinion is that it is probably better to have the hospital's lawyer on the committee than not to, but that the committee has to watch out lest the meetings become two-way conversations between the lawyer and the ethicist. If a hospital decides not to have its lawyer on the committee, then the committee should take care to consult with her or him often. Some IEC's have resolved this issue by inviting a lawyer who is not the hospital counsel. The intent here is to avoid possible conflict of interest. But most IEC members are hospital employees or staff, and it is not clear that the hospital counsel would suffer more from such conflict than other members.

Other "others" should include one or more social workers, chaplains, administrators, and members of the board of trustees. Administration attendance and support is essential. Depending on how large the committee is, it might think of inviting a member of the clergy from Jewish, Protestant, and Catholic perspectives.

There is some controversy over whether or not the committee should have a "patient advocate." This might be a "member of the lay public" or a representative from some patient advocate group or patient rights group. The argument in favor of this is that otherwise the committee can become too elitist. The argument against it is that one person from the public would be simply tokenism, and would be dominated in any case, and that a patient advocate group would see its mission as pushing strongly for one position. If a "lay member" is chosen, she or he should probably be a person of some importance within the community, acquainted with how committees work and unafraid to speak up. Though it is not exactly the same thing, perhaps a member chosen from the hospital board of trustees could help provide a "lay" perspective.

b) Physician members.

Physician members should represent various departments and divisions within the hospital. I am myself convinced that it is very important that the physician members of the committee include some of the hospital's "biggest wigs," some of its most important doctors. A top surgeon should serve. The head of medicine, or of the intensive care unit, or of the emergency room might be invited. One member almost must be on the medical executive committee, especially if the IEC is not a medical staff committee. The IEC will simply not work unless the medical staff consider it part of medical care in the hospital, just as informed consent, for example, does not work when physicians see it as a legal and bureaucratic imposition rather than as an essential and intrinsic part of good medical care. If the IEC consists mostly or only of residents with maybe a fellow or two, it will not work. However, the membership ought to include some newer members of the staff, perhaps including one of more fellows or residents.

It should be obvious that physician members who have an interest in ethics, and perhaps even some background in the area, will be of greater value than those who do not. If none of the "big wigs" give a hoot about ethics, or if most of the department heads think ethics is one more invasion of outside expertise intended to plague the doctor, then the hospital is in a muddle anyway, and the ethics committee will have a hard time of it. This should not be the case in any hospital, and my own experience has shown that good hospitals are not like this. There should, therefore, be no contradiction between the suggestion that some department heads be on the committee and the suggestion that these be physicians interested in ethics.

c) Nurse members.

Nurses are essential to the IEC. The same criteria which are true for physician members are true as well for nurses. Some of the nursing members should be the ones with clout. A nurse-administrator should be on the committee. Nurses are often the group most sensitive to ethical questions, and nurses are always involved in patient care and in treatment decisions. Nurses from different specialties should be members. Some nurse members should be floor nurses who can speak from actual day-to-day experience. There should be enough nurse members (this is why the one-third rule is important) to give them a true voice. Like the physician members, all should have an interest in ethical health care and have, or be willing to gain, knowledge in the field.

d) Chairing the committee.

One more question about the makeup of the committee is who should chair it. God, maybe. Probably not the ethicist, since usually ethicists are not long-term hospital staff personnel. If the ethicist has been a long-term hospital employee, accepted as an essential member of the health care professionals of the hospital, this might be acceptable. The chaplain is usually not a good candidate, for similar reasons. The best idea is usually to have a physician as chair, but that is a politically practical rather than a theoretically arguable decision. After the committee is established, it may be possible to rotate the chair, though this carries with it the danger that continuity and interest will flag. It is most important that the chair honestly be intrigued by ethics, and recognize the importance of the work of the committee. No one else is going to call the meetings and set up the work agenda.

e) Changing membership.

A final issue is how to handle changing membership. Inevitably some members will quit expressly, and others will simply stop coming. The committee needs to have some way of asking those whose attendance falls to leave the committee to make way for others who are more interested. One committee I work with sends out a report card of attendance at the end of each year, telling each member his or her percentage of unexcused absences. Members are asked to call the chair's office if they cannot attend. I originally wondered if professionals would find this too much like second grade, but there is little if any resentment, and I think this technique helps. Committees might require that members with more than a certain percentage of unexplained absences leave the committee.

Part Two
Function

What does the IEC do? Three principle functions are universally ascribed to ethics committees, though some committees explicitly reject the third of these. The first is education. The second is policy development. The third is case review.

1. Education.

a) Self-education.

Education is the *sine qua non* of any IEC. Without this, there is no function for an ethics committee. No IEC ought to attempt any other function until it has made a considerable start at this for itself, and has at least begun to do it for the hospital. It takes more time than is often anticipated. A good guideline is that no IEC ought to attempt policy development or actual case review for at least two years after its inception. There may be exceptions to this in cases of emergency. But hospitals have always had need for case decisions and for policy development, and the new IEC simply cannot consider itself able to develop policy and review cases until after a time of self-education.

Techniques for this are several. The hospital might provide stipends for the committee to bring in outside experts to give lectures on various aspects of health care ethics. Funds can be made available for members to attend one or more of the many symposia and brief courses and seminars on various issues given by the think-tanks. The *Hastings Center Report* usually lists these, and the Hastings Center gives a number of excellent ones. The American Society of Law and Medicine also sponsors seminars and symposia on medico-ethical and medico-legal issues. Other medical societies, such as the Society for Critical Care Medicine, are now including serious ethical discussion within their annual meetings.

Indispensable is some process whereby the committee meet on a consistent basis to read and discuss issues. The best process I have experienced of this is the procedure at St. Francis Medical Center, where books are assigned, one or two chapters at a time, to the committee. One member is assigned to report. Inevitably, focused and meaningful discussion ensues. The presence of an ethicist is helpful for this process, but even without one, the members of the committee, if required to work through the material, will educate themselves.

Beginning with a practical issue, possibly the practical issue of forgoing treatment, is a good idea. The report of the President's Commission, the Hastings Center *Guidelines,* and other similar works offer good starting points. Wider works might include Ruth Macklin's *Mortal Choices* or a good work in nursing ethics.[3] If the committee chair or one other member takes on the task of mailing copies of articles to all members, which are then discussed at the meetings, the process is helped immeasurably. Each member of the committee ought to subscribe to a journal in health care ethics; the *Hastings Center Report* is probably the best for this purpose.

The self-education process can also proceed by using cases from the several case-books now available, or by having physicians and nurses present cases for discussion. If the purpose of the case presentation is the education of the committee, however, and not case review as such, care should be taken to make sure that the committee does not know who the patient is, and also that there is no feedback to the actual people involved. Educational cases are better when some changes are made in them so that they are theoretical rather than actual cases, since the purpose is the education of the committee and not consultation as a help in resolving the case.

The self-education of the committee never ends, of course. Even after the committee has completed its self-imposed period of self-education before it begins policy development and case review, it will continue to be educated as it actually develops hospital policy and as it actually consults on cases. IEC's, like all other committees, will have changes in membership over the years. It is impossible to repeat the entire process of committee education for each new member. This poses a problem which is not really resolvable. But as the very ongoing tasks of the committee are themselves of necessity educating, new members will become more and more aware of the approach used, the terminology, the ethical issues, etc. And new members can help the committee avoid short cuts which assume things that ought not to be assumed.

b) Education of the hospital.

In addition to self-education, the IEC will involve itself in the education of the hospital community. There is no reason why this task must await completion of the committee's own self-education. Ways of implementing general hospital ethics education include grand rounds, special lectures, seminars, and even weekend symposia. Grant monies are available from pharmaceutical and other providers, and from local and national foundations, as well as from hospital sources such as auxiliaries. Mixing a vacation weekend at a resort for hospital personnel with a few sessions on ethics is a good means of establishing ongoing dialogue and education.

2. Policy Development.

The second task usually taken on by IEC's is policy development. Each hospital will have different ways of assigning this task to ethics committees. IEC's should not try to usurp the role of other hospital divisions and committees. Just because a policy involves ethics—and every hospital policy does because health care delivery is a moral enterprise at its core—does not mean the IEC is the place where the policy must be developed.[4] Hospitals may want to say that the administration or the medical staff can ask the IEC to research and develop a policy. The committee may itself decide that a policy is in need of review. If the IEC is seen not as a policing agency, but as an intrinsic part of the hospital community, this should not be much of an issue. Sometimes external agencies, such as the Joint Commission on Accreditation, will require a policy, as it now does in the area of forgoing treatment. Ethics committees may be the best places for these to be written. But this should never be done by a new IEC. IEC's are not *ad hoc* committees, and trying to short circuit their own period of self-education will be harmful in the long run.

What authority does the ethics committee have to enforce its developed policy? The best answer, I think, is none at all. IEC's should submit the proposals to the already established chain of authority within the hospital. They should not be another enforcement body. Policies which the IEC is asked to write should be submitted to the division which requested them. Usually major policies, such as the policy on forgoing treatment, will need approval by the medical staff, the administration, and the board of trustees. The IEC does not have any administrative power. It may, however, wish to inform hospital authorities of perceived problems in implementation and enforcement of policy.

3. Case Review.

The third function usually ascribed to IEC's is case review. Some IEC's explicitly reject this function. They fear, rightly in some hospitals, that case consultation will be seen as an intrusion into the physician-patient relationship. There is no total consensus on this, but I am myself convinced that at some point any good ethics committee will get involved in case review.

Though there are exceptions, the literature on this issue is in general agreement that hospitals which do this do not find that ethics committees are harmful or intrusive. Ethics committee consultations serve in ways similar to other consultations. They provide written and personal resources to the decision-makers. They provide opportunities for collaboration in prospective reviews and for education in retrospective reviews. I myself have been thoroughly edified by the degree to which physicians expose themselves in their own peer-review meetings and in morbidity-mortality case reviews to suggestions and criticism from others. Little if anything similar exists, for example, among professors in higher education. We professors don't have to present our attempts to help failing students to any review board, even when they flunk. Properly understood, ethics committee case reviews are helps in mutual decision-making, and will be accepted as such by many, probably most, physicians.

a) Initiation and recommendation.

There is a helpful way of clarifying the role of IEC's in case review. A distinction is made between the origin of the review and its outcome. The origin of the review refers to how the review is initiated and who initiates or calls it. The outcome refers to what kind of recommendation is made and how strong it is.

Either can be mandatory or optional. Mandatory-mandatory case review is the least common and the least attractive. Here certain treatment options, such as withdrawing ventilation or withdrawing nutrition and hydration, must be prospectively reviewed by the IEC—the initiation is mandatory; and the judgment of the IEC must be followed—the decision is mandated. This approach is not recommended.

The best way to set up case review is to make it optional-optional. There is no mandate for review, nor is the final suggestion which the IEC makes, if indeed it makes one, binding on the hospital, patient, physician, or family. IEC's are not supposed to be courts. Decisions about treatment are best made by the patient and the physician with the family at the bedside, that is, in the clinical setting. Case reviews and consultations by persons who have tried to educate themselves in these questions are often very helpful. In most instances the consultation will enable the patient, family, and physician to get a clearer idea of what is happening, of what the ethical and legal implications of the decisions are, and of what is the general agreement among the experts, if there is one. Individual members of the IEC may be versed in certain religious traditions and may be able to offer knowledge and solace from the patient's faith tradition. But the advice or judgment of the IEC should not be binding as such.

Another possible way of dealing with initiation and decision is to make the initiation mandatory in certain situations, but to make the recommendation optional. For example, if a hospital were to be concerned about the possibility of withdrawing medically induced nutrition from a patient in a persistent vegetative state, it might want to require an IEC review in all such cases. While understandable, this is probably a bad idea. Although an ethics review might well be very helpful in this kind of case, this decision is still one which should be made by family and physician in the clinical setting. In most states there is no law against forgoing this kind of treatment in this type of case. Still, hospital administration or legal council might want, in some few types of cases, to mandate review. If, in the wake of the *Cruzan* decision, states mistakenly begin to require clear and convincing evidence before surrogates can choose to forgo life support, IEC's may be asked to review such cases. But I am convinced that mandated review should be avoided if at all possible.

It is theoretically possible to make the initiation optional and the recommendation mandatory, but I doubt this combination is used by any IEC. It might well result in the complete disuse of case review.

b) Who calls the review?

Who should be able to initiate case reviews? Some argue that only physicians should be able to call case reviews, at least when these are to be actual consultations. But this is to miss entirely the point of ethical review. Ethical issues are not owned by physicians. Doctors and nurses have medical expertise. They do not necessarily have ethical or moral expertise. Ethical case review should be available at the request of anyone actively involved in the case. This includes the patient, the family, social workers, nurses, physicians, and hospital administrators.

If it is true that anyone actively connected with the case may initiate a review, it is necessary that patients and families be aware of the existence and role of the IEC. At St. Francis, a patient brochure is available to help with this. The ethics committee hopes this will become a part of the admissions packet. Entitled "Making Difficult Choices about Treatment," the brochure is intended for patient education about the options to choose and to forgo treatment modalities. It is written in normal English, stresses that the patient should ask questions of the physician, and informs the patient that the IEC is available for consultation should the patient or the family request its help. It is included as an appendix to this book.

c) Other issues.

There are a number of other issues connected with case review and consultation. Some brief mention of these is in order.

First, should the process even be called a consult? Some argue that there may be legal ramifications when IEC reviews are called consults which would not arise if the term is not used. I think this is not a real issue. Though IEC's are properly concerned about such legal questions, this sort of problem should not be exaggerated to the point where it paralyzes IEC's and their work. Ethical consultations are just as much a part of medical practice as any other consultation. People can sue anybody for anything. The point is not whether one can be sued, but whether the proper standards of medical care are followed. If they are, then suits are frivolous. Physicians and ethicists who spend most of their time worrying about possible litigation are sometimes likely to court it by failing in their responsibilities. Many, probably most, IEC's do actual case review consults. The consultation should be charted just like any other medical consult.

Though some have feared that IEC's might increase the possibility of lawsuits by bringing up issues otherwise ignored, it is now generally recognized that the opposite is true. IEC's are more apt to reduce litigation than to increase it. They allow patients and families an opportunity for dialogue. The right decision is more likely to be made. The presence on the chart of an ethical consult backing up the decision by the physician, after consultation with the patient and/or the family, can serve as evidence of proper procedure. The bottom line—and this is a quote from a workshop I attended several years ago run by the American Society of Law and Medicine—the bottom line is that "the best way to avoid losing lawsuits is to do the right thing in the first place." Ethics committees and ethics consults can help in reaching the right decision.

The mechanisms for actually doing ethical case review and consultation will vary from hospital to hospital.[5] In some instances it may be possible to call the whole committee to review a case. This may be true for educational retrospective reviews, and possibly for some prospective reviews where an actual charted consultation is not requested or where time is not important. In many prospective reviews, however, a sub-group of the IEC will probably actually do the consultation. Three-person teams may be called for this purpose, consisting of one nurse, one physician, and one "other." None should have been directly involved in the case. The team speaks with the attending physician, the staff physicians, nurses, and other hospital personnel. The patient and the family are actively involved, speaking to the team, or to individual members of the team if that is easier for them.

The conclusion of the consulting team can take many forms. Most of the time everyone will agree about the desired course of treatment, and this will simply be charted by the team. When disagreement persists, the ethics team may be able to help in showing exactly where the disagreement lies. Sometimes a compromise solution is available. Often an agreement is reached to wait for a time-limited trial for a certain course of treatment, after which a further meeting is held. The decision should be charted.

Confidentiality is important. Records should be kept away from those with no right to access the information. Cases later reviewed by the entire IEC for educational purposes should not include names or other data which might result in violations of the patient's right to privacy.

4. Range of Issues.

There is one final question which deserves some attention, though it must be brief. What kinds of issues are IEC's likely to get involved in, and what issues ought they stay out of? There is no easy answer to this. Theoretically, and practically, all policy issues in hospitals have ethical components. The most obvious areas, and these are of great immediate importance, are those involving decisions to forgo treatment. IEC's were first suggested to deal with this kind of question and to develop hospital policy for this. But IEC's cannot be limited to this question. Informed consent and the way it is carried out, record confidentiality, policies for treating Jehovah's Witnesses, for dealing with AIDS patients, for dialogue among nurses and physicians, discipline policies, and many other aspects of the hospital's work all have ethical ramifications. The IEC is not the only or even the most important body within the hospital to deal with such issues, but such issues may well come before it for reflection and proposed action.

The IEC also ought to educate itself and the hospital about the whole problem of allocation of health care resources, both within the hospital and at the national level. There is controversy as to whether or not the IEC ought to try to propose policy for in-hospital allocation, such as whether or not to buy this or that machine, open this or that wing, develop or drop this or that specialty. These are most often issues involving questions of justice, and are often of the highest ethical import. But they are just as clearly extraordinarily complex issues, and the IEC may decide it will not focus its own energies on policies of this kind. It ought, however, to include in its agenda the general education of the hospital about the importance of hospital and societal issues of this type.

Conclusion

With interested and energetic leadership and with a hospital community dedicated to good medical care of patients, institutional ethics committees can be of significant help. It is clear that they are here to stay. Just as clear is the fact that there is no completed blueprint. The search for better health care ethics committees is part of the search for better health care and for better medicine.

Discussion Questions

1. What experience have you had with a hospital ethics committee? Has it been positive or negative?

2. Distinguish between the IEC and other similar bodies. What are the dangers if IEC's try to do what these other committees do?

3. Which of the proposed institutional structures do you think is best? Is this based on theoretical reasons or on the situation of your hospital?

4. Discuss the role of the various members of an ethics committee.

5. Which kinds of policies should IEC's help develop?

6. Should IEC's do case review? What procedures enable them to do this best?

Endnotes

1. Sr. Maureen Lowry, at a talk on ethics committees at an ethics retreat at Mercy Hospital of Pittsburgh, Oct. 13, 1989.

2. "The Nursing Ethics Group: When the Ethics Committee Is Not Enough," *Hospital Ethics* (January-February, 1989), 15-16.

3. See the Bibliography.

4. I had to attend one meeting of the forms committee at St. Francis, to explain the new Palliative Support Care Orders Form and get it approved. If any committee could rightly escape ethical discussion, I thought, it would be this one. Wrong. I discovered that the rest of the meeting dealt with issues of honesty and of confidentiality.

5. The guidelines used by St. Francis for ethics consults are included as an appendix to this book.

Chapter Nine

Allocating Health Care Resources

The issue of scarce resources and the quality of health care concerns the problem of allocating, or rationing,[1] scarce medical resources in a just and effective way. That is, it has to do with setting up a system of health care for our nation. It is an excruciatingly complex question. Unlike some other issues in health care ethics, no consensus has arisen about allocation. In earlier chapters we have described in considerable detail the consensus which has emerged as to when and why medical treatments may be forgone for certain patients, and who makes the decision. Nothing similar has developed concerning the question of allocation.

To a considerable extent, this is a new issue for us Americans. The Roman Catholic tradition, which was virtually the only source of medical ethics up until the 1960's, scarcely mentioned the question. Over the past thirty years or so, the governing context for decisions about treatment has shifted, largely due to the growing influence of medical ethics and of the consumer movement, from that of physician paternalism to that of patient autonomy. The emphasis in recent years on informed consent is characteristic of this shift. But no sooner has patient autonomy gained general acceptance than we are confronted with the need for cost containment which threatens, at least to some considerable extent, to take decision-making power out the hands of both physician and patient, and place it in the hands of society as a whole, or of government, which now pays for 41% of the nation's health care.[2]

138

Introduction: The Problem

We Americans do not like the idea of allocating or rationing resources. We want to believe that technology will make it possible to solve health care problems at lower and lower cost. We quite rightly point to those scientific and technological breakthroughs which have enhanced medical care and have benefitted so many of us. But this proper pride has brought with it a hubris and a blindness. When Americans are asked if we think each and every American should have the same health care that a millionaire can buy, we overwhelmingly say yes. When we are asked how much we are willing to pay in increased taxes for this care, we refuse to pay the price: "Read our lips, no new taxes."

Yet the facts which confront us are forcing us at last to look at the problem. The United States spends about 11 or 12 percent of its gross national product on health care; this is more than any other nation and is more than twice what we spend on national defense.[3] We actually spend eight-tenths of one percent of the entire gross national product in intensive care units. Yet we now rank 20th in the world in infant mortality, though the data on which this commonly quoted statistic are based may be questionable.[4]

We have some 37 million persons without health insurance.[5] While it is true, as the American Medical Association points out in a recent advertisement opposing government regulation, that some other nations have waiting lists for certain surgeries which are more quickly available in the U.S., it is also true that effective access to primary care in this country is not available to all our citizens in a way which even approaches equality. Other nations do far better than we do at this. We tend to stress tertiary care at high cost to the neglect of preventive care at lower cost. The United States simply does not have a coherent national health care policy.

There are historic reasons for this. Probably the basic one is the tension which has always existed in our country between individual liberty and the common good. This tension is often a valuable one, as it has helped us avoid the extremes of anarchy and statism. Our insistence on individual liberty has doubtless been an important influence on our advances in modern medicine, which, from a technological perspective, have been unparalleled in the world. But when the stress on individual freedom is not counterbalanced by insistence on the common good, the common good suffers, and individual freedom is compromised as well.

We Americans have tried in a number of ways to avoid the issue. For example, when we were faced with the problem of deciding who should have access to scarce hemodialysis machines, we solved it when the federal government added dialysis and kidney transplant, even for those under 65, to Medicare.[6] I am not arguing that this was a wrong decision. But it allowed us to avoid facing the issue of allocation. Similarly, we have tried to avoid the issue of government health insurance by setting up a system whereby employers pay for health insurance for their employees. This seemed to protect the right of individual freedom, keep the government out of medicine, and at the same time provide decent medical care for working Americans. But this approach is now in jeopardy, as employers claim they cannot afford to continue paying for it. Economists say that global markets make this approach impossible. Strikes are now as apt to be about health insurance as about salary. And large numbers of Americans are without health insurance.

There are a number of experts who continue to claim that allocation within health care is unnecessary. The main argument here is that the United States is a very rich and powerful nation. Statements are often made that if we can bail out the Savings and Loans or build another aircraft carrier we can afford all the medical care we want for all our many diseases.[7] While it is easy enough to show that health care resources are in fact limited, it is harder to show why they cannot be extended. Why can't we double our health care expenditures and spend a trillion instead of 650 billion? Are we not ethically obliged to do so? Surely the needs of the sick outweigh our desire for gadgets and entertainment. That would solve the problem.

I would like to think that this is true. But I am compelled to the judgment that it is not. There are serious difficulties with the argument. Ethically, it suffers from theoretical and practical problems which will be explored later in this chapter and in more detail in the next. And there are economic problems as well. Economists tell us that we could increase the share of our wealth and productivity which goes to health care, but add the all too obvious warning that we would have to reduce the monies and energies spent on other pursuits which we also value and which serve to sustain American productivity. At some point such an increase becomes logically and economically impossible. The global economy of today's world also restricts the portion of economic energy our nation can afford to devote to any one sector.

Nor would shifting allocation within the federal budget solve the problem. Even if we were to reduce those portions of the federal budget which go to other areas, to the military for example,[8] we would still not be able to absorb the growing health care portion of the budget. Other cost-containment mechanisms such as HMO's and DRG's, which are already in place, are not doing the job. These measures are themselves ethically problematic, and the savings they realize have probably reached their peak and are now flattening out. Health care costs are rising so fast that these measures are, and would be, inadequate.

Thus a constellation of factors, including international economics and the ever-expanding portion of the U.S. economy devoted to health care, when seen in the context of other services also required in a just society, force us, despite our reticence, to face up to the fact that some limitation of, and allocation within health care is needed.

Allocation is, of course, already a major factor in the way we deliver health care. I am convinced that we are already rationing health care resources and that we are not doing it in an ethically justifiable way. Present allocation mechanisms restrict access for the poor, deemphasize prevention and education, and often fail to be cost-effective. We ought to try to do it better.

I am equally convinced that there is no one perfect way to allocate health care resources, and that those who make the claim that there is are simply unaware of the complexities involved and of the deficiencies which are apparent in all of the attempts made by various nations thus far toward dealing with this problem. Despite this, however—despite the fact that no one perfect system is apparent, or perhaps in some way because of it—it is clear that ethical principles and moral virtues must play a central role in the national debate toward and construction of a system of health care resource allocation.

This chapter will have five sections. The first will locate the question by distinguishing it from other issues in the medical ethics of forgoing treatment. The second will summarize some of the reasons why allocation arguments are so very difficult to make in a convincing way and will suggest a way to improve them. The third section will briefly address two kinds of visions of who people are and show how these two visions lead to different ways of resolving the issue. The fourth will speak about rationing on the basis of age. The final section will summarize a general approach for a more just health care system.

Part One
Allocation and Forgoing Treatment

Allocating or rationing scarce resources means that certain treatments are withheld or withdrawn. They are forgone because they are scarce; there are not enough to go around. But there is another context for forgoing treatment, one where a general agreement has emerged in our nation that it is right to forgo. While this other context overlaps with the context of rationing, it is different from it.

The kind of forgoing treatment with which we are familiar, which is not done for purposes of rationing, has been a major focus of this book. It is based on the emerging consensus we have described. This consensus is based first on a recognition that not all treatments which prolong biological life are truly beneficial to the patient (in Catholic ethics this is the distinction between morally ordinary, mandatory treatment and morally extraordinary, optional treatment); second on the general agreement that there is a moral difference between killing (euthanasia) and allowing to die; and third on the legal concepts of autonomy, privacy, and liberty to refuse unwanted treatment. Together these three bases are the pillars on which the present consensus has been built.

We have already reviewed the distinction between morally ordinary and morally extraordinary medical treatment. We noted that the proportion of burdens and benefits of the treatment was central to the distinction. Though the distinction is not generally used in the context of allocation, it is worth noting that one of the burdens which the Catholic tradition mentions is the burden of cost. It is morally right, says the Catholic tradition, to choose to forgo costly treatments if we have better things to do with the money. A parent might rightly choose to forgo expensive treatment, even if it would be effective, in order to give the money to children for education. It is true that this tradition was developed long before the advent of third party payors. Today the burdens and benefits most usually considered are those for the patient him- or herself.[9] But third party payors are not always involved, and even when they are, some restrictions for cost containment are justifiable. In any case, the Catholic tradition is clearly open to the possibility that a treatment may rightly be forgone in order to help others with the resources saved.

How can the consensus which has emerged be differentiated from the issue of the allocation of scarce resources?

It is clear that there is some overlap between the two issues. The more that treatment is forgone as based on the three accepted pillars of the present consensus, the less money is spent on it, and the more resources are available, at least theoretically, for other purposes. And it is possible that patients, families, and health care providers may have the scarce-resource question in the backs of their minds when making some decisions to forgo treatment.

Despite instances of overlap, however, when resource allocation is a factor, usually a hidden or implicit one, in decisions to forgo, there is an easy way to distinguish decisions to forgo treatment when they are made on the basis of the three pillars we have already discussed—reasonable and unreasonable treatment, killing and allowing to die, and patient autonomy—from decisions to forgo based on allocation of resources. The former decisions, the ones we make all the time in hospitals, are ones we ought to make even if resources were infinite. The reason we do not treat pneumonia in a patient with metastatic cancer is that the patient does not want the treatment, and we ought not treat. The reason we are morally and ethically justified in removing ventilator and nutritional support from a patient in a persistent vegetative state is that this treatment is not in that person's best interests (as decided by the patient before lapsing into unconsciousness, or as decided by the surrogate who expresses what the patient would have said if he or she could). We would be ethically justified in forgoing the treatment despite any scarcity of resources. Thus, though the areas overlap, they are not the same.

Part Two
The Problem with Allocation Arguments

Allocation decisions inevitably mean at some point that we are going to spend less on one worthy project and more on another. Arguments like this seem very seldom actually to convince us. This is partly due, as I have already suggested, to our resistance as Americans to the idea that we cannot, as free individuals, have it all and have it all right now. Our resistances are due to greed—each of us wants access to everything and few of us want our taxes to go up so that others can have it, too—and to our delight with technology.

In addition to these resistances, there are also problems with allocation arguments themselves. I must confess that these problems are not always taken seriously by those who, like me, argue for a better national health system with a more equitable allocation. The next chapter will treat these difficulties in greater theoretical detail, but some brief overview is helpful here.

A first problem is why we should cut back on this surgery or on that ICU bed instead of on this school or on that bomber. Or why should we not outlaw television or opera or medical schools or houses costing more than $100,000 or vacations to Hawaii and spend the resources saved on housing the poor and feeding the Third World? Does the moral obligation to share mean that just about any expense on personal or family pleasure or comfort is morally wrong? Sometimes writers and speakers give us that impression, and we rightly resist it. Ultimately such questions cannot be answered in an entirely satisfactory way; despite this, they do need to be raised and thought about.

A second problem is the difficulty we all have, and ought to have, I think, in deciding to let one named person die in order to free up resources for larger unnamed groups. This child will die in the well, or from heart disease, unless we spend millions. Yet the millions of dollars could save thousands of children if we bought them food. Another aspect of this problem is the issue of family relationships. We do have obligations to our families that we do not have to strangers. Yet this cannot mean that we have no responsibilities to share resources beyond our families. Simple answers to this problem are not forthcoming.

We often hear in this context that a human life, by which we usually mean the life of this or that named individual, is of infinite value. Implied in this is the idea that we ought to spend whatever it takes to save that one life. But we forget that what we ought to mean when we say that human life is of infinite value is not that it is worth an infinite number of dollars but that it cannot be measured by dollars, few or many. And we also forget that measuring a named individual life in this way means that we undervalue many other human lives.

A third problem is the complexity of economics. Things are seldom as simple as spending on this person or on those persons. Monies saved here may go there, or they may not. Monetary systems, supply and demand, incentives, taxes, and other similar complex matters are all part of allocation decisions. They are excruciatingly difficult issues to deal with, so we avoid them as long as we can. Allocation arguments are very difficult to make in a convincing way.

In the context of these difficulties, there is, I believe, at least one way to make allocation arguments better, i.e., more convincing. We ought to be able to argue with at least some strength that those medical procedures which are very expensive and which are at best of questionable benefit to those who get them should not get public funding, except as limited experimental research. Now this seems reasonable, but it is hard to convince people that this means there should be little or no public funding for certain health care measures. Once the application is made to this or that health care expenditure, those representing these or those patients or this or that research project are quick to insist on the need of the patients and the worthiness of the project.

Part Three
Competing Visions of Who People Are

There are two competing visions about who people are as we relate in society. One vision says that we are basically isolated individuals, and the only reason we care about each other, at least in large groups beyond the family, is that we have to keep others from hurting us. This vision of humankind tends to think that we don't owe anybody anything except what we actually contract to give them. It denies the existence of positive rights and insists that no one has the right to be helped, merely the right to be left alone. Certain libertarian and contractarian theories of justice tend in this direction.[10] Justice thus becomes something we decide on rather than something we discover to be true and try to live up to. Allocation systems are just, according to this first vision, if reasonable and free individuals agree to them. Whatever social contract we agree to set up becomes right by the very fact that we agree to it.

But this ignores the real social situation of real people. The second vision proposes that we are social beings, that we thrive only in society. This vision proposes that we do owe others real help, that nations do have a moral obligation to spend resources on the poor, that systems which allocate without recognizing these obligations are unjust systems. Now there is no doubt but that many who subscribe to this second vision, as I do, are all too often ready to proclaim unworkable allocation solutions. They are too likely to love centralized planning and to think they can eliminate sin just as many Marxists thought they could eliminate nationalism. But at least this vision challenges us with something which approaches the notion of civic virtue. We cannot simply sit around and *posit* a system of allocation and call it fair. We are going to have to sit around and *discover* a system of allocation, and try to discover one which *is*, more or less, fair. There is not only one fair solution. There is no perfect solution. But we must do better than we are doing now.

Part Four
Rationing on the Basis of Age

Perhaps the most engaging and developed attempt to propose allocation of health care resources by a limitation of life-prolonging measures based on age is that made by Daniel Callahan, co-founder and director of the Hastings Center, in his book *Setting Limits: Medical Goals in an Aging Society.*[11] His proposal, startling as it may be at first reading or first hearing to many, deserves serious study.

Callahan argues his proposal from two perspectives. The first is the problem we have already noted of increased health care costs. In an appendix to his book, Callahan cites statistics showing that health care costs for the aged will rise to $200 billion dollars by the year 2000, in addition to inflation, and that pension and health care costs for the aged alone would, by the year 2040, be 60% of the entire federal budget.[12] This is due both to increased costs of health care and to the increased number of elderly among us, especially of the very old, that is, those over 85 or so.

But Callahan's argument is not mainly one of statistics. Callahan's major argument depends on our understanding of the meaning of life. He wants us to see life as biography and not just as biology. He points out that our conception of medicine has shifted from one primarily of caring to one of caring and curing. We actually can cure illnesses, something we used not to be able to do. This advance in turn has led to a change in our understanding of health, from one connected with fate and luck to one open to active medical intervention. Sometimes it even seems as if we might medically conquer death and never die.

In such a context, says Callahan, we need to discover again that the goal of aging is not as such to defer dying but to live old age well. The goal of aging is not individualistic disengagement from the lives of others and from social responsibility but is rather active transmission to the young of the lessons learned through a long life. A social system which sets a goal of indefinitely extending life acts to erode the social sense that there is meaning to old age. It would be better for the old, says Callahan, if such a system were not available. Then old age might better understand itself as a valid stage in the living process rather than as a time when, unfortunately, science will at some point fail to win a victory over the defeat that is death. He thus makes his proposal: "I want to argue that medicine should not be used for the further extension of the life of the aged, but only for the full achievement of a natural and fitting life span and thereafter for the relief of suffering."[13]

Callahan tells us what he thinks is a "tolerable death":

> My definition of a tolerable death is this: the individual event of death in a life span when (a) one's life possibilities have on the whole been accomplished; (b) one's moral obligations to those for whom one has had responsibility have been discharged; and (c) one's death will not seem to others an offense to sense and sensibility, or tempt others to despair and rage at the finitude of human existence.

"Note," he goes on to say, "the most obvious feature of this definition: it is a biographical, not a biological definition."[14]

Thus we see the two bases of Callahan's argument: first, the fact of limited resources, and second, a biographical understanding of life and of a tolerable death. Though the two bases of Callahan's argument work together, he implies that the argument from the meaning of life as biography would be sufficient by itself, even were resources not limited, to support his proposal that treatment funding for the elderly be limited.[15]

As a philosopher, Callahan wants to see our society reinstate what he calls a "thick" as opposed to a "thin" theory of the good. Now this is heady, and very controversial. It would mean a society in which we *agreed* that the meaning he proposes for old age and for a tolerable death would be the anthropology acceptable to all of us, so that we actually *support* the idea of medicine ceasing its attempts to extend our life span beyond the biographical optimum, and so that we would continue to support this even if resources were unlimited. Our agreement on this would thus be similar to our general agreement to forgo treatments which are of great burden or of little benefit. We would come to agree that old age as such is a sufficient criterion, from the social perspective, to make it burdensome and of little benefit to extend life further.

But people in fact do differ about what life means and about what makes it worth living. Though we have generally agreed that some treatments for some patients in some conditions are of little or no human benefit, we have not agreed that age by itself makes this the case. In this context we tend to have a "thin" theory of the good, that is, at the worst, that the good is what individuals claim it to be,[16] or, at best, that the federal government cannot be in the business of imposing one notion of what old age should mean on others who disagree.

I very much doubt that Callahan's "thick" theory will take hold, and I am not sure that I want it to. The "individualism" of which Callahan speaks is often clearly pernicious in our society. But it is not merely a dirty word. It has important positive ethical implications.[17] It serves to counterbalance a move toward absorption of the individual in some sort of state-imposed or society-imposed soup. On the other hand, it must be admitted that it is this same "thin" theory that is one of the reasons for the "ennui" or "alienation" so many old people experience. We simply do not know what old age means, and so we go on trying to extend it indefinitely in the hope that of course it is important that it be extended.

As important and as central to his argument as Callahan's insistence on life as biography is, it will probably never by itself be able to sell the proposal of denying funding for life-extending treatment for the very old. Too many of us might disagree that the meaning of old age requires that medicine stop despite the fact that it can extend our lives and let us live what we as individuals and what those around us might think to be a meaningful and fulfilling life. Though most of us would surely insist that we do not want to live forever, this may well be due mainly to our not wanting to be biologically alive but severely handicapped, perhaps bedridden and dependent on machines. That is what we probably mean when we say we do not want to live forever. I am much less sure that we would refuse if we were offered a treatment which would promise us eternal earthly life with healthy bodies and the potential for growing wisdom and greater experience.[18] As long as we think medicine might someday bring us this gift, I very much doubt that *this* part of Callahan's argument will persuade.

But the other basis of Callahan's argument is still with us. Even if we never agree on a "thick" theory of the good, even if we never agree on what old age ought to mean, or that it ought to mean we should stop trying to extend longevity, we will still have to deal with the limited-resource problem which faces us. Insisting on extending our own lives means inevitably that we have fewer resources left to enhance the lives of those younger than we. At some point we simply must let go and give others a chance at living.

What are we to think, then, about the moral rightness or wrongness of restricting health care expenditures on the basis of age? Can we make an argument that age is a morally irrelevant factor and that it is simply wrong to discriminate this way, as it would be wrong (and here a consensus has emerged) to discriminate on the basis of race or sex or on the basis of social contribution? We have agreed, generally at least, in issues of immediate microallocation (who of three people gets the organ or the bed) that race and sex and religion and even past or future social contribution are factors which must not be included. Only medical need and benefit and random choice are valid factors. The person medically most in need and most likely to benefit is chosen; if there are more than one, flip a coin, or first come first served. Can we rule out age?

I think the answer is no. Age is unlike morally irrelevant factors like race, gender, religion, or national origin. There is a very easy way to show this. Age is a factor which does not exclude any living person. We all have a chance of growing old. I will never be Black, or a woman, or Italian. To restrict treatment on bases such as these would allow me to escape the restriction; it would discriminate against *others* while leaving *me* untouched. That is the reason behind the heinousness of race and sex discrimination. The discriminators gain while the oppressed lose. The oppressors need not worry that the restrictions they enact will restrict their own access to what they want.

But age does not necessarily entail this kind of injustice. Of course that does not mean that age should be used as a basis for just any kind of restriction. It means that age may rightly be used as a basis for those restrictions where it can reasonably be shown that it is morally relevant. Age can reasonably be shown to be morally relevant when it comes to flying commercial airplanes. Those under 21 and those over 70 or so ought not be allowed to do it. We do not recoil morally from such restrictions.

Callahan and a good number of others are therefore proposing that age is a morally relevant basis for restriction, not of life-enhancing treatments, but of life-extending treatments. Since resources are better spent elsewhere, since there is no way of increasing these resources to the point where the problem of allocation would disappear, since this is not the same kind of invidious discrimination as that based on race, sex, and similar criteria, and since there is at least a plausible argument that the meaning of old age is not enhanced by life-extending treatment, therefore such restriction is morally justified.

Callahan's proposal has, needless to say, come in for considerable criticism.[19] According to one theory of justice, it is never right to deny resources to the neediest among us; they must get priority.[20] Surely the very old, especially those who are sick, are among our neediest. Restricting resources allocated to their health care is thus unjust. In a recent article, Robert Veatch, while disagreeing with Callahan on certain matters of philosophical theory, agrees with his basic conclusion that age may be used as a basis for restriction.[21] Veatch suggests a way to answer the criticism that the old are the most in need. He says that while this is true from a "slice-of-time" perspective—those old who are sick are, right now, very much in need—it is not true from an "over-a-lifetime" perspective. Over our lifetimes, we who get very old are actually quite well off indeed. We are among the least needy, when compared with others who have been less fortunate. Veatch thus concludes, like Callahan, that while it would be immoral to refuse to *care* for the old, to relieve suffering, to include them—and that means us when we get there—in meaningful social relationship, it may well be right to exclude them—and that means us when we get there—from expensive life-extending technologies. Norman Daniels makes a sophisticated book-long philosophical argument for a similar position.[22]

Though age as a criterion for allocation cannot be ruled out *a priori*, there remain serious political and ethical obstacles to its actual practical implementation. We may well decide not to use age as a criterion, at least not explicitly. But we will have to decide on some criteria and we are morally obliged to make sure that these criteria are indeed just, or at least that they do indeed approach justice.

Part Five
Toward a Better Health Care System

We have noted a number of times that there is no consensus about the question of how to allocate resources. But there is, at least among some who are studying the question, a growing convergence toward the acceptance of some basic parameters. This last section will point out features of such a system.[23]

First, our health care system must have some form of national health insurance, paid for by tax dollars, which guarantees all of us, regardless of wealth or employment, access to primary care. This would include those whose disease process is such that no cure is possible. We should try as much as possible to eliminate the cost-containment which now occurs by rationing against this access to basic care. That means a system like Canada's or England's on this level. Doctor's visits and procedures such as check-ups, inoculations, basic health education, and the drugs and medicines needed for primary care should be available to all of us and paid for by taxes. Some minimal deductible or co-payment might be acceptable as a hedge against misuse, but even this should be waived for the very poor.

In addition, and still on the level of primary care, we must allocate more dollars to educational attempts at prevention of illness. Prenatal and well-baby programs are morally obligatory and will almost certainly be cost-effective as well.

Second, the same health insurance program should cover most medical procedures which are reasonably likely to return patients to health. This second requirement is consistent with my argument earlier that we ought not spend resources on procedures which are unlikely to benefit those who get them or to benefit the specific population at which they are aimed, even though they may benefit the individuals who receive them. This second requirement is also consistent with the argument of Callahan and others that age may rightly serve as a criterion for denying public funding for life-extending technologies. A national health insurance program should cover most medical procedures which offer a decent likelihood of returning patients to a reasonably healthy state.[24] There may well be exceptions. Some procedures may be so expensive that we will simply decide not to pay for them for anybody. This will be very hard to do, but it is not unjust. What is unjust is to go about our business as usual, rationing in hidden ways against the most defenseless. The first and second levels imply as well that we should continue to pay for basic medical research.

Third, we ought to continue to allow the wealthy to get any treatment they desire. Though it can be argued that an individual might, in some cases, act wrongly when requesting such treatment, it is better for all of us to allow this freedom to individuals. Such a free market will maintain incentive for creation of new procedures, and will enable us to keep a share of the health care system somewhat free of government regulation.

Such an approach would be far from perfect. These are its barest outlines. At least we can claim that in the past few years we have begun to take a look at what will be the most important issue in health care ethics for the next generation.

Conclusion

At the risk of repetition, I want to conclude by reiterating the major thesis I have made in this chapter. Ethicists like Callahan insist, and in this they are quite right, that we are already rationing our health care dollars. But this "soft rationing," as Callahan calls it, is less explicit than "hard" rationing, where legislators and voters actually decide where and how to allocate resources. We simply do not want to engage in hard rationing. It is easy to see why. Those excluded or restricted will fight back. Yet soft rationing clearly results in the reduction of resources to those who are not organized, to those who have little or no voice, to the poor for whom access to health care is so often limited. And poverty cannot justly be a basis for exclusion when health care is distributed.

Scarce-resource arguments are notoriously hard to make. They usually leave us unconvinced, and for good reason. We would prefer not to have to face them at all. Yet our society is already rationing its medical care. We must look at how we do it and try to do it better.

Discussion Questions

1. What do you think is the difference between forgoing treatment based on the best interests of individual patients and forgoing treatment to allocate resources? Is allocation of this kind ever right? If not, how will we pay for medical care?

2. Do you agree with Daniel Callahan's proposal of rationing life-extending technologies for the very old? Would you be willing not to have them available for yourself? Would you be willing to pay more in taxes so that everyone could have them?

3. How should the United States balance individual liberty and the common good in this area? In general, what kind of a health care system should we have?

Endnotes

1. Some authors distinguish these two terms. Allocation means deciding on the basis of disease or other medical criteria; rationing means deciding which person or persons of equal need get a limited resource, or deciding on the basis of age or other criteria not considered to be strictly medical. Though the distinction is helpful, I am not persuaded that the two can be completely distinct, or that, as some argue, we ought to allocate but never ration.

2. Charles J. Dougherty, *American Health Care: Realities, Rights, and Reforms* (New York: Oxford Univ. Press, 1988), p. 16. On how to respond to this new governing context no consensus has emerged.

3. Dougherty, p. 16.

4. Dougherty, p. 4; *Newsweek*, April 9, 1990, p. 78. The problem stems from a claimed difference in what counts as a live birth as opposed to a miscarriage among the nations compared. I have been told that American statistics count as live births premature fetuses who cannot survive, and who are considered miscarriages in other nations. Different American states may come up with their data differently. This would affect not only infant mortality figures but life-expectancy figures as well. I have no idea how much this kind of discrepancy affects the final rankings, or even how much discrepancy exists. The final figures are simply quoted

in the literature with no explanation of whether or not the data on which they are based are comparable. Garbage in, garbage out. My own sense is that the incomparability of the data base, to the extent it does exist, would not be enough to put the U.S. at the top of the infant mortality list. But issues like this do make it clear that comparative statistics are only as good as the figures on which they are based.

5. Dougherty, p. 11. See also Larry R. Churchill, *Rationing Health Care in America: Perceptions and Principles of Justice* (Notre Dame, IN: Univ. of Notre Dame Press, 1987), p. 10, who cites figures from 1983 of 25 million at any one time, and 34 million at some period during a year. The 37 million figure is the most recent I have seen (*Newsweek*, April 23, 1990, p. 47).

6. See Tom L. Beauchamp and James F. Childress, *Principles of Biomedical Ethics*, 3rd. ed. (New York: Oxford Univ. Press, 1989), p. 291.

7. Ronald Bayer made statements to this effect at the First International AIDS and Ethics Conference in San Francisco, June 27, 1990. His argument was in attempted refutation of Daniel Callahan's talk the day before, where Callahan insisted that, while AIDS is a special disease, some prioritization of funds to various aspects of preventing and treating it is morally justified.

8. We should clearly take advantage of the current geopolitical situation and reduce our military spending. This will make some further monies available for health care, for debt reduction, and for other purposes. But it will not solve the health care problem.

9. A counter-position is now taking shape which argues that the interests of the family ought to be given equal weight to those of the patient even when decisions are made by surrogates. See John Hardwig, "What About the Family?" *Hastings Center Report*, 20, No. 2 (March/April, 1990), 5-10. According to this position, the criteria of patient autonomy and patient best interests should be rejected or radically changed. While it is true that the Catholic tradition has insisted on the moral rightness of a patient deciding for him- or herself to forgo treatment in order to help others, this criterion is far more problematic when the decision is made by surrogates and is based on their own interests. Possibly some reconciliation between the generally accepted "best interests of the

patient" standard and Hardwig's insistence that the best interests of the family be given equal weight would result from recalling the flexibility of the "ordinary-extraordinary" distinction and its moral nature. Doubtless much treatment which would be rejected "in the best interests of the family" would also be rejected if the "best interests of the patient" were given primacy, but were interpreted humanly, not biologically or medically. But Hardwig's proposal is fraught with danger if it means that families could override the patient's interests in favor of their own. The *Cruzan* decision worries about the precise kind of danger Hardwig's proposal seems to risk.

10. For lengthy development of these issues see Dougherty, *American Health Care,* and Churchill, *Rationing Health Care.*

11. Daniel Callahan, *Setting Limits: Medical Goals in an Aging Society* (New York: Simon and Schuster, 1987).

12. Callahan, p. 227.

13. Callahan, p. 53.

14. Callahan, p. 66.

15. Callahan, p. 53.

16. This is a kind of metaethical positivism. We spoke of this in chapters four and five.

17. I have developed some of these in "Individualism and Corporatism in a Personalist Ethic: An Analysis of Organ Transplants," in Joseph A. Selling, ed., *Personalist Morals: Essays in Honor of Louis Janssens* (Louvain: Univ. of Louvain Press, 1988), pp. 147-166.

18. Recent development of human growth hormone as a way to slow down or even temporarily stop or reverse many symptoms of the aging process is a case in point. This expensive treatment will surely be in great demand. If it works, it will improve the quality of life for the aged, and may extend that life as well. Few of us will voluntarily choose to reject it. Will we, and should we, demand that public funding be allocated to treat all of us with this potentially "miraculous" medication?

19. For one rejection of the entire position, and for citations of many authors on both sides, see John F. Kilner, "The Ethical Legitimacy of Excluding the Elderly When Medical Resources Are

Limited," *The Annual of the Society of Christian Ethics, 1988* (Washington, DC: Georgetown Univ. Press, 1988), pp. 179-203.

20. The basic position is made in John Rawls, *A Theory of Justice* (Cambridge, MA: Harvard Univ. Press, 1971).

21. Robert M. Veatch, "Justice and the Economics of Terminal Illness," *Hastings Center Report*, 18, No. 4 (August/September, 1988), 34-40.

22. Daniels makes his argument from the basis of what he calls a "prudential lifespan account." All have a right to an "age-relative normal opportunity range." Working from a contractarian approach where prudent deliberators must choose a just system for their society, Daniels argues that this just system may rightly include restrictions of life-extending technology to the old. This is not a question of discriminating among birth cohorts, that is, between different people born in different years, but of discriminating among age groups, that is, among the same people at different times in their lives. Prudent deliberators will choose to postpone some expenses in order to save for old age, but they need not postpone enough to enable them to extend their lives beyond a "prudential lifespan." See Norman Daniels, *Am I My Parents' Keeper: An Essay on Justice between the Young and the Old* (New York: Oxford Univ. Press, 1988).

23. The basic approach here is from Dougherty, *American Health Care*, pp. 125-127.

24. Inevitably people will differ as to what "reasonable health" means. But I prefer this phrase to the one used by Charles Dougherty, who wants national health insurance to provide funding for treatments "likely to preserve or restore functioning typical for a normal member of the species" (*American Health Care*, p. 189). This might mean no funding for any treatment whatsoever for anyone less than "normal" mentally or physically. We ought rightly avoid the extreme of vitalism, which insists, for example, on treating all handicapped newborns regardless of severity of illness or of quality of outcome. But we surely ought to continue to fund the kinds of simple surgery which allow infants born with Down's Syndrome to live. Similarly, nursing home care and personal care services needed by many partly disabled elderly ought to be funded even though "normal" functioning might not be possible.

See Norman Daniels, *Am I My Parents' Keeper?* (New York: Oxford Univ. Press, 1988), p. 79, pp. 103-116.

Chapter Ten

The Use and Misuse of the Allocation Argument

Allocation-of-resource arguments can take many forms, and there are a number of important systemic questions involved in the larger context of such arguments. They demand for their solution a complete system of justice. No such attempt can be made here. Those attempts which have been made, for example that of John Rawls, have met with mixed reviews and leave open in any case the specific kind of question I want to explore in this chapter.[1] While the applications here will be limited to medical ethics, which is the focus of this book, the methodological questions obviously have implications for other areas of social ethics as well.

This chapter will deal with the allocation-of-scarce-resource argument as that argument occurs explicitly or implicitly in the following form: It is morally wrong to spend x money on A while situation B exists on which the x money ought to be spent instead. This form of the allocation argument distinguishes what I want to explore from another, easier question, one usually considered an issue of "microallocation." This other question concerns who of a limited number of named potential recipients should receive the organ, the machine, or the hospital bed. The issues here have not been completely resolved either, but there is agreement concerning at least some of the factors which may rightly be included (medical factors, time on the list, randomization) as well as those which should not, at least usually, be considered (race, gender, social worth).[2]

In the first section of this chapter I will note a number of reasons why the allocation argument in the form "x money should not be spent on A as long as situation B exists on which the money should be spent instead" is so often unpersuasive. In the second section, I will advance a suggestion for making it more persuasive by arguing that it can take on a more directly normative quality—that is, it can more persuasively lead to the conclusion that spending the money on A really *is* wrong—if it is combined with an argument about the benefits or lack of benefits of doing A in the first place. The chapter will conclude with an application of this "combination-argument" to the current procedure in medicine of using artificial hearts as bridge devices to human heart transplants.

Resistance to Allocation Arguments

Why is it that the allocation argument in the form in which we will examine it—it is wrong to spend x money on A while situation B exists on which the resource ought to be spent instead—sounds so good at first reading or first hearing but so often fails to be persuasive? We recognize its importance, know that it urges us to attend to the gross inequalities of our world, and accept it, even proclaim it as a countervailing exhortation to materialism and selfishness. But when it comes to a normative application of this form of the allocation argument, so that we might *really* accept the idea that we "ought" to stop spending money on A and spend it on B instead, the argument often fails to convince. For example, while it seems correct to urge that more health care dollars and energies be allocated to prevention, and less resource, relatively speaking, be allocated to cure, when it actually comes down to choosing which cures will no longer be available, the allocation argument leaves us unconvinced.

We do ration our health care dollars, of course, as we have noted in the last chapter. But, to use again Daniel Callahan's term, we do it "softly." And "soft" rationing is usually unjust because it tends to follow the path of least resistance, which means that those who have the greatest moral claim on resources, because they have the least powerful voice, are the ones least likely to get them. Yet "hard" rationing, such as the attempt in Oregon to reduce state funding for transplant surgery in order to make funds available for other purposes, or the recent Oregon attempt to prioritize treatments for funding, while theoretically a far better way to make these kinds of decisions, is itself fraught with difficulties. It is simply very hard to be convinced that some named individual person will have to die (monies ought not be spent on A) in order that some other goal may be achieved (while situation B exists on which the money should be spent instead). Why does this form of the allocation argument so often fail to lead to concrete normative conclusions which people are actually willing to carry out?

There are a number of reasons. Some of these are problematic aspects of the argument itself. Others are resistances which the argument is intended to address and which it urges us to overcome. These latter are surely powerful. The first set of resistances can be summarized as the human resistance to the good, which is a part of the theological doctrine of original sin. We don't allocate our resources more justly because we do not want to. We like to spend our money as we do. Selfishness, greed, lust for money and power all play a role.

A second set of these resistances is our reliance on technology, our hope that technological answers to the allocation questions will be found by eliminating the scarcity of resources which makes allocation necessary. This is the hope in superconductivity and in cold fusion. We would prefer not to face the allocation issue which might require us to make hard choices. And surely technology can and does, in many instances, alleviate scarcity and thus reduce the need for allocation. Rejecting technology is not the answer. Physicians and nurses should not want to reject CT scans and heart monitors any more than authors will want to reject computerized word processing.

Unfortunately, however, this very reliance on technology too often increases the scarcity we hope to reduce. So much is spent on high-tech procedures that less is left for other purposes. It is true that the original microallocation question of who gets the dialysis machine was "solved" by eliminating the scarcity through federal funding. The technology has been literally a life-saver for many persons, and I would certainly not want to reject it. But the "solution" has meant that these monies are not available for other purposes. Reliance on technology tends to exacerbate the problem of scarcity at least as much as it alleviates it.

Problems with the Allocation Argument

These factors—greed and selfishness and a too eager reliance on technology—are powerful forces contributing to our reluctance to accept specific normative conclusions from the allocation argument. But there are problematic aspects to the argument itself. Even if we overcame our selfishness and agreed to rely less on technology, problems would remain. When faced with determining exactly which expenses we ought not make, or how much money is indeed greedy, we find ourselves often without firm norms.

Catholic moral theology is a case in point. Whereas it has been quick, too quick in my judgment, to make absolute normative applications in areas of sexual ethics, and in those areas of medical ethics which deal with reproduction or which otherwise can be "solved" by the physicalist analysis of the traditional principle of double effect, the Catholic tradition has not, at least not usually, attempted to make similar applications in the area of allocating resources. Is it morally wrong to get a heart transplant? What about a second one? Official Catholic teaching prohibits direct sterilization, but there is no norm against expensive neonatology, no insistence that the money be spent instead on prenatal care. No general consensus has emerged in Catholic ethics concluding to the wrongness of driving a six- or an eight-cylinder car, or of taking a European vacation, or of buying a CD player to play Mozart, though it might be implied from many more general statements about consumerism and the unequal distribution of resources that such conclusions would follow.

Why are such conclusions not more often derived from the allocation argument, and why do they seem so unpersuasive, at least to so many? I think it is because the allocation argument itself is problematic in too many ways, and I want to note five of these ways.

First, the argument is too open-ended. "A" (the purpose for which spending money is said to be wrong because "B" should get it instead) can be virtually anything which can be seen to be of less importance than "B." The general argument that we ought to redress the imbalance in our health care policies where too much is spent on expensive cures for the few and too little on prevention for the many is one to which I subscribe. I think this is clear, for example, when comparing the monies spent on expensive peri- and neo-natology with those spent on pre-natal preventive care, especially for the poor. But how is the argument convincing that it is the neonatal monies which should go to prenatal prevention and not the funds spent on eight cylinder cars, European vacations, and CD players? While most of us would agree, I think, that we should spend more on prevention of illness than we do, it is very hard to provide adequate justification for where the funds should come from. It is easy to identify situation "B." It is far harder to provide warrants for identifying "A."[3]

Since "A" can be almost anything, the allocation argument in the form we are examining makes it wrong to do almost anything! "A" can analogously be almost (not quite but almost) any human activity. Surely food for the starving is more important than teaching Shakespeare. Does this make literature classes and summer Shakespeare festivals morally wrong uses of monies? Surely not. But it is very hard to begin with the allocation argument and show *why* not. Even were we to accept the idea that other expenses more properly fit into category "A" than Shakespeare festivals (the monies spent on gambling or on prostitution, for example), how could we justify going ourselves to Shakespeare just because others go to Nevada? Sure, they should spend the money on the poor instead of on the tables, we might say, but just because they don't would not relieve us of the presumed obligation to give up on Shakespeare.

The second problematic aspect of the argument is the question of guilt.[4] The allocation argument, because of its relative inability to exclude almost any resource-expending pleasurable human activity from category "A," threatens to create false feelings of guilt. If indeed it is morally wrong to take a vacation while monies are needed for food, then we ought not do it. If we do, we are guilty of a wrong action, and possibly of a sin. But this, it would seem, must be extended to any human action which might fit category "A." After we have eliminated European vacations, eight-cylinder cars, and CD players, what next? It would seem there is no end.

The traditional distinction between the so-called positive and negative norms of the natural law, where the former were said to oblige, but not to oblige continuously, while the latter were said to oblige always, has been quite correctly criticized by today's moral theologians as minimalist and often physicalist. Yet the distinction at least had the advantage of allowing that the positive norms came to an end somewhere. It may be difficult to avoid all deliberate sexual stimulation of thought, word, and deed until married, but at least the obligation is located and limited. If "A" is as widely extended as it would seem to be, then the scrupulous person—indeed, on the presumption that the allocation argument and its implied normative conclusions are correct, the good, virtuous person—is caught in an ethical bind from which there might seem no escape save severe poverty, or even death. If so many human activities are judged to be wrong uses of resources, then moral uprightness becomes equated with an almost extreme asceticism. Those of us who have counselled people tortured with scrupulous consciences in the area of sex ought to be slow to develop other devices of inflicting similar pain.

Anne Patrick points out the dangers of inflicting guilt, using images which many of us can identify with:

> Moral theology, we must admit, is not everyone's favorite subject. The knowing laugh that humorist Garrison Keillor evokes when he refers to . . . "Our Lady of Perpetual Responsibility" says much about moral theology. . . . Moral theology has provided more than one generation with sweaty brows and clammy palms as they examined their consciences and worked up the courage to confess hard-to-name sins in dark confessional boxes around the country. Moral theology, in short, has supplied the peculiarly Catholic variety of guilt so prominent in the literature of parochial school nostalgia. . . . The phrase "moral burnout" is not too strong to describe a syndrome suffered by devout persons who identified all the opinions published in official Catholic books or uttered by religious authority figures as clearly and certainly God's opinion too, and then tried to live in their God-given bodies in the real world.[5]

At this point a counter-argument is often made. The allocation argument, it is claimed, is not intended to apply to individual expenses such as vacations and cars and heart transplants. It is intended to point to structural flaws within the national and international economy, flaws we ought to work to eliminate. In the meantime, even though it is true that spending monies on "A" means that "B" is not funded, it is of course morally right to do so, since individuals cannot be required to give up "A." I am not exactly sure what to do with this. I agree entirely that the basic intent of allocation arguments, and of redistributive justice generally, is to enact structural change. But I am not sure how the argument, if it is accepted in the form we are examining, can exempt individuals from being bound to stop spending on "A" simply because the perfect economic system has not yet arrived. Perhaps part of this is that I do not think such a system will arrive.

The third problematic aspect of the argument has been noted in the literature. The argument as it stands can be criticized for failing to attend to the more complex aspects of real world economics. It is at least possible, and often likely, that doing away with "A" will not make more funds available to "B." This problem is more apparent when dealing with social policy than with individual decision, of course. If an individual decides not to buy a car but to buy food for a poor neighbor instead, that person can be relatively certain where the money goes. Still, the complexities of economics get in the way of making normative conclusions from the allocation argument. Redistribution is not possible without continuing productivity. Continuing productivity requires at least some restriction on the breadth and the quantity of egalitarian distribution. These issues are far too vast for further pursuit here. They necessarily involve the debate between capitalism and socialism with the possibility of some third alternative which might reduce the evils of both. It is enough here simply to say that the economy as it is poses problems for the allocation argument which that argument cannot transcend and which make normative conclusions drawn from it less persuasive than they would otherwise be.

A fourth problem has been pointed out in feminist ethics, though in a much different context than is my own here. It concerns the issue of relationships. Carol Gilligan argues that Lawrence Kohlberg's stages of ethical development are inadequate, and one of her reasons is that they give too little weight to relationships. They are too abstract, too universal, she argues, and women in Kohlberg's scheme are seen too often to be fixated at a lower, less mature level of moral development (the third stage in Kohlberg's six stages) because women's moral reasoning tends to emphasize personal relationships more than abstract concepts such as equality based on justice and human rights.[6] Stressing attachment, and seeing individual autonomy and separation as an "illusory and dangerous quest,"[7] women, says Gilligan, emphasize care and connectedness. Women's patterns of moral decision-making reach judgments which are not universalisable in the traditional sense, but which nonetheless offer insights and validity often missed in the more logical male emphases on abstract principles of utility and justice as fairness.

In a recent article Virginia Black continues Gilligan's argument in the context of the family bond, which she extends to any congregation marked by "exceptional emotional involvement; more generous than usual give-and-take and often willing sacrifice; . . . attachment to memories, traditions, lineage, heritage, ancestry and bequests;" and other criteria which can be summarized in the concept of bonding.[8] Black argues that "universalisability is not necessary . . . for many kinds of judgments we make about, and within, family type relationships."[9] "Fairness in close relationships," she says, "rests on our capacity to discern non-resemblance and non-repeatability for it consists in moving in on those nuances of influence and identification that make the other know we care."[10]

I will not try to develop here the relationship between this approach to ethics and the more usual insistence on universalisability. As Black herself points out, some universalisable rules apply within family groups, and the principle of universalisability properly requires that some degree of specificity of morally relevant circumstances be included in norms and rules.[11] It may well be that the argument Gilligan and Black make will result more in the reorientation and clarification of the universalisability principle than in the exemption of family morality from its demands.

For our purposes, however, it is clear that feminist ethics has something to say about the inadequacy of the allocation argument stated in the form I have suggested. The allocation argument in this form is precisely the kind of abstract argument from justice which some feminist ethicists are criticizing. It may well be that it *is* morally right to spend money on "A" even though, in the abstract, situation "B" demands more than "A" does. It is difficult if not impossible to give a thoroughly convincing justification for two quite correct moral judgments: first, that it is morally wrong for a physician or a scholar to attend a medical or an academic conference while his or her own child is at home with no food in the house, but second, that it is morally right to attend that convention, despite the expense, while thousands die of hunger in our world. Relationship does count toward responsibility. Allocation rules which ignore this are, for that reason, often unconvincing.

A fifth and final problem with the allocation argument is similar to the problem of relationship, and has received some attention in ethical scholarship. It is the problem of how to decide concerning the moral relevance of the distinction between identified and named individuals and more vague and unnamed groups. In the allocation argument, "A" may be an identified named person, while situation "B" is wider, but less easily identified. Should identified little girls be left in wells to die so that the energy and expense of saving them can be transferred to larger populations who are likewise in desperate need, but whose names are not known?

In medical ethics, the traditional physician-patient relationship establishes a bond of obligation between a doctor and the patients he or she happens at accept. But it leaves far less easily determined the obligations the physician has to sick people whom he or she has *not* accepted as patients.[12] Thus it has become an acceptable practice—indeed it is often seen by transplant surgeons to be obligatory—that a second, third, and subsequent organ be transplanted in cases of organ rejection, even though other candidates are equally in need, and may even have greater potential to benefit. This practice seems in conflict both with utilitarian and with fairness approaches to justice, at least theoretically, and may well be wrong when proposed as an absolute. Yet it would doubtless be humanly very difficult, if not impossible, for transplant teams to abandon patients after the first rejected transplant.

This fifth factor, like the other four, is a complex issue, and is not easily open to rational "solution." But it is one more reason why we are reluctant to find the allocation argument convincing when we try to apply it to specific cases so that we might draw from it concrete norms for our conduct.

Before turning to my own suggestion for strengthening the allocation argument, I want to mention one recent attempt to apply it directly in medical ethics, an attempt which I think fails. In his article in a 1988 issue of *Ethics and Medics*, "IVF and Social Justice," Donald DeMarco argues that *in vitro* fertilization is immoral because it is "a violation of distributive justice. . . . The extraordinary cost incurred in operating fertility centers which offer a relatively small number of people a relatively small chance of having their own children is inconsistent with society's more general obligation to provide all its citizens with basic health care."[13]

Now there is much reason to worry about fertility centers and IVF. Many centers fail to inform couples of the real, often very low, likelihood of success. There are a number of ethical questions which urge hesitancy. Indeed, if it can be shown that the population served by IVF is indeed not truly benefitted by the procedure, then the allocation argument would become the "combination-argument" which I will propose shortly and would, I think, justify the judgment that IVF ought not be done, or at least that it ought not receive public funding. But DeMarco's argument as it stands is inadequate.

This becomes even more apparent later in his brief essay when DeMarco states:

> Society has a duty to respond to people's health needs, since people have a right to have these needs met. Basic needs are universal and as such are appropriately discussed in the framework of rights. Wants, on the other hand, are private rather than universal. An individual may have any number of wants which are peculiar to him. These wants, no matter how intensely he experiences them, are not the same as needs and consequently are not the subject of rights. An individual may want a high income, pleasurable vacations, and a second car. [Why not a first car—is it only a second one which is a want while a first is a need—if so, why is a pleasurable vacation a want and not a need?] He may also want contraception, sterilization, and access to an *in vitro* fertilization program. At best, these are privileges rather than rights. But when society allows the medical profession to deprive some people of their basic rights to health care in order to try to satisfy the wants of others, the issue of social justice is brought into sharp focus. Social justice demands that rights be met before wants are satisfied.[14]

The problematic nature of this argument should be clear from what we have already said. DeMarco puts contraception, sterilization, and *in vitro* fertilization into his category "A" along with pleasurable vacations and a second car. He calls them privileges, but then, especially for IVF but at least implicitly for the others, he argues that they are immoral because the resources spent on them ought to go instead to true health care needs. It is clear, of course, that his choice of the medical procedures to be rejected is influenced considerably by the fact that they are condemned by physicalist Catholic medical ethics. And his distinction between "wants" and "needs" lacks criteria. This kind of application of the allocation argument will convince only those searching for further support of an ethical judgment already made on other grounds, grounds which proscribe the procedures in question as morally wrong apart from any problem of allocation. In the absence of such grounds, the allocation argument advanced here fails to convince, for the reasons we have already proposed.

Improving the Allocation Argument

What, then, is left? Is the allocation argument utterly useless? The first answer to this would probably be no, and I think this answer is intuitively correct. Even in the form examined in this paper, the allocation argument has merit. Most obviously, it has merit as exhortation. Even if it is hard to apply convincingly to individual cases—that is, even if it is hard to identify "A"—the allocation argument properly urges us to worry about distributive justice. It *is* a scandal that there is in our world both great wealth and great poverty. Though the allocation argument may not be conclusive in concrete instances, it does make us pause; it gets at us. It points out to us the necessity of at least imagining a better way. If it is utopic, even utopian in the common meaning of that term, the society urged upon us by the argument for a just allocation is nonetheless a society toward which struggle, prudent and cautious perhaps, but struggle nonetheless, ought to be exerted.

In this, the allocation argument is not unlike other principles, principles often derived from theology, which are seen to be important in medical ethics. As was noted in chapter one, these theological principles, for example, the principle of God's dominion over human life, have often been misused in medical ethics when it is implied that they can solve medical ethical issues. But these principles act more as hermeneutic themes than as norms and rules. They give us hints. They make us pause and think. The allocation argument does this well, and for this reason alone ought not be abandoned. It reminds us that we are not isolated individuals, that we have obligations to others, even to unnamed others in vague far-away groups, that we do not have absolute rights to private property, that wants and needs, even if not easily distinguished, are not identical either. As exhortation, as hint, as caution, the allocation argument is of significant importance.

But there may be even more. Perhaps the allocation argument can be helpful in leading to normative conclusions. I will make a proposal which might allow us, in some cases, to *combine* the allocation argument as such with *another* claim which, while not of itself conclusive, might, in combination with the allocation argument, actually provide moral warrant for judging that spending the money on "A" is morally wrong. I propose that the allocation argument, when combined with the empirical claim that "A" is at best of dubious benefit for those on whom the money is spent, properly serves as a basis for the moral judgment that the funds ought to be spent elsewhere instead. Though the combination argument is not directly helpful in identifying "B," and though it does not answer problems three, four, and five enumerated above, it can help in identifying "A," and this opening toward an answer to problems one and two might enable us, tentatively at least, to derive normative judgments on the basis of the demand for allocation.

Artificial Heart Implants

I think the best way to develop what I mean by this "combination argument" is to apply it to a specific issue in medical ethics, the use of the artificial human heart. What follows here has already been published, and I have proposed it to various groups, to very mixed review.[15]

Theoretically the artificial heart would seem to be an ethical as well as a technological advance over cadaver transplants. A permanent artificial heart would eliminate that portion of organ scarcity which results from too few donors. It is quite likely that the costs would decrease if more hearts were made. The problem of rejection, and thus the cost of immuno-suppressant drugs, would seem to be less than with human or animal hearts. It might be easier to "fix" and to "do maintenance on" a human-made heart than an organic one.

But there has thus far been little success with the permanent artificial heart. This is true, of course, in the early stages of most medical techniques, and some are of the opinion that despite the present difficulties there is sufficient hope of benefit to patients to permit the procedure as a therapy of last resort. But is there such a hope? At present, it seems that there is no likelihood of real benefit to the recipient of a permanent artificial heart. Recipients are tied to machines which radically inhibit mobility. They suffer from consistent periods of physical and mental incapacity. Catholic tradition has not required the use of "extraordinary means" of preserving life. The mere fact of continued life is not sufficient reason to warrant the use of any means at any cost.

In the absence of any real hope of success, experimentation with permanent artificial hearts must be strictly limited. If there are patients whose hearts offer them no hope of survival, and for whom human heart transplants are and will remain impossible, limited experimentation with permanent artificial hearts would seem to be ethical, provided all the requirements of informed consent are strictly adhered to, provided there is indeed no other way to gain the needed knowledge, and provided the experimental protocol is properly designed and approved. Assuming that these experiments continue to be of little or no real benefit to recipients, then if and when it is determined that they are not advancing vital knowledge, no more should be attempted.

But what about the *temporary* artificial heart? Would not this solve the problem by permitting patients to wait for permanent human heart transplants? Unfortunately, major ethical problems arise even with the temporary artificial heart. Instead of costs being reduced, as might be true for permanent artificial hearts, costs are increased, as a second expensive procedure is added. The scarcity of organs is not alleviated. Indeed, since more patients will be alive to need them, the scarcity problem is increased. Thus temporary artificial hearts as a therapy for heart disease ought not be attempted, at least for the present. As long as there are too few cadaver hearts, the temporary artificial hearts only add to the list of those needing them without adding to the list of donors. This would change if enough human hearts should become available, but for now the procedure is of no benefit to heart patients as a whole. Potential recipients without artificial hearts are passed over in favor of those with them, who would otherwise already have died. Since this is done at great cost, and since it merely shifts the outcome of who will live and who will die from one group to another within the population of those needing heart transplants, it does seem to be a morally wrong procedure.

As in the case of permanent implants, temporary implants might be done ethically on a restricted experimental basis. Important knowledge might be gained leading to a successful permanent device. The problem of limited human hearts remains, however, and the criteria for deciding who receives them demand constant vigilance.

Morally, then, it seems that as long as there is a shortage of human hearts for transplant, artificial implants should be limited to a restricted number of experimental procedures. Widespread therapeutic use of implants, whether permanent or temporary, seems unethical. The reason for this conclusion is a combination of general criteria for the just allocation of resources together with the claim that there is a lack of any real benefit to the individual recipient of a permanent implant or to the population of potential recipients when the implant is temporary.

A very difficult problem remains. Who is obliged to reject this expense? On whom does the obligation for a better allocation rest? Theoretically it rests on all of us. The medical profession should not, for the present, use artificial heart implants as a standard treatment modality for patients with end-stage heart disease. Public funding should not support it. And dying patients should not consent to it. But, given the inherent difficulties with allocation arguments, it is perhaps arrogant and overreaching to conclude that individuals are obliged to refuse artificial hearts. Theoretically that conclusion may be justified. But practically it will be better for our society to work toward a better system of health care delivery, one where such expenditures are not publicly funded, and one where all citizens are aware of the social nature of medicine and of its costs.

Conclusion

Despite the difficulty we often encounter in coming to precise conclusions about how we should allocate our resources, we do need to worry ourselves about this issue. If we believe that humans are one in God's creative love, then we need to be concerned about all humans, not just about the ones in our own hospitals or offices. And this concern must be one of the reasons why we will reject procedures which are not only expensive but which are at best of dubious benefit to the few whom they are supposed to help.

Discussion Questions

1. What is the extent of the obligation to resist spending on one need or desire in order to spend on another? What is the limit of this obligation?

2. Discuss the problem of relationship. To what extent does our obligation to care for those near to us relieve us of obligations to others farther away?

3. What do you think should be the basic approach our nation takes to growing technology?

4. Discuss the issue of artificial heart implants. Is this one of the areas where we should cut back on expenses? If not, suggest some others.

Endnotes

1. This last point is noted briefly by Walter Kaufmann, *Without Guilt and Justice: From Decidophobia to Autonomy* (New York: Dell, 1973), p. 91. General systems of justice often leave specific questions unanswered. For a system of justice similar to Rawls' but differing in some details and critical of Rawls on some counts, see James P. Sterba, *The Demands of Justice* (Notre Dame, IN: Univ. of Notre Dame Press, 1980), esp. pp. 29-62. Sterba argues for a "basic

needs minimum" which he says is less demanding than that required by Rawls' maximin principle. But Sterba points out the requirement that persons contribute to the basic needs of future generations and distant peoples. Although he applies this to a rejection of abortion on demand, and states that his system requires considerable sacrifice (p. 151), he does not explicitly state the kinds of expenses which must be forgone or the amount of wealth which is immorally high. Another approach to distributive justice is suggested by Alan Gewirth, who derives it from his "principle of generic consistency" (*Reason and Morality* [Chicago: Univ. of Chicago Press, 1978]). On Rawls, see John Rawls, *A Theory of Justice* (Cambridge, MA: Harvard Univ. Press, 1971); Norman Daniels, ed., *Reading Rawls: Critical Studies of A Theory of Justice* (New York: Basic Books, 1974); Robert Paul Wolff, *Understanding Rawls: A Reconstruction and Critique of The Theory of Justice* (Princeton, NJ: Princeton Univ. Press, 1977).

2. One interesting aspect of this "easier" issue which is probably impervious to an acceptable solution is the question of how many "American" organs should be made available for "foreigners." One figure often used is 10%. This seems to many to be an acceptable compromise between the danger of making so many organs available to the wealthy from foreign countries who are rich enough to come to the United States that many Americans are in effect shut out and the strange notion that only Americans are worthy to get American organs. But why 10%? Why not 5% as the American Society of Transplant Surgeons has proposed as the maximum. Or 20%? The National Task Force on Organ Transplantation made that suggestion (see Olga Jonasson, "Commentary, Case Studies: In Organ Transplants, Americans First?" *Hastings Center Report*, 16, No. 5 [Oct. 1986], 24). The American Society of Transplant Surgeons proposed a maximum of 5% (Jonasson, p. 24). The 10% figure is supported by John Kleinig in his "Commentary," p. 25. Why is any limitation just? No theoretically acceptable solution is apparent. In this, the problem is similar to the one explored in this chapter.

3. I think this is true even if "A" is identified as military spending, which it very often is. Unless it can be argued persuasively that military spending is in itself either unnecessary or otherwise morally wrong, the problem occurs even when "A" is military ex-

pense. We must, of course, strive for the kinds of international structural changes which would reduce our reliance and the reliance of other nations on the military. I am convinced that at least some, and perhaps much, American military expenditure is unnecessary and even dangerous. This is becoming more and more true in light of the recent changes in Europe and the Soviet Union. Military expenses are morally wrong when they are not necessary. But I cannot accept the argument that all of the defense budget is in this category. And, as has been noted already, even the elimination of the entire military budget, which would be immoral, would not ultimately solve the problem of scarce resources. Nations which spend far less on their defense than the United States also spend less on health care. An exploration of this question depends, of course, on a complex series of analyses which is impossible here.

4. See Walter Kaufmann, *Without Guilt and Justice*, esp. pp. 66-96, 112-137. Kaufmann tends at times to reject altogether the notion of justice in order to get rid of guilt, a proposal I do not accept (p. 112, e.g.). Still, he makes many excellent points not easily answered.

5. Anne E. Patrick, "Conscience and Community: Catholic Moral Theology Today," *Warren Lecture Series in Catholic Studies* (Tulsa, OK: Univ. of Tulsa Press, 1989), p. 3.

6. Carol Gilligan, *In A Different Voice: Psychological Theory and Women's Development* (Cambridge: Harvard Univ. Press, 1982), p. 18. The third stage, says Kohlberg, emphasizes "trying hard," "pleasing others," and relationships, and does not yet demonstrate the universality of principles of justice found in stages five and six. For a development, see Ronald Duska and Mariellen Whelan, *Moral Development: A Guide to Piaget and Kohlberg* (New York: Paulist Press, 1975), p. 46, pp. 58-64, 87-88.

7. Gilligan, p. 48.

8. Virginia Black, "Is Universalization Universal? Subjectivity in the Family Bond," draft typescript of paper in progress, pp. 3-4.

9. Black, p. 3.

10. Black, p. 10.

11. Black, p. 3 and p. 7.

12. This area has been examined lately in the context of a physician's duty to care for AIDS patients. See Benjamin Freedman, "Health Professions, Codes, and the Right to Refuse to Treat HIV-Infectious Patients," *Hastings Center Report*, 18 (April-May 1988), Special Supplement, pp. 20-25; John D. Arras, "The Fragile Web of Responsibility: AIDS and the Duty to Treat," pp. 10-20; George J. Annas, "Legal Risks and Responsibilities of Physicians in the AIDS Epidemic," pp. 26-32.

13. Donald T. DeMarco, "IVF and Social Justice," *Ethics and Medics*, 13, No. 7 (July, 1988), 1.

14. DeMarco, pp. 2-3.

15. See my "Artificial Hearts: An Ethical Solution to the Donor Shortage?" *Health Progress*, 68, No. 3 (April 1987), 24-26; also "Ethical Aspects of Heart Transplants," *Bulletin of the Allegheny County Medical Society*, 75 (1986), 438-439; also "Individualism and Corporatism in a Personalist Ethic," pp. 147-166.

Appendix A

Forgoing Treatment Policy

Recognizing that the usual DNR policy is not sufficient, St. Francis Medical Center asked its Ethics Committee to draw up a more sophisticated policy on forgoing treatment. The policy rejects the usual classification of patients into three or four categories and uses instead a "Palliative Support Care Orders" form to specify in a more precise and therefore more flexible way which treatments will be initiated and which withheld or withdrawn.

The policy was developed and proposed to the hospital by the Ethics Committee; its basic drift was written by Mark Schmidhofer, MD. The policy was approved by the ethics committee, the medical executive committee, the hospital administration, and the board of trustees. A series of educational programs, assisted by the year-long full-time presence of a resident ethicist, informed the hospital staff of this policy and its implications. The Policy and the Palliative Support Care Orders Form are included here.

St. Francis Medical Center
Pittsburgh, Pennslyvania

I. Introduction

The development of sophisticated means of life support mechanisms has sometimes led to the circumstance in which life is prolonged without seemingly providing additional meaningful time to an individual's existence, and which can, in some instances, prolong the process of death without restoring health. Both patients and health professionals are, with increasing frequency, distinguishing between cognitive, sapient existence where there is

177

the possibility of pursuing the purpose of life, and a mere biologic survival. It becomes clear that in some instances, certain forms of treatment should be forgone in order to avoid an agony laden delay in the inevitable demise of the ravaged physical being.

Legal guidelines concerning the withholding or withdrawal of treatment are not clearly defined, though an increasing number of decisions affirm the acceptability of the process in certain circumstances. The purpose of these guidelines is to provide a framework which can be used to approach this decision-making process in clinical situations. By so doing it is hoped that a reasonable degree of consistency of application can be maintained throughout the health center, and that this difficult decision-making process can be facilitated for both the patient and the health care team.

II. General Principles

The principles underlying the formation of these guidelines stem from both ethical and legal considerations and, among others, include:

A. Autonomy.

Individuals have the right to make important decisions concerning the course of their lives, and this includes the choice of whether or not to accept any given mode of treatment. This assumes that the patient is in possession of decision-making capacity and sufficient grasp of the facts and alternatives to permit an informed decision; when the patient lacks decision-making capacity, for any reason including age, this is done for him of her by an appropriately chosen surrogate.

B. Beneficence and Nonmaleficence.

Morality requires not only that one refrain from harming others, but also that one contribute to the promotion and maintenance of their welfare (*the principle of beneficence*). This tenet is fundamental to the doctor-patient relationship and embodies the concept that the role of health care is patient benefit. In general, this results in there being prejudice toward treatment, though it is recognized that in some instances the patient's interest are not best served by the continuation of old or application of new procedures. Related to this is the principle of nonmaleficence, summarized by the time honored treatment aphorism, "First of all, do no harm."

C. Justice.

1. The first obligation of the health care professional is to the patient. In some instances, patient care may be affected by the needs of others when community resources are not unlimited. The principle of justice demands that all members of society have equivalent care, and that access is not limited as a result of inappropriate utilization by particular individuals or groups. However, individual caregivers should not make specific patient decisions based on economic considerations or the perceived need to ration scarce resources. This risks the implementation of arbitrary and unfair decisions which are not uniformly applied throughout the health care system.

2. In only partially related fashion, the principle of justice relieves the health care professional of the obligation to provide treatment which is clearly futile.

D. Integrity.

Health care professionals must act within the standards of their profession. They must, among other things, respect the rights and human dignity of their patients and act accordingly. However, if a patient request violates the religious or ethical commitments of the health care provider, that individual is not required to comply. In this instance, it may be necessary to transfer the patient to another health care provider (*physician or institution*); care must be continued until such satisfactory transfer has been made.

E. Judicial Review.

In the majority of instances, the decisions surrounding whether or not to forgo treatment, and who should be the surrogate for a patient who lacks decision-making capacity, can and should be made without involving the judicial system. Such involvement adds expense, delays the decision-making process, and serves to make public difficult and disturbing decisions which are better left private. However, in certain instances judicial review will be necessary if appropriate consensus cannot be achieved.

F. Ordinary and Extraordinary Means.

Within the Roman Catholic Tradition, the concepts of ordinary and extraordinary means have been developed as a way to distinguish between those treatments which persons are obliged to use in preserving their lives (*ordinary means*) and those which they may rightly forgo (*extraordinary means*). The distinction is *moral*, not technological or medical. That is, it depends on relative burden and benefits, not on whether or not the procedure is routinely applied in medical practice. A treatment which would be "ordinary means" when used in caring for a person whose chance of recovery is great would become "extraordinary" in the care of a patient who has no or little chance of recovery. The one patient is obliged to use the treatment; the other may rightly forgo it. Thus even the use of medically induced hydration and nutrition might well be an extraordinary means in some cases (*e.g.*, those in persistent vegetative state).

G. The Concept of Proportionality.

Recent criticism of the "ordinary/extraordinary" distinction has pointed out that these terms are too often confused with the medical concepts of "ordinary medical practice" and "experimental procedure." Since the traditional distinction, as accepted by Catholic moral theology, depends on relative burden and benefit, many suggest that less confusing terms for the same approach are "reasonableness" or "proportionality." Patients ought to accept reasonable or proportional treatments in preserving their lives; they may rightly forgo unreasonable or disproportionate treatments. The concept of proportionality is used to critically examine any and all treatments for the benefits they offer and the physical and psychological cost they entail. Treatment is offered if the benefits outweigh the costs; it is recognized that not all patients utilize the same metric in the determination of these weights.

H. Direct Killing and Allowing to Die.

Catholic Tradition is quite clear that all "direct" or "active" euthanasia is forbidden; American law is similarly clear that such actions are criminal. Nothing in this policy implies that any action may be taken which directly kills a patient. Catholic Tradition does not, however, consider withdrawal of extraordinary or disproportionate treatments to be a "direct" killing. Nor is the use of sedatives or analgesics needed for pain relief considered killing, even though they may suppress respiration and hasten death. The disease kills the patient in such circumstances, not the medication needed for comfort. Similarly, the forgoing of medical nutrition and hydration, including its withdrawal, is not considered direct killing provided the treatment is truly extraordinary or disproportionate. Great care must be taken to insure that the patient is never "abandoned." Palliative and comfort measures are *always* obligatory; if medically induced hydration or nutrition are deemed necessary for patient comfort, it must be given.

III. Specific Considerations.

In the application of the above principles to the decision of whether or not to forgo treatment, certain particularly important concepts emerge.

A. Early Review.

Many dilemmas arise because the wishes of the patient or surrogate have not been elicited prior to the occurrence of a life-threatening emergency whose treatment must be immediately instituted if an untoward outcome is to be averted. There is frequently no time for consultation until after the therapy has been administered. One may find that a patient has been inappropriately treated or resuscitated. One can frequently determine that there is a relatively high degree of likelihood of such an occurrence before it happens, and these questions should be discussed with the patient or surrogate at that time, perhaps shortly after admission to treatment, rather than awaiting the catastrophic event, when the decision may need to be made under greater duress, and at which time a previously decision-capable person may no longer have the capacity for meaningful expression of his or her feelings.

B. Withdrawal Versus Withholding of Treatment.

There is no ethical distinction between the withholding of an inappropriate treatment not yet begun and the cessation of an ongoing treatment if it is deemed to be similarly inappropriate. The term "forgoing" includes both withdrawing and withholding. While there is not an ethical distinction between withdrawing and withholding, from a practical standpoint there is generally a psychological difference, particularly when the discontinuation of treatment can be expected to culminate in the patient's immediate demise. This observation reinforces the advisability of early review of a patient's status and wishes, so that some such situations can be averted by never actually beginning the treatment.

C. What Constitutes Treatment.

Traditionally, consideration of forgoing treatment was given only to advanced and complex modalities such as measures of advanced life support, dialysis, and the like. However, all therapies are appropriately viewed within the proportionality framework, and as such may be forgone in certain circumstances. Though measures such as intravenous hydration and nasogastric feedings may superficially seem humanitarian and inviolate, they, too, can sometimes impose a burden to the patient which is disproportionate to the attendant benefit, and as such may be subject to discontinuation.

D. Role of the Ethics Committee.

During the decision making process, the ethics committee is available to play the role of consultant. It does not make binding decisions, but can offer advice and help insure that avenues of communication are open and utilized, that sufficient information has been obtained and disbursed, and that appropriate alternatives have been explored and offered. The committee's input can be requested by patients, their surrogate, or any member of the health care team. Upon admission to the hospital, all patients will be notified of this committee's existence and purpose and the mechanism by which it can be contacted.

IV. Procedure

When consideration exists that some degree of forgoing of treatment might be appropriate, certain procedures should be pursued.

A. Early review.

Such review of circumstances should take place as soon as it is considered even possibly appropriate. Failure to do so may result in the application of treatment on an emergency basis which, if more carefully thought out, might have been forgone.

1. Great care must be taken to explore relevant issues in detail with the patient, family, and surrogate, and to guard against assumption of commonality of values and goals, especially but not

exclusively when dealing with patients of different ethnic and religious background.

2. If a given treatment modality is discussed and forgone, that decision applies to the discussed treatment alone, and to no others. It is not to be considered an irrevocable decision, and it should be periodically reviewed as a patient's condition changes. In particular, measures to insure patient comfort and dignity should continue or even be increased, with great care being exercised to insure that the patient and family recognize that they are not being abandoned because certain treatments are being withheld or withdrawn.

B. Patient Autonomy.

It is the patient's right to decide what treatment will be accepted or refused; the patient is the true and appropriate source of authority. It is the role of the health care team to act not as an adversary, but as a knowledgeable and trusted consultant in the process. It is the team's role to provide adequate information and understanding such that an informed decision can be made by the patient.

1. It is to be recognized that the process of communication is difficult and perceived differently by the various participants. It is made the more difficult in the medical setting because of the time required to present patients with information that is probably new and unfamiliar. Health care professionals too often view this education process as less important than the action of the physical delivery of care, and thus relegate it to a less important position. The discomfort of health care professionals in acknowledging and discussing matters of death and their relative impotence in its prevention can substantially interfere with open discussion, and should be confronted by each individual; attempts should be made to improve the ability to deal with this difficult situation. In describing therapeutic alternatives care should be taken to avoid the use of poorly understood jargon; terms which are simple and carry the emotional impact of what is to be conveyed should be sought and tailored to the background of the patient. In an effort to convince a patient or family of the appropriateness of a given modality, stringent efforts should be made to avoid playing upon the fears of the patient; accurate descriptions of attendant discomfort should be made, and undue optimism or pessimism concern-

ing like outcome of treatments should be avoided. One must remember that if inappropriate expectations are raised and are unfulfilled, subsequent proclamations and suggestions made by the health care team might understandably be met with a modicum of suspicion and distrust.

2. If at any time during the course of discussion it is felt that the lines of communication are insufficiently open and smooth, prompt consideration should be given to the enlistment of a facilitator. This person could be a physician, nurse, social worker, cleric, or knowledgeable friend whose purpose is to aid in the establishment of more optimal levels of rapport, and who may be better able to communicate relevant facts necessary for informed decision-making. If conflict between the patient and health care teams arises and cannot be satisfactorily resolved with the aid of facilitators, the ethics committee should be consulted. If this is unsuccessful in obtaining adequate resolution of the conflict, the hospital attorney should be consulted in expectation of the possible need for judicial review.

3. It is to be emphasized that decision-making is a process rather than an event; it occurs over time rather at an instant in time, and includes at least three elements:

a. Recognition of the existence of the problem, its ramifications, and its implications.
b. Appreciation of the alternative solutions with their relative advantages and disadvantages.
c. Selection of desired solution.

4. Time-limited trials. An under-utilized approach to some treatment questions is the time-limited trial in which a given treatment is instituted for a specified purpose. Upon completion of the trial period, results can be assessed, and a new decision made about whether or not to continue, based upon relevant clinical parameters. The utility of this technique is fundamentally dependent on the acceptance of the premise that the withholding and withdrawal of treatment are ethically identical.

5. Information should generally not be withheld. Exceptions might occur in two instances:

a. When the disclosure of information to the patient poses an immediate and real threat to the patient's well-being, the health care team is obligated not to inflict that information on the patient; an appropriate surrogate should be fully informed, and the patient should be provided with information deemed not to be harmful. This situation is not to be easily presumed; truth-telling usually does not pose a threat to the patient.

b. If a given patient is made aware of his or her rights and chooses to give them up or reassign them, that decision should be honored, but an appropriate surrogate should, again, be fully informed.

c. In either case, the reasons for withholding information from the patient should be documented in the chart.

C. Patients Lacking Decision-Making Capacity.

1. In some instances, the patient may be felt to be lacking in decision-making capacity. It is to be recognized that there is a difference between "competence" in the legal sense of the word which, in part, refers to the ability to manage one's financial and legal affairs and what is herein called "decision-making capacity." In some instances, "capacity" exists in the absence of "competence." These patients' preferences should be heard, and, when appropriate, their wishes should be followed. In order to be considered to have decision-making capacity, patients must demonstrate the ability to:

a. communicate their choice to the health care team.
b. understand the relevant information germane to the issue being decided.
c. appreciate the situation and consequences of their decisions.
d. manipulate information rationally and reach conclusions logically consistent with their starting principles.

2. It is the role of the health care team to decide if the patient has decision-making capacity; psychiatric consultation may be useful, but is not mandatory.

3. If it is deemed that the patient lacks decision-making capacity, a surrogate should be appointed. In many instances, when a number of the family members are present, consensus can be achieved, and it is not necessary to formally select a single in-

dividual as surrogate; even when that selection is made, it is advisable not to segregate that decision-maker from other concerned family members, but rather to attempt to allow decisions to be made in concert, if possible. Surrogate appointment is usually made without judicial intervention, though that may become necessary if disagreement or acrimony exists. If no obvious surrogate exists, the attending physician, in concert with the hospital ethics committee, may act as surrogate, but judicial approval is necessary before this occurs.

a. Unless there are circumstances strongly indicating that other choices should be made, the following, in order of priority, are generally chosen to act as surrogate:

(1) guardian, if one exists
(2) spouse
(3) adult child
(4) parent
(5) adult sibling
(6) other close relative or friend

b. Decisions of the surrogate should be followed only as long as they are reasonable and appropriate.

4. Advance Directives. As noted elsewhere, many problems surrounding the issue of forgoing treatment can be averted if questions are addressed at an early date, when a patient still retains decision-making capacity. The subject should be broached and decisions made at the earliest possible date. Matters can be further simplified if such sentiments are formalized in the form of an advance directive, a document which takes effect when the patient loses decision-making capacity and which gives directions about the future medical care. It can take one of two forms.

a. A treatment directive, such as a living will, allows persons to indicate which treatments they wish to have, and which they wish to forgo.

b. A proxy directive, also known in some states as a durable power of attorney, allows individuals to appoint a proxy decision-maker (*surrogate*) to make decisions in the event that they lose decision-making capacity.

c. Advance directives should be written documents which are signed and preferably witnessed. Since it is a manifestation of the patient's wishes, it should be given the same weight as would an oral declaration. If it is disregarded, it should be done based on more than speculation concerning the validity of the document or expressed wishes contained within it.

D. *Any physician or health care worker may refuse to comply with patient requests under certain circumstances.*

1. If the request is in serious violation of the health care worker's ethical or religious belief, it need not be granted.

2. If the requested treatment is clearly futile or non-beneficial, it need not be provided.

3. In the event of this occurrence, it may be necessary to transfer the patient to the care of another physician or institution; care must be continued until that transfer has been effected.

E. *Orders*

1. When it has been decided that certain treatments are to be forgone, it is the responsibility of the attending physician or his or her designate to record in writing that decision in the medical record; given the possibility of misinterpreting or transcription error, a telephone order is generally not acceptable, but when time is of the essence and the attending physician is not immediately available a telephone order can be accepted. The physician should also discuss the decision with appropriate members of the health care team in order to minimize the possibility of misunderstanding.

2. The physician can specifically designate on the order sheet which therapies are to be forgone, and which continued; in addition, a check list is to be completed in order to facilitate communication with the various members of the nursing staff. The use of such a check list serves to overcome some difficulties encountered in interpreting categories such as "All but CPR" and "No Extraordinary Measures."

3. At the time the order is written, a progress note should be entered into the chart containing at least the following information:

a. diagnosis

b. prognosis

c. patient, family, and surrogate wishes

d. assessment of the patient's decision-making capacity and the means by which the decision was made, along with the names of those involved in the decision-making process.

V. Procedure Synopsis

What follows is a brief description of the procedure to be followed within the St. Francis Medical Center when it is felt that forgoing (withdrawing or withholding) medical treatment may be appropriate. For a more complex discussion on the concepts behind the procedure, the main body of this document should be consulted.

A. Early review.

It can often be anticipated early in the course of a patient's hospitalization that the prognosis is poor, and that a variety of treatment interventions may not realistically be expected to meaningfully prolong the patient's life. As soon as this is recognized, these issues should be explored with the patient by the physician of record, and an acceptable plan of treatment should be outlined. This early review can frequently prevent a situation in which undesired therapies are instituted in response to emergency situations which do not allow reasoned deliberation.

1. Relevant information must be discussed with the patient and other involved individuals in terms appropriate to their levels of education and sophistication.

2. If it is decided that a given treatment modality should be forgone, such decisions apply to discussed modalities only, and may not be extrapolated to others without further deliberation. Measures to provide comfort, hygiene, and human dignity must always be continued.

B. Patient Autonomy.

Patients have the right to decide which therapies they will accept and which they will reject. Health care providers have the task of giving patients sufficient information, in terms they can understand, so that they can then make the decision most appropriate for themselves.

1. If at any time during the course of decision-making it is felt that the lines of communication are not sufficiently open or smooth, prompt enlistment of a facilitator should be considered. This can be another physician, nurse, social worker, cleric, or knowledgeable friend, whose role is to help communicate options and choices between patient and health care team.

2. If conflict between patient (*or surrogate*) and health care teams arises and cannot be satisfactorily resolved with the aid of facilitators, the ethics committee should be consulted. If this is unsuccessful in obtaining adequate resolution of the conflict, the hospital attorney should be consulted in expectation of the possible need for judicial review.

C. Patients Lacking Decision-Making Capacity.

1. Patients are considered to have decision-making capacity if they have the ability to:

   a. communicate their choices
   b. understand information relevant to the decisions at hand
   c. appreciate their situation and the consequences of their choices
   d. manipulate available information rationally and reach conclusions logically consistent with their starting principles.

2. The health care team decides if the patient has decision-making capacity; this decision may benefit from, but does not require, psychiatric consultation.

3. If the patient lacks decision-making capacity, a surrogate should be selected. Ordinarily, judicial review is not necessary for surrogate selection, who is generally appointed, in order of priority, as follows:

   a. guardian, if already appointed
   b. spouse
   c. adult child
   d. parent
   e. adult sibling
   f. other close relative or friend

4. If a patient has formulated an advance directive prior to loss of decision-making capacity, those wishes should be carried out. If

a durable power of attorney has been granted, the directions of the appointed surrogate should be followed.

5. The decisions of the surrogate should be followed only so long as they appear reasonable and in the best interest of the patient.

D. Any health care provider may refuse to comply with patient requests under certain circumstances.

1. If the request is in serious violation of ethical or religious beliefs, it need not be granted.

2. If the requested treatment is clearly futile or non-beneficial, it need not be provided.

3. In the event of this occurrence, it may be necessary to transfer the patient to the care of another physician or institution; care must be continued until that transfer can be effected.

E. Orders

1. When it has been decided that certain treatments are to be forgone, it is the responsibility of the attending physician to record in writing that decision in the medical record; a telephone order is generally not acceptable, but when time is of the essence and the attending physician is not immediately available a telephone order can be accepted. The physician should also discuss the decision with appropriate members of the health care team to minimize the possibility of misunderstanding.

2. The physician can specifically designate on the order sheet which therapies are to be forgone, and which continued; in addition, a checklist is to be completed in order to facilitate communication with the various members of the nursing staff.

3. At the time the order is written, a progress note should be entered into the chart containing at least the following information:

    a. diagnosis
    b. prognosis
    c. patient, family, and surrogate wishes
    d. assessment of the patient's decision-making capacity and the means by which the decision was made, along with the names of those involved in the decision-making process.

PATIENT NAME _____ DATE _____

PATIENT'S DIAGNOSIS _____

The following are orders established for the medical care of this patient by Dr. _____

after consultation and in accordance with the wishes of the patient and/or surrogate _____

	YES	NO	NOT APPLICABLE
Mask to Mouth Resuscitation without Intubation	_____	_____	_____
External Chest Compression	_____	_____	_____
Electrical Ventricular Defibrillation	_____	_____	_____
Chemical Ventricular Defibrillation	_____	_____	_____
Intubation without Mechanical Ventilation	_____	_____	_____
Intubation with Mechanical Ventilation	_____	_____	_____

IF ANY OF THE ABOVE SIX (6) ARE CHECKED (√) YES, A CARDIAC ARREST MUST BE CALLED.

Inotropic and Vasoactive Support	_____	_____	_____
Electrical Cardioversion for Atrial Tachyarrhythmia	_____	_____	_____
Transfer to ICU	_____	_____	_____
Dialysis	_____	_____	_____
Transfusion	_____	_____	_____
IV Support	_____	_____	_____
Enteral Nutrition	_____	_____	_____
Antibiotics	_____	_____	_____
Chemotherapy	_____	_____	_____
Radiation Therapy	_____	_____	_____
Radiologic Studies	_____	_____	_____
Laboratory Studies	_____	_____	_____
Other	_____	_____	_____

_____   _____

PATIENT'S SIGNATURE   ATTENDING PHYSICIAN'S SIGNATURE

_____   _____

PATIENT SURROGATE OR RELATIVE   WITNESS

This order should ordinarily be reviewed on a weekly basis and signed by M.D. However, it will remain in effect unless superseded by a subsequent order. If the patient is discharged and readmitted, these orders must be rewritten.

Weekly review dates and physician's signature:

Date _____ _____ M.D.   Date _____ _____ M.D.

Date _____ _____ M.D.   Date _____ _____ M.D.

St. Francis Medical Center
PALLIATIVE SUPPORT
CARE ORDERS

DISTRIBUTION CODE:
WHITE   -   PATIENT'S CHART
YELLOW   -   CHAIRPERSON, ETHICS COMMITTEE
                      I.C.U. OFFICE. NORTH 4500

FORM: H-1648

Appendix B

Making Difficult Choices About Treatment

As St. Francis began to implement its new Forgoing Treatment Policy, it became clear that early review of patient wishes was essential. Toward this end, the Ethics Committee decided to draw up a brochure which would be given to patients, informing them in accessible language of the issues involved, of their right and responsibility to ask questions of their physicians, and of the availability of consultation with members of the Ethics Committee.

The brochure was written by Stacey Hinderliter, M.D., a pediatrician at St. Francis and a member of the Ethics Committee. As this book goes to press, the brochure is being "field-tested." The Ethics Committee hopes it will be approved for general hospital use and be included in the admissions packet.

St. Francis Medical Center
Pittsburgh, Pennsylvania

Introduction

St. Francis Medical Center is dedicated to providing the best medical care available to all of our patients. We believe that part of providing good medical care is making sure that patients know about their illness and understand what is happening to them. We have written this pamphlet so that you will know how to get answers to your questions about your medical care.

Everyone has the right to make choices about medical treatment.

Some of the choices are easy. You can choose which hospital or which doctor you go to see. Or you can choose not to see anyone at all. Other choices are much harder. Someday, you may be asked to decide about treatment that could keep you or someone close to you alive. This pamphlet was written to answer some questions you may have about this.

What is "life or death" treatment?

Sometimes when a person is very sick, certain treatment can keep that person alive. This is called "life-sustaining treatment" or "life or death treatment." This can mean putting someone on a ventilator or a breathing machine. It can mean trying to restart the heart if it stops beating. It can mean giving special medicines or using special intravenous (*in the vein, IV*) lines. It can mean using special ways to feed someone. It can sometimes mean having an operation or another special procedure, such as a kidney machine.

In some cases, the choice may be whether or not to start some treatment. In other cases, the choice may be whether or not to stop a treatment.

The same treatment can be "life-sustaining" for one person and not be "life-sustaining" for another. Sometimes, if a person is so sick that there is almost no chance that the person will get better, "life-sustaining" treatment might not be worth doing. Each situation is different.

Who will tell me if treatment is "life-sustaining" or not?

The doctor who is in charge of your medical care (*the attending physician*) is the person who should give you this information. He or she should tell you what the problem is and all the different ways to deal with this problem. If the illness is serious, the doctor should also tell you if some treatment is "life-sustaining" or not. The doctor should tell you about the risks and side-effects of treatment, and what the chances are of the treatment working. The doctor should also tell you what the chances are of you getting better and being able to leave the hospital. The doctor may also give you advice about what he thinks is the best treatment for your problem.

You should ask your doctor questions about the problem. If there is any treatment that you don't understand, *you should ask about it.* You can only make good choices if you know enough about the problem, so *don't be afraid to ask.*

There are other people who may also be able to answer questions. These include your nurse, the hospital social worker, and members of the Hospital's Ethics Committee.

Who makes choices about "life-sustaining" treatment?

In most cases, you decide what medical treatment you should have. Sometimes, the person who is sick may be unable to make these choices. The person may be unconscious or the illness may prevent the person from being able to make choices. The doctor in charge (*attending physician*) will usually decide if that person is able to make choices or not. Sometimes, the attending physician may ask for help from other doctors to make that decision (*ask for a consultation*).

If a patient is unable to make his own choices, these choices are then made by someone else. This special decision maker is called a "surrogate." This person may be a close relative, a group of family members, or a friend. Sometimes, it may be a doctor or nurse whom the patient had asked earlier to be the surrogate. For children, the parents usually are the surrogates.

Just as the doctor would tell the patient about his illness and his choices about treatment, the doctor will tell the surrogate about the illness and the choices about treatment.

Can choices about "life-sustaining" treatment be made in advance?

Although these kinds of choices are hard to think about, everyone should try to think about these problems before they happen. Some people may have already thought about some of these choices, and may have already decided what kind of treatment they want or don't want. If they have written their decision down on paper, this is called an "advance directive." It doesn't have to be written in a special way, or be called a "Living Will." It doesn't even have to be witnessed. It just has to be written clearly and it should be signed by that person.

The choices written in the advance directive will be followed as long as they are within the standards of medical care and are not against the law.

You can also decide in advance who you want to be your surrogate, if one is ever needed. This should also be written down and signed.

What if I change my mind?

You or your surrogate are always free to change your mind about the treatment. Sometimes, the illness may change, and what is "life-sustaining" treatment today may no longer be "life-sustaining" treatment the next day. Sometimes, the chances of getting better and being able to leave the hospital may change. The doctor will let you know about any new information or change in the illness. If there is something that you want to know, you should ask about it. You or your surrogate should discuss the problem with the doctor as often as you need to.

Will I be told everything about my illness?

Most of the time, you or your surrogate will be told everything that is known about your illness, so that a good choice can be made about treatment.

If there is something you don't want to know about your illness, and you tell that to the doctor, then you will not receive that information. You will have to let your doctor know about this in advance.

If the doctor thinks that certain information about your illness would cause serious harm to your health or life, he may not tell you about it. When he feels that the information is no longer harmful, he will then tell you about it.

Who else can help me with making these choices?

These choices are between you or your surrogate and the doctor in charge (*attending physician*). Sometimes, you may want more help to understand things. There are other people in the hospital who may be helpful, including administrators, psychiatrists, and other doctors. You may want to speak with someone from the Hospital's Ethics Committee. Members of this committee know a lot about making "life or death" choices and may be able to help you get the information that you need to make a good choice. If you would like to speak to a member of the Ethics Committee, ask your doctor, nurse, or social worker.

What if I have more questions about this?

It is best for you to ask your doctor about your medical care. He or she knows your illness best and is most able to tell you about your problems.

You may also want to speak to your nurse or the social worker. If you want to speak to a member of the Ethics Committee, ask your doctor, nurse, or social worker.

Remember, you can never ask too many questions. Don't be afraid to ask when you don't understand something. The staff of St. Francis Medical Center is here to give you the best medical care available. We also want you to feel that you understand your illness and medical treatment.

Appendix C

Guidelines for Ethics Consultations

Three brief documents are included here. The first, "Procedural Guidelines for Ethics Consults," is a quick review for the use of the three-member consult team from the Ethics Committee. The second is a worksheet for their use while consulting. The third, "Calling an Ethics Consult," has been distributed within the Hospital to help remind staff of the availability of consults and how to call one.

St. Francis Medical Center
Pittsburgh, Pennsylvania

Procedural Guidelines for Ethics Consults

I. Initiation

1) Anyone actively involved with the patient may request a consult by contacting the Chair of the Ethics Committee, currently Dr. Hoyt, or the co-Chair, currently Dr. Daly.

2) If the Chair and co-Chair are not available, and if time is of the essence, any other member of the Ethics Committee may be contacted. ICU personnel will assist in making this contact.

3) The Chair, or the member contacted, will gather a Team of three members of the Committee who are available and who are

197

not directly connected with the case; one will be a physician, one a nurse, and one member will be neither physician nor nurse.

4) The initiating person(s) should attempt to discuss the anticipated consult with the patient's primary attending physician.

5) The Chair, or the member contacted, shall in all cases contact the patient's primary attending physician.

II. Process

1) The three member Team will assemble and decide on how to proceed. Ordinarily all three members of the Team will speak to the patient unless the patient is not able to communicate; to the family members, who should be invited to speak to the Team, and to any guardian or surrogate; to the attending physician and any others who may have important information to give; to the nurses who are involved in the patient's care; and to other personnel, such as social workers, attorneys, or psychiatrists or psychologists, when this is helpful.

2) The Team will deliberate on the case and reach a decision. This decision may be to postpone any charted notes until further consultation with persons not immediately available. When a decision is reached, the Team will enter its suggestions on the patient's chart.

III. Charting the Result of the Consultation

1) The Team will ordinarily reach consensus, and the following are usually entered on the chart, using a standard consultation form, and adding the words "ETHICS CONSULT" at the top for easy identification:

a) A brief summary of the process the Team used.

b) A brief description of the facts of the case.

c) The Team's opinion on the issue in question.

2) The Ethics Committee has no authority to require that any treatment decision be carried out. It is consultative. It's language will reflect this. Phrases such as "may," "might," "is appropriate" are often better than "must," "should," etc.

3) The charted results will always include a description of the wishes of the patient/surrogate.

4) If the Team does not reach consensus, a majority and minority opinion may be charted. In this case, the person requesting the consult may wish to consult with other members of the Ethics Committee.

5) The Team members will send a copy of the charted entry to the chair of the Ethics Committee.

6) An Ethics Consult Worksheet is available to help the Team in their deliberations.

Aspects to Keep in Mind

Members of the Ethics Consult Teams will be drawing on the education the Committee has given itself and on their own understandings of these and other issues involved in making these decisions. This list is intended to be of help, but is not sufficient. Members should be familiar with the Forgoing Treatment Policy. Videotapes of Dr. Kelly's course and Grand Rounds lectures are available and may be helpful.

The Consult Team will want to keep the following in mind:

1) The wishes of the patient. This is often of primary importance.

2) The wishes of the surrogate(s), and, if there is disagreement among them, which side is more in keeping with the patient's wishes, if these are known.

3) The burden which proposed treatments would impose, and the benefit they would possibly bring, as well as the probability of benefit.

4) The patient's comfort. Patients are never abandoned. Care and comfort measures are always required. It is often helpful to make note of this in the charted entry.

5) The emotional content of language when speaking to the patient/surrogate(s). Phrases which mean one thing to health care professionals may mean something different to others. Try to ask questions which will ensure understanding and always allow time for questions and for repetition.

6) The distinction between medical futility, whose definition is quite restrictive, and where the physician makes the decision to

forgo; and human, moral, quality-of-life, or burden-benefit futility, which is the more usual case, and where the patient/surrogate makes the decision whether or not to forgo.

7) The fact that allocation of resources is not ordinarily germane to the decision. Emergency situations where beds are immediately needed might be an exception, but here great caution must be exercised that the patient's care is not unduly jeopardized and that the desires of the patient/surrogate are given significant weight.

8) The difficulty of distinguishing between being an advocate for the patient and being simply a communicator of the surrogates' wishes. This occurs most frequently when it is clear that in requesting aggressive treatment surrogates are not acting in the patient's interests . There is no easy answer to this. In some very rare cases it may be necessary to suggest that legal action be taken. More usually, a period of time will help establish the facts and allow the surrogates to be at ease with the proper decision. Remember that these decisions to forgo treatment may not be made unilaterally by physicians (unless it is a case of medical futility in the strict sense) or by the Team.

9) The ethical and legal principle that surrogates may never opt to forgo treatment which is in the best interests of the patient. In some very rare cases, it is possible that a patient may have left a clear directive that treatment which would otherwise be considered in the patient's best interests (morally ordinary, that is, morally required treatment) be forgone. But this kind of evidence is legally questionable and usually requires a legal analysis. In such an unlikely case the Hospital Attorney should be consulted.

Ethics Consult Worksheet

Patient's Name:

Name of Person Initiating Consult (Enter on Consult Form):

Purpose of Consult:

Patient's Diagnosis and Prognosis:

Family Member(s)/Surrogate(s)/Persons with Durable Power of Attorney:

Health Care Professionals Involved (M.D., R.N., social worker, pastoral care, psych., attorney, etc.):

Problem (if different from Initial Purpose of Consult):

Pt's Wishes:

Surrogate(s)' Wishes:

Results of Deliberation by Team (Include minority opinion, if any):

Calling an Ethics Consult

I. Purpose

The Ethics Consult Service provides a Team of people from the Hospital's Ethics Committee to assist in discussing and advising on ethical questions concerning the care of an individual patient at St. Francis. These questions often concern the issue of forgoing aggressive treatment, but ethics consults may be called concerning other areas of ethical concern as well. There is no policy requiring such a consult.

II. Rationale

Frequently a physician, nurse, patient, or family may be involved in making an ethical decision where the solution is not easily seen. Consulting members of the Ethics Committee have experience in dealing with this kind of issue and may be able to assist in clarifying treatment options and patient prerogatives from an ethical perspective, offering advice and suggestions for possible solution.

III. Initiating the Consult

1) Anyone actively involved in the case may request a consult by contacting the Chair of the Ethics Committee, currently Dr. Hoyt, Director of the Medical Intensive Care Unit, or Dr. Daly, currently co-Chair of the Ethics Committee.

2) If the Chair and co-Chair are not available, and if time is of the essence, any other member of the Ethics Committee may be contacted. ICU personnel will assist in making this contact.

3) The Chair, or the member contacted, will gather a Team of three members of the Committee who are available and who are not directly connected with the case; one will be a physician, one a nurse, and one member will be neither physician nor nurse.

4) The initiating person(s) should attempt to discuss the anticipated consult with the patient's primary attending physician.

5) The Consult Team will want to speak with those involved in the case, including the family or other patient surrogates, as well as the physicians, nurses, etc. If possible, the initiating person(s)

should attempt to assure that these are present when the Team arrives. A member of the Team will assist in coordinating this if necessary.

Appendix D

Condoms and AIDS in Catholic Hospitals

This brief essay, which I wrote a few years ago, will be of importance only to Catholic hospitals. For this reason, and because it is not directly germane to the central focus of the book, I have decided to include it as an appendix instead of as a chapter.

One of the issues connected with AIDS prevention is the question of the use and distribution of condoms. The issue is complex, involving technical, psycho-social, and moral aspects. The first two of these are factors in investigating the third.

The technical issues deal with the effectiveness of condoms in reducing the transmission of the virus. Those who oppose condom use tend to emphasize their ineffectiveness; supporters claim they are effective. There is truth on both sides. Condoms do not turn unsafe sex into "safe sex," but they do make it "*safer*" than it would otherwise be. The AIDS virus is considerably smaller than human sperm; for this reason "natural" condoms (lamb intestines) are particularly ineffective, since their microscopic holes let the virus through. Spermicides may increase protection against viral transmission. A reputable latex condom properly used from start to finish will significantly reduce the risk of transmission. But it is not foolproof. User failure and method failure combine to lessen actual effectiveness.

One psychological and social question which must be considered in arriving at a moral judgment is the question of whether or not condom awareness and availability increases non-marital sexual activity, especially among teenagers. Claims are made on both sides of this issue. Statistics are usually said to show that the availability of condoms does not increase sexual activity among our youth, but many are not convinced. They argue, and quite plausibly, that teenagers are more likely to have sex in a society where contraceptives are accepted as part of their environment. But trying to determine whether increased contraceptive availability is an independent variable causing increased teenage sex or whether both are in fact dependent variables caused by other social influences is virtually impossible. I find the second opinion more plausible, though I cannot prove it to be true.

If we try to speculate on how teenagers might respond to the availability of condoms, we will conclude that there are probably some whose reluctance to have sex is based on fear of pregnancy or of disease, and who, in fact, do decide to have sex because condoms are easy to get. But there are certainly also some teenagers whose rush into sexual experimentation is slowed by the very decision-making process that goes into contraceptive preparation. Teenagers who prepare responsibly to reduce the likelihood of pregnancy and disease have at the very least thought through one aspect of their decision. Perhaps as a result of this process some of them may come to think through other aspects as well, and conclude that it is morally wrong for them to engage in premarital sex. This is the kind of moral decision-making process we should encourage, not discourage.

May Catholic health care facilities and health care professionals morally inform patients about condoms and distribute them in the hope of reducing transmission of the AIDS virus? In my judgment, the answer is yes.

The question can be approached from a number of different angles. Perhaps the simplest instance is the case of a married couple of which one spouse, but not yet the other, has contracted the virus. The couple is faced with a choice. They may choose to abstain from sexual intercourse. For some couples this is indeed a morally right choice. But surely it cannot be demanded as the only possible right choice for all married couples in this situation. The spouses may wish to continue their sexual lives together. They consider, quite rightly, that sex is a sacramental expression of their love; perhaps they even feel that to stop it now would imply an abandonment of the infected spouse and of the marriage. They want to avoid transmission of the disease to the other spouse and, if it is the woman who is infected, to prevent a pregnancy which carries a severe chance of causing AIDS in the baby. In such cases the spouses are not only morally permitted to use condoms, they are morally *required* to use them.

Catholic hospitals and health care workers ought to provide such couples with the necessary counselling, and may rightly dispense the condoms. In most cases it is not at all a question of preventing pregnancy. Where contraception *is* intended—to prevent AIDS in the baby—the purpose surely is not "selfish contraception" or a "contraceptive mentality." Indeed, in such cases contraception is only *one* of the purposes for condom use; it is not the only purpose. Even those who believe that direct contraception is always immoral ought to allow condom use in this case, just as other medical treatments which prevent pregnancy have been permitted by the tradition of Catholic moral theology when their primary purpose is something medically helpful, as in the use of anovulant drugs for the purpose of regulating the menstrual cycle. This is an indirect contraception, and the prevention of AIDS transmission is sufficiently important to give it moral warrant.

But what about patients who are not married? Here the contraception aspect of the problem is less of an issue. In the United States, at least at present, the greatest incidence of AIDS is among male homosexuals. The traditional condemnation of condoms as direct contraception no longer applies. Opposition to their use has to be based on something else, and that something else is the worry that condom education and distribution will give the impression that society condones immoral sexual activity, thus increasing its incidence. (Some religious leaders add to this the notion that AIDS is a divine punishment for homosexual perversion and a proof that the end of the world is near. This kind of theological ugliness would lead us to the conclusion that medical research toward preventing AIDS ought to be stopped because it undermines divine vengeance!)

The argument that condom availability and condom education lead to increased immorality is tenuous at best. Nor can those providing such information and devices be presumed to be in moral agreement with their patients' sexual activity. The attempt of Catholic hospitals and Catholic health care professionals to reduce the spread of this serious disease will, I believe, be seen as an attempt to heal, not as a relaxation of moral standards. And if some do make that charge, Catholic hospitals ought to answer that this is part of the criticism that comes to those who are doing the work of the Gospel.

An analogy can be drawn to the question of sterile needles. In some Catholic statements on this issue, there is more openness to the possibility of distributing sterile needles to drug users at risk for AIDS than to the possibility of distributing condoms. This is so despite the fact that it is harder to argue that the use of mind-altering illegal drugs is morally right than it is to argue that some cases of non-marital sex, as for example among committed homosexuals, is morally right. Yet the analogy, despite this difference, is still informative. Those who support education about sterile needles need not support the destructive use of drugs. Those who support education about condoms need not support the destructive use of sex. But if we can be open to the idea of sterile needles, as I think we can, then we must also allow for the possibility that condom education and distribution is morally right.

There is one final approach we can take in investigating condoms and AIDS, an approach familiar to Catholic hospitals and Catholic medical ethics. It is a complex approach, and impossible to detail here. The Catholic tradition allows for something called "indirect," "remote," or "material" cooperation with an immoral act or procedure. I am not myself convinced that warning people to sterilize needles (even though their drug use may be immoral) or warning them to use condoms (even though their sexual activity may be immoral) or warning them to use seat belts (even though their driving habits may be immoral) ought to be considered "cooperation" in an immoral action. In this kind of case it is more accurate to see the warning as a right action intended to reduce the negative consequences of a wrong one than to see it as cooperation in the evil act. But perhaps those who oppose condom education on the grounds that it identifies the educator with immorality or that it implies cooperation with moral evil might accept the notion that this kind of cooperation is at most a "remote" or "indirect" cooperation.

For moralists and others interested in the traditional technical proof of such a thesis within the principle of double effect, it would go something like this (other readers can skip it). 1) The distribution of condoms is not itself intrinsically immoral. Even those who argue that all direct contraception is immoral must admit this, since condoms have other uses than direct contraception, and in this context the contraceptive motivation is either non-existent or indirect. 2) The good effect (saving lives) is not caused by the bad effect (immoral sex, even assuming that this is "caused" by condom education, which I doubt; or the prevention of pregnancy, even assuming this is one of the effects, which it very often is not). 3) The hospital or health care professional has no formal connection with the sexual acts. They do not will them; they do not intend or delight in any bad effects. 4) The proportion of effects is sufficient to warrant the cooperation.

God calls us to heal. Health care providers ought to tell their patients that condoms reduce the risk of catching and transmitting the AIDS virus, but that they offer no guarantee against the disease. The distribution of condoms and of prophylactic information in this context is morally right.

The opposition by many members of the American hierarchy to condom education and distribution is unfortunate. In many ways it parallels the opposition by the USCC to the withdrawal of nutrition and hydration in the *Cruzan* case which we noted at some length in chapter three. In both cases, bishops have spoken contrary to their own tradition. In the *Cruzan* brief they forgot or implicitly rejected the Catholic tradition of permitting the withdrawal of morally extraordinary treatment. On AIDS they have forgotten or implicitly rejected the Catholic tradition permitting indirect contraception and remote cooperation with evil. They did the former, as I have shown, because they fear being identified with any movement toward legalized euthanasia and abortion. They have done the latter because they do not wish to be seen as in any sense condoning contraception or homosexual relations. I believe that this kind of approach will actually support the developments the bishops fear. And neither position is true to traditional Catholic medical ethics.

Bibliography

Ashley, Benedict M., and Kevin D. O'Rourke. *Health Care Ethics: A Theological Analysis*. 3rd ed. St. Louis, MO: Catholic Health Association, 1989.

Beauchamp, Tom L., and James F. Childress. *Principles of Biomedical Ethics*. 3rd ed. New York: Oxford University Press, 1989.

Benjamin, Martin, and Joy Curtis. *Ethics in Nursing*. 2nd ed. New York: Oxford University Press, 1986.

Callahan, Daniel. *Setting Limits: Medical Goals in an Aging Society*. New York: Simon and Schuster, 1987.

Callahan, Daniel. *What Kind of Life: The Limits of Medical Progress*. New York: Simon and Schuster, 1990.

Churchill, Larry. "Reviving a Distinctive Medical Ethic," *Hastings Center Report*, 19, No. 3 (May-June 1989), 28-34.

Daniels, Norman. *Am I My Parents' Keeper: An Essay on Justice between the Young and the Old*. New York: Oxford University Press, 1988.

Dougherty, Charles J. *American Health Care: Realities, Rights, and Reforms*. New York: Oxford University Press, 1988.

Drane, James F. *Becoming a Good Doctor: The Place of Virtue and Character in Medical Ethics*. Kansas City, MO: Sheed & Ward, 1988.

Flynn, Eileen P. *Hard Decisions: Forgoing and Withdrawing Artificial Nutrition and Hydration*. Kansas City, MO: Sheed & Ward, 1990.

Gula, Richard M. *What Are They Saying About Euthansia?* Marwah, NJ: Paulist Press, 1985.

The Hastings Center. *Guidelines on the Termination of Life-Sustaining Treatment and the Care of the Dying*. Briarcliff Manor, NY: The Hastings Center, 1987.

Kelly, David F. *The Emergence of Roman Catholic Medical Ethics in North America: An Historical, Methodological, Bibliographical Study.* New York: Edwin Mellen Press, 1979.

Lynn, Joanne, ed. *By No Extraordinary Means: The Choice to Forgo Life-Sustaining Food and Water.* Bloomington: Indiana University Press, 1989.

Macklin, Ruth. *Mortal Choices.* Boston: Houghton Mifflin, 1987.

Maguire, Daniel C. *Death By Choice.* Garden City, NY: Doubleday, 1973.

May, William F. *The Physician's Covenant.* Phildelphia: Westminster, 1988.

Meisel, Alan. *The Right To Die.* New York: John Wiley & Sons, 1989.

President's Commission for the Study of Ethical Problems in Medicine and Biomedical and Behavioral Research. *Deciding to Forego Life-Sustaining Treatment: A Report on the Ethical, Medical, and Legal Issues in Treatment Decisions.* Washington: Government Printing Office, 1983.

Shannon, Thomas A., and James J. Walter. "The PVS Patient and the Foregoing/Withdrawing of Medical Nutrition and Hydration," *Theological Studies,* 49 (1988), 623-647.

Veatch, Robert M. "Generalization of Expertise," *Hastings Center Studies,* 1, No. 2 (1973), 29-40.

Index

Abortion 3, 5, 11, 37, 38, 44, 45, 55, 76, 80, 89, 91, 94, 174, 208
Active euthanasia 8-12, 16, 21, 24, 25, 29, 49-51, 69, 89
Addiction 113
Advanced directive 50
Advertising 77, 81, 82
AIDS viii, 110, 135, 155, 176, 204-208
Allocation of resources vii, viii, 63, 72, 76, 91, 92, 96, 136, 138, 139, 140-147, 151, 154, 159-170, 172, 200
Allowing to die, see Killing
AMA 81
American Academy of Neurology 28, 30, 35
American College of Physicians 28, 35
American Medical Association 28, 35, 73, 139
American Society of Law and Medicine 129, 134
American Society of Transplant Surgeons 174
Anencephaly 69
Annas, George J. 31, 34, 176
Appendicitis 13, 79
Aquinas, Thomas 85
Aristotle 85
Artificial heart 145, 170-173
Ashley, Benedict M. 103
Assisted suicide 8, 9, 47, 51
Atheism 107
Attempted suicide 17
Autonomy 1, 13, 21, 28, 43-46, 55, 58, 66, 68, 73, 74, 105, 120, 138, 142, 143, 155, 166, 173, 178, 183, 188

Baby-Doe Regulations 120, 121
Banez 17
Bayer, Ronald 155
Beauchamp, Tom L. 155
Benefit/burden 7, 9, 14, 15, 32, 41, 45, 46, 65, 148, 180, 182, 199, 200
Best interests 14-17, 21, 41, 47, 50, 56, 113, 116, 143, 154-156, 190, 200
Bible 82, 85, 98
Black, Virginia 150, 166, 175
Blackhall, Leslie J. 71
Blood transfusions 27, 46
Bloom, Alan 86
Brain death vii, 6, 57, 68-70
Brennan 40, 71
Brody, Howard 71
Brophy case 22, 23, 25-27, 29, 31

Brother Fox case 27
Burden, see Benefit

Cahill, Lisa Sowle 103
Callahan, Daniel 147, 154-156, 160, 209
Canada 32, 152
Capacity 13-15, 21, 26, 27, 29, 41, 44, 46, 48, 50, 53, 113, 166, 178, 179, 181, 185, 189, 190
Capital punishment 3, 11
Capitalism 80, 165
Case review 128-134, 136
Cathell, Daniel Webster 76, 86
Chaplain 114, 116, 127
Chart 134, 185, 187, 190, 198
Childress, James F. 155, 209
Chiropractic 81
Christ, see Jesus Christ
Churchill, Larry R. 86, 155
Clear and convincing evidence 39-42, 48, 50, 133
Clergy 66, 89, 105, 114-117, 126, 189
Codes 73, 75-78, 81, 88, 101, 176
Coma 21, 22, 26, 28, 30-32, 69, 70
Combination argument 170
Comfort (measures) 25, 51, 70, 144, 180, 181, 183, 188, 199
Committee of the person 49, 53
Common good 45, 100, 139, 140, 154
Common law 18, 27, 43, 48, 52, 55
Communication 66, 67, 71, 115, 182-184, 188, 189
Competence (see also Capacity) 26, 37-39, 48-50, 53, 185
Condoms 93-95, 204-208
Confidentiality 135, 137
Conflict 49, 57, 65-67, 125, 167, 184, 189
Connery, John R. 103
Conroy case 56
Consequentialism viii, 97
Constitution 37, 39, 43-45, 48, 55
Consultation 61, 67, 125, 129, 130-135, 134, 182, 189, 192, 197-199, 201, 202
Contextualism 80, 83
Contraception 55, 89, 91, 93, 94, 99, 168, 169, 205, 206, 208
Contractarian (theory of justice) 146, 157
Cost 7, 63, 65, 66, 69, 72, 138, 139, 141, 143, 152, 168, 171, 172
Cost containment 63, 66, 72, 138, 141, 143, 152

Court (see also Supreme Court) vii, 1, 9, 11-13, 21-23, 26-30, 36-43, 48, 50, 52, 53, 56, 63, 65, 67, 81, 82, 87, 120, 122, 134
CPR (coronary pulmonary resuscitation) 59, 63, 65, 71, 80, 187
Cranford, Ronald E. 30
Cronin, Daniel A. 34
Cruzan case vii, 1, 9, 13, 18, 21, 26, 27, 31, 34, 36-48, 50, 52, 54, 55, 61, 62, 65, 120, 133, 156, 208
Curran, Charles E. 18, 103

Daniels, Norman 151, 157, 158, 174
Dehydration 30
DeMarco, Donald T. 168, 169, 176
Death, moment of 6, 21, 69, 113; readiness for 7, 9; tolerable 148
Deontology viii, 97
Diagnosis 22, 30, 57, 63, 64, 66, 79, 93, 121, 122, 188, 190, 191, 201
Diagnostic related groupings 66, 141
Dialysis 58, 59, 140, 161, 182, 191
Direct (see also Indirect) 1, 3, 8-11, 21, 24-26, 28, 33, 37, 38, 47, 50, 59, 82, 94, 117, 162, 180-181, 206, 208
Divine sovereignty 2, 98
DNR (do not resuscitate) 71, 177
Double effect 8-11, 32, 94-97, 102, 162, 207
Dougherty, Charles J. 87, 154
Drane, James F. 31, 86, 209
DRG, see Diagnostic related groupings
Durable power of attorney 39, 40-42, 49, 50, 53, 54, 186, 190, 201
Dying process 2, 11, 12, 24, 120

Early review 53, 66, 181, 182, 186, 188, 192
Ecclesiastical positivism 100
Ectopic pregnancy, abortion in 38, 95
Edmund D., Pellegrino 87
Eichner case 35
Emotivism viii, 80, 83, 88
England 58, 73, 152
Enlightenment 82, 90
Epistemology 74, 78, 79
Ethical relativism 74
Ethics committee viii, ix, 23, 27, 28, 67, 116, 119-128, 130-137, 177, 182, 184, 186, 189, 192, 194, 196-199, 202
Etiquette 75, 76, 78, 81, 88
Eucharist 22
Euthanasia 1, 2, 8-12, 16, 18, 20, 21, 24-26, 28, 29, 34, 38, 44-47, 49-51, 56, 69, 89, 91, 94, 117, 142, 180, 208, 209; legalization of 11, 12, 47, 51
Extraordinary treatment, see ordinary treatment

Feminism 165, 166
Fetus (see also Abortion) 37, 95

Flynn, Eileen P. 31, 209
Foundationalism 82
Fourteenth amendment 39, 55
Futility vii, 29, 57, 59-64, 66, 67, 70, 71, 116, 179, 187, 190, 199, 200

Gastrostomy tube 20, 23-26, 43
Generalization of expertise 58, 70, 210
Genetics 91
Gewirth, Alan 174
Gilligan, Carol 165, 166, 175
God's dominion over human life 15
Greed 41, 109, 144, 161, 162
Griswold v. Connecticut case 55
Gross national product 139
Guardian 23, 67, 198
Gula, Richard M. 103

Hardwig, John 155, 156
Hastings Center 17, 18, 28, 30, 31, 34, 35, 70, 72, 86, 87, 119, 129, 147, 155, 157, 174, 176, 209, 210
Health insurance, see Insurance
Heart transplant (see also Artificial heart) 33, 162
Hinderliter, Stacey viii, 192
Hippocrates 89
HIV (human immune deficiency virus) 110, 176
HMO (health maintenance organization) 66, 141
Homeopathy 81
Hospital lawyer 125, 184, 189
Hoyt, John W. ix, 197, 202
Humanae Vitae 99
Hydration vii, 16, 20-22, 25, 26, 28-34, 38, 39, 47, 51, 60-62, 69, 70, 132, 181, 182, 208-210
Hysterectomy 38

In vitro fertilization 168, 169, 176
Incompetence (see also Capacity, Competence) 18, 47, 48, 51, 71, 81
Indirect (see also Direct) 3, 9-11, 38, 94, 206-208
Individualism 16, 46, 72, 73, 74, 149, 156, 176
Infallible 100
Infant Care Review Committee 122
Infant mortality 139, 154, 155
Infants 5, 14, 69, 120, 122, 157
Informed consent 46, 55, 57, 66, 76, 105, 126, 135, 138, 171
Institutional Review Board 7, 122
Integrity of the medical profession 12, 179
Intent, intentionality 24, 25, 32, 86, 120, 125, 165
Intraprofessional medical ethics 88, 90
Intraprofessional relativism 74, 100
Irreversible coma 22, 32

Insurance 72, 81, 139, 140, 152, 157

Jane Doe case 26
Janssens, Louis 16, 72, 156
Jecker, Nancy S. 71
Jehovah's Witness 27, 35
Jesus Christ 3, 4, 82, 101, 107, 110, 115
Jewish 16, 31, 90, 126
Job, book of 18, 78, 110, 112, 141
Jobes case 26, 33
Jonsen, Albert R. 16, 71, 86, 103
Just war 3

Kaufmann, Walter 173, 175
Kelly, David F. 1, 2, 86, 102, 103, 199, 209
Kelly, Gerald 25, 31, 32
Kevorkian, Jack 55
Killing/allowing to die 1, 2, 4, 5, 8-12, 16,
    20, 21, 24, 26, 28, 29, 33, 38, 43, 45-47,
    55, 94-96, 142, 143, 180, 181
Kohlberg, Lawrence 165, 175

Leake, Chauncey 75
Libertarian (theory of justice) 146
Liberty 1, 13, 18, 21, 27, 28, 39, 43, 44, 47,
    55, 139, 142, 154
Life-sustaining treatment 28, 35, 37, 38, 40,
    72, 115, 209, 210
Liguori 17
Litigation 8, 134
Living will 33, 50-53, 186, 194

Macklin, Ruth 19, 129
Magisterium 99, 100
Maguire, Daniel C. 18, 56, 210
Maine 28, 40, 42
Massachusetts 22, 23, 26, 27, 61
May, William E. 33, 86
McCartney, James J. 34
McConnell case 26
McCormick, Richard A. 31
Medical association 28, 35, 73, 139
Medical insurance 75
Medical morals committee 122
Meisel, Alan 18, 31, 35, 55, 56, 210
Mental reservation 95
Metaethical absolutism 82, 85, 98
Metaethics viii, 74, 78, 79, 82, 86-88, 98
Missouri 26, 28, 36, 37, 39, 40, 42, 50
Mistakes vii, 31, 55, 57, 63-65, 79
Murphy, Donald J. 71

National Conference of Catholic Bishops,
    see United States Catholic Conference
National health insurance, see Insurance
Natural death act 52
Natural family planning 93, 94
Natural law viii, 16, 82-85, 88-90, 93, 98-
    103, 163
New Jersey 23, 26, 27, 33, 56

New York 16, 18, 26-28, 31, 40, 42, 50, 86,
    87, 103, 154-158, 173-175, 209, 210
Non-cognitivism 80, 82-84
Nursing associations 74, 88
Nursing ethics 74, 75, 78, 85, 88, 123, 129,
    137
Nutrition vii, 16, 20-23, 25, 26, 28-34, 38-
    40, 43, 45, 47, 51, 60-62, 69, 70, 132, 181,
    191, 208-210

O'Connor case 26, 34
O'Rourke, Kevin D. 34, 103, 209
Ordinary and extraordinary treatment 2,
    6-9, 13-15, 17, 18, 20-23, 25, 26, 28, 32-
    35, 41, 43-47, 53, 56, 96, 142, 156, 168,
    171, 180, 200, 208, 210
Original sin 82, 109, 161
Overtreatment 64, 65

Pain vii, viii, 2, 7-10, 13, 21, 30, 61, 96, 105-
    114, 117, 164
Palliative Support Care 137, 177, 191
Paris, John J. 17, 31, 71
Pastoral medicine 90, 91
Paternalism 57, 58, 73, 74, 120, 138
Patrick, Anne E. 164, 175
Paul VI 99
Pennsylvania vii, 26, 33, 52, 177, 192, 197
Percival 75, 86
Persistent vegetative state (PVS) 16, 21, 22,
    30, 32, 33, 35, 36, 47, 60-62, 70, 71, 132,
    143, 210
Personalism viii, 96, 102
Physicalism viii, 32, 93-99, 102, 162, 164,
    169
Physician-patient relationship 131, 167
Pius XII 6, 99
Pope John XXIII Medical-Moral Research
    and Education Center 33
Positivism, see Rational positivism, see Ec-
    clesiastical positivism
Positron emission tomography 30
Poverty 40, 47, 54, 62, 109, 141, 144, 146,
    152, 153, 163-165
Power of attorney 39, 49, 50, 53, 54, 201
President's Commission 28, 35, 129, 210
Privacy 1, 13, 17, 18, 21, 23, 28, 43-47, 55,
    135, 142
Probability of success 61-63
Process theology 108
Professional adjustments 74, 78, 88
Professional associations 75, 77
Prognosis 57, 63, 64, 66, 79, 122, 188, 190,
    201
Proportionalism 97
Proportionate 17, 20, 103, 180, 182
PVS, see Persistent vegetative state

Quality of life 4, 5, 15, 16, 29, 60, 62, 70,
    71, 156, 200

Quality Review Board 122
Quinlan case 22, 23, 27-31, 55, 61, 120

Racism 109
Rahner, Karl 104, 117
Rational positivism 83, 88, 100
Rationing (see also Allocation) 138, 139, 141, 142, 147, 152-156, 160, 179
Rawls, John 157, 159, 173, 174
Redistribution 165
Rehnquist, Justice 40, 41
Relativism (see also Ethical relativism) 73, 81
Resuscitation 24, 61
Right-to-life 36, 37
Risk Management Committee 122
Roe v. Wade case 37, 55

Saikewicz case 27
Salpingectomy 38, 95
Salpingostomy 95
Sanctity of life 5, 15, 45
Scalia, Antonin 39, 40
Scarce medical resources 138
Schmidhofer, Mark 177
Schneiderman, Lawrence J. 71
Sedation 9, 11, 21, 113, 180, 181
Sexism 41, 109
Sexual ethics 89, 162
Sexuality 75, 99
Shannon, Thomas A. 16, 30, 210
Shaw, George Bernard 76
Situationalism 80, 83
Socialism 80, 165
Society for Critical Care Medicine 129
Sowle Cahill, Lisa 103
Specialization ix, 121
SSM Health Care System 45, 46
St. Francis Medical Center vii, viii, ix, 129, 133, 137, 177, 188, 191, 192, 196, 197, 202
Starvation 30
Sterba, James P. 173, 174
Sterilization 3, 25, 91, 94, 162, 168, 169
Stevens, Justice 40
Stewardship 2, 4, 15-17, 21, 41, 50, 56, 116
Suffering 2-5, 8, 9, 12, 15, 30, 45, 50, 98, 106-112, 117, 148, 151; redemptive 3, 98, 112

Suicide (see also Assisted and Attempted suicide) 5, 8-10, 17, 18, 21, 44, 47, 51, 55
Supreme Court (see also Court) vii, 1, 9, 21, 23, 26, 27, 36-40, 42, 43, 48, 52, 65, 81
Surrogate 13-17, 21, 28, 38, 41, 46, 54, 57, 58, 60, 61, 65, 67, 70, 72, 143, 178, 181, 182, 185, 186, 188-191, 194-196, 198-201

Technology 41, 120, 139, 144, 157, 161, 162, 173
Terminal illness 8, 31, 32, 113, 157
Theodicy 106, 107, 110-112, 117
Theological principles 3, 4, 97, 98, 169
Third party payors 17, 63, 72, 143
Thomasma, David C. 87
Time-limited trials 66, 184
Tomlinson, Tom 71
Toulmin, Stephen 16, 86, 103
Transplant 33, 69, 72, 91, 140, 160, 162, 167, 172, 174

Undertreatment 64, 65
United States Catholic Conference 43, 45, 46, 55, 208
Universalisability 166
Utilitarianism 97, 103

Vatican II 89, 91, 92, 95, 96, 101
Veatch, Robert M. 56-58, 70, 72, 87, 151, 157, 210
Ventilator 8, 23-25, 29, 33, 45, 132, 143, 191, 193
Vitalism 5, 37, 157

Webster case 37
Withdrawing 9, 10, 16, 20, 21, 24, 31, 33, 39, 117, 132, 178, 181, 183, 184, 188, 209, 210
Withholding 9, 10, 20, 21, 24, 28, 34, 39, 117, 178, 181, 183, 184, 188
Wolf, Susan 18

Youngner, Stuart J. 59, 71

Zaner, Richard M. 55